PC
3304
T6

Topsfield, L
Troubadours and love

DATE DUE			
JUN 1 76		FEB 02 88	
APR 4 1982			
AUG 2 1985			

TROUBADOURS AND LOVE

To Valerie

TROUBADOURS AND LOVE

L. T. TOPSFIELD

Lecturer in Provençal and French in the
University of Cambridge and
Fellow and Tutor of St Catharine's College

Qui aquestz digz estiers enten,
si mielhs hi dis, non lo·n repren,
quar s'a trops sens una razos,
mout m'es mieller quan quecx es bos.
Anon.

CAMBRIDGE UNIVERSITY PRESS
Cambridge
London · New York · Melbourne

Published by the Syndics of the Cambridge University Press
The Pitt Building, Trumpington Street, Cambridge CB2 1RP
Bentley House, 200 Euston Road, London NW1 2DB
32 East 57th Street, New York, NY 10022 USA
296 Beaconsfield Parade Middle Park, Melbourne 3206, Australia

© Cambridge University Press 1975

Library of Congress Catalogue Card Number: 74–14440

ISBN: 0 521 20596 4

First published 1975

Printed in Great Britain by The Anchor Press Ltd
and bound by Wm Brendon & Son Ltd
both of Tiptree, Essex

CONTENTS

PLATES

(between pages 72 and 73)

ACKNOWLEDGMENTS

THE CHAPTER ON Guilhem IX of Aquitaine reproduces material from 'The burlesque poetry of Guilhem IX of Aquitaine' in NMi, LXIX (1968), pp. 280–302, and from 'Three levels of love in the poetry of the early troubadours, Guilhem IX, Marcabru and Jaufre Rudel' in *Mélanges de philologie romane dédiés à la mémoire de Jean Boutière* (Liège, 1971), pp. 571–87. The chapter on Jaufre Rudel is reprinted with additions and amendments from '*Jois, Amors* and *Fin' Amors* in the poetry of Jaufre Rudel', NMi LXXI (1970), pp. 277–305. The sections on Peire d'Alvernhe, Raimon de Miraval and Guilhem de Montanhagol also contain paragraphs which have appeared in *Mélanges offerts à Charles Rostaing* (Liège, 1974), MLR, LI (1956), pp. 33–41, and FS, XI (1957), pp. 127–34, respectively. References to these articles will be found in the notes, and full details are given in the bibliography. I thank the editors of these journals and collections of studies for their permission to use this material.

I am also greatly indebted to all the scholars who have worked on editions of the troubadours whom I have discussed; to the Syndics and Officers of the Cambridge University Press, and especially to Mr Michael Black, Miss Diane Speakman and Mr Jay Bosanquet, for their kindness and helpful suggestions. I also thank Mrs M. Anderson for doing the general index and Mrs Susan Church, Mrs Ruth Hebblethwaite and Miss Iris Little for their invaluable help in transforming my manuscript into legible material.

January 1975   L.T.T.

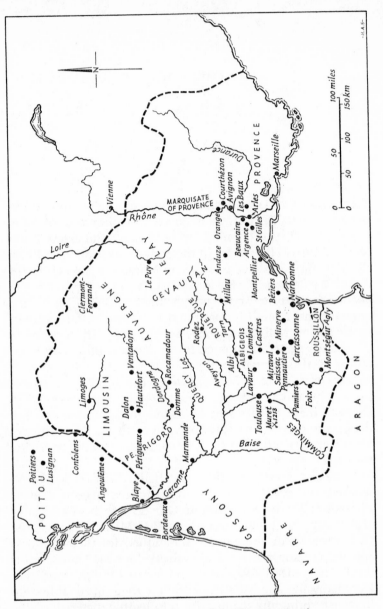

The South of France at the time of the *Albigensian Crusade*.

The approximate limits of the sovereignty of the Counts of Toulouse extended along the Baïse in the west to Marmande, Rocamadour, Millau, Anduze, the Rhône, the coast, the river Agly and the Pyrenees. They also had rights in the Marquisate of Provence. The broken line marks the approximate linguistic boundary of Provençal at this time.

INTRODUCTION

THIS BOOK IS an attempt to understand the poetry of the troubadours and their ideas on love. It is not concerned with any view of troubadour poetry as a uniform phenomenon or the illustration of a rigid, isolated doctrine of Fin'Amors or 'courtly love'. It aims to show, through individual studies of certain troubadours, the ways in which their ideas on love, social behaviour, and the quest for happiness evolved from one generation to another and varied from one troubadour to another in the same generation. It tries also to bring out the poetic qualities of these troubadours and to show how love and joy, folly and reason could not have the same meaning for troubadours who composed in a 'dark' allusive style as it did for courtly poets who sang in the clear, easy style of the trobar leu,* on their single plane of worldly experience.

The troubadours who have been chosen for inclusion in this work were all famous in their day and exercised a strong influence on later poets, and they also exemplify the division between reflective and courtly poetry which is a feature of troubadour poetry in the twelfth century. They all show a strong sense of individuality in their poetry, and, to judge from their work and what we know of their lives,[1] they were all, in some degree, in a state of conflict with themselves, with the noble society in which they lived, and with courtly, conventional ideas on love. Some major troubadours have had to be omitted; the greatest of these is Guiraut de Bornelh, whose significance in the evolution of the troubadour love lyric appears to lie more in the manner and the style rather than the substance of his work.

* This and other technical terms are defined in the glossary on p. 256.

I

Troubadour poetry has been compared to a flower which appears from the earth without root or stalk. Although the comparison is very probably untrue, the flower imagery is itself apt, for, to our eyes, troubadour poetry buds, opens out and blooms, in perceptible stages, in the South of France in the twelfth century, and in its flowering, and its decline in the thirteenth century, it encourages and enriches the poetry of Western Europe in marked and lasting fashion. Troubadour poetry, as it exists in about fifty MSS.,[2] flourished actively for nearly two hundred and fifty years, and this is the span of time which is covered in this book, from the end of the eleventh century, when Guilhem IX Duke of Aquitaine began to compose, until 1323 when seven citizens of Toulouse, forefathers of the nineteenth-century Felibrige, founded the Consistory of *Gai Saber* in the hope that they might revivify Provençal poetry with the literary concourse of the *Jocs Florals*.[3]

In this long period of poetic development four main stages can be discerned. In the first half of the twelfth century we find a primarily experimental and seeking type of poetry which is centred on the court of Poitiers and its dependencies. This early poetry, which is not normally tied down by courtly ideas of behaviour, is often more abstract than worldly in intention and is concerned more with the personal quest for joy and the absolute ideal of an ultimate happiness than with conformity to social convention. In the second 'stage' from about 1150 to 1180, which may correspond to the period of influence at Poitiers of Eleanor of Aquitaine, there appears to be a widespread strengthening of courtly doctrine in the South of France and a clash for some of the greatest and more individually minded troubadours between the demand from their noble audiences for poetry of 'courtly love' in the light, easy style and their own inclination towards the composition of more reflective poetry. This conflict appears to be resolved in the period from about 1180 to 1209, by the victory of the 'light', courtly type of poetry, but not before troubadour song has reached its finest flowering with Arnaut Daniel. By this time, the focal point of patronage has moved south from Poitiers to Toulouse and Carcassonne, Montpellier and Narbonne, and is diffused among the myriad minor courts of Languedoc, the marquisate of Provence, and Auvergne. In 1209, at the moment of greatest poetic richness and social splendour, the axe of the Albigensian Crusade falls on the noble society of the South. Courtly society in many areas is decimated, and in the changed world of the late thirteenth century love for the courtly lady or domna is transformed into love for the Virgin. Troubadour poetry has travelled its full cycle, reaching in its end and beginning towards a happiness outside earthly existence.

This book is primarily concerned with the poetry of the troubadours, and it is not part of its purpose to look for the 'roots' and 'stalk' of their song, although account has been taken of classical, Christian and medieval thought which may have influenced their ideas. The 'roots' of the courtly system of moral values based on profane and not religious love appear to extend back to the thought of Greece and Rome and Moorish Spain, and to have been nourished more immediately by Christian and feudal doctrine. Music and the technique of composition came to these poets most probably from the Church and from medieval Latin verse, and perhaps from Hispano-Arabic sources.[4] But the 'stalk' of the flower was the inspiration which flowed from the traditions and life of the court of Poitiers into which the first known troubadour, Guilhem VII Count of Poitou, IX Duke of Aquitaine, was born. This court had been famous for its civilised interest in letters and learning since the days of Guilhem the Great, III Count of Poitou and grandfather of the troubadour.[5] During his reign, from 993 to 1030, he held splendid court and won renown for his wisdom. He was keenly interested in the religious issues of his day and was on good terms with Odilon of Cluny and Fulbert of Chartres, whom he persuaded to accept the treasurership of the cathedral at Poitiers. This connexion between the court of Poitiers and the school of Chartres, which continued after Fulbert's death,[6] may have provided a vital link between the lay world of the court and the new humanism of Chartres which was based on a return to the study of the classics, especially the Platonic writings of Cicero, and Boethius, and may also have acted as a focus and filter for the 'new' ideas on science, on astronomy, arithmetic, algebra and navigation, and on love, which were flowing to France from Moorish Spain.

To this growing interest in the things of the mind at the court of Poitiers in the eleventh century there should be added the civilising influence of the remarkable women who ruled this court. It is probable that these women were partly responsible for the refinement of social manners and the system of courtly values and virtues which existed when the first troubadour began to compose. The greatest of these women was Agnes of Burgundy, third wife of the ageing Guilhem the Great, mother of two successive Counts of Poitou and of Agnes who married the Emperor Henry III in 1143. Well travelled in Germany and Italy, Agnes of Burgundy put her imprint on her day almost as decisively as did her descendant Eleanor of Aquitaine, Queen of France and England, and Blanche of Castile, Queen and Regent of France, and mother of Saint Louis.

What was a troubadour? The word *trobador* comes from *trobar*, the Provençal equivalent of *invenire*, which in classical Latin rhetoric meant 'to discover, invent or devise'.[7] The troubadour, who might be of noble, bourgeois or peasant birth, was responsible for inventing the words, the scheme of versification, and the melody for his song. A courtly audience would esteem him for his poetic and musical craftsmanship, his voice and courtly accomplishments, and for the individual inspiration which he, if he were a great troubadour, would bring to his work. The *joglar*, on the other hand, was not a creative poet or musician but a minstrel who lived by singing the troubadour's songs. If he learnt to compose songs and to refine his manners, he might rise to the status of a troubadour. If he were down on his luck, he might earn his keep as an acrobat or juggler, with a performing bear or monkey, like his ancestor the Roman *joculator*.

The supreme genre of troubadour poetry was the *canso*, which treated of the highest subject, love, in the highest style, which was free from base words and thoughts, and demanded a fresh scheme of versification for each new composition.[8] The early troubadours gave the name of *vers* to love songs and moralising poems alike, possibly taking this word from the paraliturgical *versus*, a form of medieval Latin trope which was widely practised in Aquitaine in the eleventh century and which may have provided the first troubadours with rhyme schemes and melodies.[9] By the mid-twelfth century the term *sirventes*[10] was used for poems of blame and praise and deeds of war, and the word *canso* came to be applied generally to the love song. Other genres in troubadour lyric poetry include the debate forms of the *tenso*, and the *joc partit* or *partimen*, in which a choice of argument was offered to one's adversary, the *alba* or dawn song, the *pastorela*, which was a poem about the attempted seduction of a shepherdess, and the *planh*, a lament on the death of a king, a great personage or poet.

Troubadours, and especially *joglars*, travelled widely through the courts of France, Italy, Spain, Germany, Hungary, Cyprus, Malta and the Holy Land, and their songs, in subject matter and style, exerted a profound influence on the poetry of Western Europe. Many Italians, Catalans and poets of other nationalities composed in Provençal, which in the early thirteenth century was described by a Catalan, Raimon Vidal, as the supreme language for the composition of the love song or *canso*.[11] Some idea of the spread of troubadour poetry can be gained from the fact that about one-quarter of the four hundred and sixty[12] troubadours known to us, of whatever nationality, composed in countries outside the South of France about a quarter of all the poems which have survived.[13] The troubadour *canso* exerted a varying but direct influence on the *trouvères* of Northern France such as Gui de Coucy and Gace Brulé, on Catalan and Spanish poets, the poets of the *dolce stil nuovo*, the Sicilian school, Dante, Petrarch and his imitators, and through them the sixteenth-century French poets of the school of Lyons. Troubadour ideas on love and courtliness which were absorbed and distilled in the *Roman de la Rose*, and in the great Arthurian romances of Northern France in the twelfth and thirteenth centuries, influenced through them the literary traditions of Germany, Spain and England.

The poetry of the troubadours was meant to be sung, and works on their music are included in the bibliography. Their poetic language, which remained remarkably stable during the two centuries of their main creative activity, is rich in vowel sounds and rhymes, and can be appreciated more fully if it is read aloud or recited. The rules of pronunciation, so far as we understand them, are not difficult,[14] and the variations in orthography, which are mostly due to the regional peculiarities of the scribes, can be ignored. The vowel sounds resemble those of modern Spanish and Italian, and Vulgar

Latin. They have an open and closed quality, resulting in most cases from their Latin derivation: *a* is normally open (as in *patte*) but is close when followed by unstable *n*, e.g. *ma* (*man*) and is pronounced as in *âge*; *e* open (always in diphthongs) as in *mère*, *e* close (usually close before a consonant) is pronounced as in *été*; *o* open as in modern French, *o* close can be pronounced as *ou*; *u* usually as in *lune*, or possibly as *ou*; *i* as French *i*, or semi-vowel, e.g. in *Blaia*, pronounced as in French *payer*. Diphthongs and triphthongs usually count as one syllable in the verse line, although each vowel should be pronounced separately. The approximate English equivalents of some common diphthongs are: *au* as in 'cow'; *ai* as in 'try'; *ei* as in 'hay'; *eu* as in Cockney 'fell' and *oi* as in 'joy'.

Enclitic forms are common in Provençal poetry. They may be monosyllabic: *no·n* for *non* + *en* (very frequent), *no·m* for *non* + *me*, *els* for *en* + *los*, *el* for *en* + *lo*; or diphthongs: *qu'ie·m* for *que* + *ieu* + *me*; or triphthongs: *ie·us* for *ieu* + *vos*.

The consonants in medieval Provençal can be pronounced as in English, with some exceptions:

c before *e* or *i* is pronounced *ts* (or sometimes *s* regionally).

ch is *tch* as in 'watch'. As a final sound it can be written with a *g* or an *h*: *fug*, *fuh*.

g before *e* and *i*, and *j*, which is often written as *i*, are like English *j* in 'Jack', e.g. *Lemoges*, *domnejaire*.

l palatalised as in Italian *egli* or Spanish *ella* is found written down as *ll*, *lh*, *il*, *ill*, *li*, and the *i* in these forms is merely an indication of palatalisation.

n palatised as in French *gagner* can be written as *gn*, *nh*, *ing*: e.g. *loing*, *lonh*.

q is always occlusive *k*, whether written as *c*, *q* or *qu*.

r is rolled as at the present day in Spain, Italy and parts of Southern France.

s intervocalic is pronounced as in modern French *voisin*.

z final is pronounced as *ts*. This sound may also be written down as *tz*: e.g. *toz*, *totz*.

Our present-day patterns of thought and our 'visual' imagination[15] make it difficult for us to appreciate troubadour poetry to the full. Our hearing and mind are indifferently attuned to words which in themselves form a separate entity of sound and sense, and also to poems in which theme, vowels, consonants, rhyme and music and the structure and interconnexion of stanzas are bound together as integral parts of the poet's creation. And we also need to take account of the part played by a troubadour or *joglar*, who with intonation or gesture was freer to evoke a response from his audience than is now possible for the poet who speaks through un-changing print. Yet, in spite of such limitations and the occasional inevitable uncertainty of textual correctness and attribution, it is hoped that this book will give some under-standing of the troubadours and their ideas, and that it will lead to enjoyment of the exceptional quality of their poetry.

Early Troubadours

Guilhem IX of Aquitaine and the quest for joy

THERE MAY HAVE been earlier troubadours than Guilhem IX Duke of Aquitaine, VII Count of Poitou, who lived from 1071 to 1127, but if they existed, the manuscripts ignore them, and they were overshadowed by the versatile genius of this descendant of the kings of France and direct ancestor of Eleanor of Aquitaine, Marie de Champagne and Richard Cœur de Lion. His character, to judge from his deeds and poetry, was many-sided. He was violent, passionate and impulsive, and at the same time detached, ironical and educated, keenly aware of his own interests in everyday matters but looking beyond them for new adventure, excitement and happiness. A man, as he says, who desired what he could not have, who never enjoyed what he loved and whose heart told him at the moment of action that all is vanity.

His Provençal biographer, writing probably in the thirteenth century, says:

Lo coms de Peitieus si fo uns dels majors cortes del mon e dels majors trichadors de dompnas, e bons cavalliers d'armas e larcs de dompnejar; e saup ben trobar e cantar. Et anet lonc temps per lo mon per enganar las domnas...[1]

The count of Poitou was one of the most courtly men in the world and one of the greatest deceivers of ladies, and a fine knight in deeds of arms, and generous in wooing; and he knew well how to compose and sing. And he travelled for a long time throughout the world in order to deceive ladies...

Orderic Vitalis calls him brave and loyal, but an extreme lover of pleasure who with his amusing ways surpassed all those people whose profession it is to entertain others. On his return home from the First Crusade, after praying at Jerusalem, 'since he was gay and joyful in character [*jocundus et lepidus*] and happy with good living, he took delight in singing of the miseries of his "captivity" in rhythmical verse and pleasing melodies, in the presence of kings, great men and Christian audiences.'[2]

This reference to Guilhem's lost poems about his Crusading experiences is taken up by William of Malmesbury:

a buffoon and a man so inclined to evil that he indulged in all manner of vices before his return from Jerusalem and did not see the hand of Providence in the misfortunes that befell him, believing that chance and circumstance were responsible for everything...He took nothing seriously, he turned everything into a joke and made his listeners laugh uncontrollably.[3]

Geoffrey of Vigeois says that his achievements were impaired by his excessive love of women and another scholar calls him the enemy of all chastity and all feminine virtue.[4]

These attacks by clerics who must have been dismayed by the ribaldry of Guilhem's burlesque poems and his rebellious and unrepentant attitude to the Church must be set against the equally one-sided flattery of those who praised his military prowess, his physical beauty, his studiousness, generosity and compassion for the wretched.[5]

Guilhem reacted with impulsive violence to what he considered as infringement of his interests by the Church. William of Malmesbury describes the scene at his first excommunication in 1114. Peter of Poitiers was about to pronounce sentence in the Cathedral when Guilhem, beside himself with anger, seized him by the hair and brandishing his sword cried out 'Now you shall die if you do not absolve me.' Then the bishop, pretending to be afraid, but seeking an opportunity to speak, was released and pronounced the formula of excommunication. When he had performed this office, he extended his neck expecting martyrdom, and invited Guilhem to strike. To which Guilhem replied: 'I hate you too much to consider you worthy of my hatred, and you shall never enter Heaven with the help of my hand.' When Guilhem learned of the miracles performed by the bishop after his death in 1115 he regretted that he had not despatched him earlier 'since he was clearly so happy in Heaven'.

At his second excommunication by the papal legate Giraud bishop of Angoulême, for refusing to renounce his mistress the viscountess of Châtellerault, Guilhem defied the bald prelate with the words: 'The comb shall curl your wayward hair before I give up the viscountess.'

Individual impulse and interest counted more for Guilhem than the movements of mass religious enthusiasm, such as that of Robert d'Arbrissel, which swept through his wide domains.[6] When Urban II arrived to preach the First Crusade, Guilhem received him at Clermont and entertained him richly at Poitiers, but he did not take the Cross. His reluctance was probably political as well as individual. In 1094 Guilhem had made a marriage with Philippa, the young widow of the king of Aragon, which offered dazzling prospects. She was the only surviving child of Guilhem IV of Toulouse and possessed undoubted rights of inheritance to the Toulousain. As the king of Aragon had not lived to assert these rights, the chance now fell to Guilhem of Aquitaine, and after the departure of Raimon de Saint-Gilles with the First Crusade, Guilhem marched his forces into Toulouse and the parts of the Toulousain to which his wife laid claim.

Guilhem's seizure of the Toulousain gave him immense power, and could have affected the history of England and France, but he was, as Raimbaut d'Aurenga described himself, 'a man of fine beginnings', for whom the moment of action was thrilling but the results of action valueless. Failing to consolidate his triumph, Guilhem left Philippa, or Mathilda as she came to be called, in power in Toulouse, and sought new adventure fighting in Normandy on the side of William Rufus. His restlessness reached a climax at the news of the capture of Jerusalem in July 1099. He took the Cross, bartered his wife's rights with Bertran de Saint-Gilles and equipped a splendid army. He assembled 30,000 men at Poitiers and lost them in an ambush in Asia Minor, reaching Antioch and Jerusalem with a handful of companions. He forfeited Philippa's rights of inheritance for good when he tried to reassert them in 1113 with a fresh occupation of the Toulousain. His remaining years were spent in governing his wide territories, in incessant and successful fighting against the turbulent vassals of Aquitaine, especially Lusignan and Parthenay, and in assembling and leading an army of six hundred knights to the help of the king of Aragon against the Almoravides and a share in the victory at Cutanda in 1120.

The eleven poems by Guilhem which have survived include five of burlesque inspiration (I, II, III, V and VI), five love lyrics (IV and VII–X) and the *congé* *Pus mos chantars* (XI).[7] Although there is verbal interplay between the burlesque poems and the love songs[8] and they have in common the theme of physical love, they belong to contrasting genres which are composed with a quite different poetic intention. For this reason they should be considered separately, and we will make a beginning with the burlesque poetry.

When Guilhem IX says that *Companho faray un vers . . . covinen* will contain more folly than wisdom:

> Et aura·i mais de foudaz no·y a de sen

he helps us to understand the construction not only of this particular poem but of his other works of burlesque inspiration which depend for their effect on the interplay of *sen* and *foudatz*. In these poems the *sen* lies in a theme which is presented in a nominally serious way and the *foudatz* or 'folly' in a burlesque treatment of this theme which may vary from an incongruous choice of subject-matter to a parody of conventional social or literary attitudes, and may culminate in bawdiness. In this interweaving of a 'serious' theme with a mocking whimsicality and in the progression in these works from apparent seriousness to licentious folly, Guilhem follows an ordered method of composition, mixing *sen* and *foudatz* in a calculated way, for, like other early troubadours, he writes according to a 'lay' rhetoric of poetry, which in its essentials was probably borrowed from the medieval and hence classical teaching of rhetoric.[9]

Guilhem offers the clearest example of this intentional progression from *sen* to *foudatz* in the poem *Ben vuelh* (VI) in which he boasts in the fashion of the *gap* of his prowess on three levels. He begins with poetic skill:[10]

> Ben vuelh que sapchon li pluzor
> D'est vers si's de bona color,[11]
> Qu'ieu ai trag de mon obrador:
> Qu'ieu port d'ayselh mestier la flor,
>   Et es vertaz,
> E puesc ne traire·l vers auctor
>   Quant er lassatz. (1–7)

I want people to know whether this poem that I have brought forth from my work room is finely coloured; for in this craft I wear the laurels, and this is the truth, and I can cite this poem, when it has been bound up, as evidence of this.

He continues with his social aptitude, his ability to distinguish wisdom from folly, shame from honour, the need for boldness or timidity and the better side to choose in a debate on love. He praises his discernment with regard to other men, especially those who wish him well or ill. 'If men of excellence find pleasure in my company, I am quite aware that I must in return desire their trust and their entertainment.'

> Conosc assatz
> Qu'atressi dey voler lor fi
> E lor solatz.   (19–21)

If the opening three stanzas were intended to gain the trust of his hearers, the rest of the poem is intended for their *solatz*, for the next three stanzas (IV–VI) represent a transitional stage describing Guilhem's skill at games, in which 'coloured' words open the way to the ribald dicing imagery in the last two stanzas and *envois*. To cap the jest Guilhem throws in a self-mocking hint of his sexual inadequacy, a common-place usage, possibly a corollary to the *gap*, which was taken up later by Raimbaut d'Aurenga.

Guilhem is also satirising his own methods of composition. He uses the jargon of a rhetoric of poetry, *bona color* (2), *obrador* (3), *mestier* (4), *auctor* (6) and *lassatz* (7), in order to beguile his listeners into expecting a serious song written at the highest level of his poetic technique, and this illusion persists for the first three stanzas. By then driving his subject-matter downhill below the level even of the *humilis* style[12] Guilhem excites amusement by his use of the grotesque and unexpected, but he also makes mock of too serious a conceit about poetic style and imagery. When he claims:

> Qu'ieu port d'ayselh mestier la flor (4),

he is not referring necessarily to his supremacy in the art of poetry but to his skill in the art of colouring his song with levels of meaning which he then binds together. In this poem he uses this art in an increasingly ribald way. At first his coloured words have a serious air; *partir un juec d'amor* means to have a courtly debate about love and merely hints at the levels of gaming and sexuality which will soon appear:

> Mas ben aya sel qui·m noyri,
> Que tan bo mestier m'eschari
> Que anc a negu non falhi;
> Qu'ieu sai jogar sobre coyssi
> A totz tocatz;
> Mais en say de nulh mo vezi,
> Qual que·m vejatz.   (22–8)

But blessed be the man who reared me and endowed me with such good skills that I never failed anyone; for I know how to play on a cushion (pillow) at all the winning games. I know more about them than anyone around me, whatever my outward appearance may seem to be.

He moves from his skill at the gaming table – with sensual undertones – to self-praise as master in the art of physical love. No one who seeks his advice will be turned away (32–5):

> Qu'ieu ai nom 'maiestre certa':
> Ja m'amigu'anueg no m'aura
> Que no·m vuelh'aver l'endema;
> Qu'ieu suy d'aquest mestier, so·m va,
> Tan ensenhatz
> Que be·n sai guazanhar mon pa
> En totz mercatz.   (36–42)

For I have the title of undisputed master. My love will never have me one night without wanting to have me the next day, for in this art I am, and I boast of it, so accomplished that I know very well how to earn my bread in all the market squares.

Guilhem has closed the rhetorical framework which began with praise of his poetic art, and he finishes with a sexual romp and bawdy puns on gaming and sex.

Guilhem's reputation for being *fatuus et lubricus . . . nimium-que jocundus* may also have been strengthened by his amusing poem *Farai un vers pos mi sonelh* (v) on the ancient theme of the traveller seduced by beautiful women.

Guilhem, travelling as a pilgrim in Auvergne, is greeted by Lady Agnes and Lady Ermessen:

> La una·m diz en son latin:
> 'E Dieus vos salf, don pelerin;
> Mout mi semblatz de bel aizin,
> Mon escient,[13]
> Mas trop vezem anar pel mon
> De folla gent.'   (19–24)

One of them said to me in her own speech: 'May God keep you, my lord pilgrim. By my troth, you seem to me to have a very fine character, for we see too many foolish (and immoral) people travelling about the world.'

The irony of this attack on folly is sharpened by the pilgrim's undisguised addiction to *foudatz* at the end of the poem and the lascivious intentions of the ladies when Guilhem feigns dumbness, muttering only 'Babariol, babariol, Babarian'. 'We have found what we are looking for. Sister, let us give him shelter for the love of God, for he is truly dumb and our plan will never be revealed by him' (31–6). Guilhem is warmed by their hospitality:

> A manjar mi deron capos,
> E sapchatz ac i mais de dos,
> E no·i ac cog ni cogastros,
>   Mas sol nos tres,
> E·l pans fo blancs e·l vins fo bos
>   E·l pebr' espes.   (43–8)

They gave me capons to eat, and I tell you there were more than two of these; and there was no cook there or scullion, but only we three, and the bread was white and the wine was good and the pepper thick,

a parody of the epic style of the *chanson de geste*.

As a trial of his dumbness a red cat *mal e felon* is to be dragged by the tail along his side. Guilhem waits in trepidation:

> N'Agnes anet per l'enujos,
> E fo granz et ab loncz guinhos:
> E eu, can lo vi entre nos,
>   Aig n'espavent,
> Q'a pauc non perdei la valor
>   E l'ardiment.   (55–60)

My lady Agnes went to fetch the wretched animal, and he was large and with long whiskers, and I, when I saw him among us, felt such terror that I almost lost both courage and boldness.

He survives the test – 'even if they had killed him, he would not have spoken' – and stays eight days with the ladies, accomplishing deeds of prowess which almost destroy him.[14]

In the full jocund mood of *foudatz* Guilhem ironically offers a progression from serious theme to bawdy deeds in three stages: an introduction in which he propounds a *sen* (I–II) (in the version in MS. N); his reception by the ladies (III–VIII); his torment and revenge, described in an Oliver-like *gap* (IX–XIV). As *envoi* he offers the throw-away jest about the *malaveg* or illness which then afflicted him.

The *sen* or serious theme which Guilhem lightly puts forward is the traditional rivalry in love between cleric and knight. He acts out in rudimentary form the topic of the knight who assumes a clerical disguise in order to seduce his lady, and in this double role he is the precursor of his namesake Guillaume de Poitiers in the Northern French romance of *Joufrois* and of the 'perfect' knight and lover, Guillem de Nevers, in *Flamenca*.

The light-hearted *Companho, faray un vers* (I) has already been mentioned. Part debate and part riddle, it is developed in an ordered sequence. The introduction (I and II) is followed by Guilhem's problem about the two horses (III and IV) whose qualities he amplifies (V, VI and VII) before calling for judgment from an arbiter and revealing his *foudatz* and the ribald explanation of his verse in the sudden twist in the last line of the poem – the three following lines, which occur in MS. E only, being a form of *tornada* or *envoi*.

This is the only example among Guilhem's extant poems in the burlesque genre which has no quasi-serious theme to serve as a cover for *foudatz*. The only hint of *sen* is contained in Guilhem's proverbial summing-up of his 'dilemma':

> Greu partir si fa d'amor qui la trob'a son talen (6).

It is hard to part from love, if one finds a love to one's liking.

Guilhem acknowledges this absence of a *razo* or theme:

> Et aura·i mais de foudaz no·y a de sen (2)

and since this poem has no recognisable *razo*, Guilhem explains his work in the next line:

> Et er totz mesclatz d'amor e de joy e de joven.

And the whole of it will be mixed with love and joy and youth.

If the expressions *amor*, *joy* and *joven* are given their 'courtly' sense, which will be discussed in a moment, this line appears to mean the opposite of line 2, and it has been suggested that this contrast was intentional.[15] On the other hand the line can be understood differently. *Mesclatz* has complex meanings. It can mean 'many-coloured' and it also has sexual connotations: Levy in *SWB*, V, 248, translates *se mesclar* as 'geschlechtlichen Umgang haben', meaning here perhaps 'adulterated'. *Amors* has a variety of meanings in early troubadour poetry and can be applied to Ovidian sensual love, as in Marcabru's *Dirai vos senes duptansa* (XVIII):

> Amors vai com la belluja
> Que coa·l fuec en la suja
> Art lo fust e la festuja,
> — Escoutatz! —
> E non sap vas qual part fuja
> Cel qui del fuec es gastatz.[16] (13–18)

Love acts like the spark that nourishes the fire in the soot; it burns the wood and the straw. Listen! And the man who is ravaged by the fire does not know in which direction to flee.

This may be the meaning of *amors* intended here by Guilhem. Joy means not only the joy to be found in love, but the positive pursuit of happiness, even 'the outgoing approach to life'. *Joven* can mean 'générosité d'âme' but also 'youthfulness, youthful high spirits and delight' (*SWB*, IV, 227–8).[17] Guilhem may be saying that the poem will be a coloured mixture of sensual love, of the search for happiness and youthful pleasure. It would appear to be more likely, however, if we consider Guilhem's stylistic methods, that he is deliberately turning upside-down the routine sequence of ideas associated with the presentation of a poetic theme or *razo*. Instead of *sen*, he offers *foudatz* (line 2) and, elaborating on this idea, instead of a serious theme with interwoven nuances of *foudatz*, he offers *foudatz* with an added mixture of *amor*, joy and *joven*. If *mesclatz* is used here with its pejorative meaning of 'adulterated', Guilhem can be seen to be jesting at the conventional acceptance of these courtly expressions as literary topics, as Raimbaut d'Aurenga jests about *gaug entier*, the perfect enjoyment of a distant, spiritual love, in *Lonc temps ai estat cubertz* (see p. 147), and, in this case, the terms *amor*, joy and *joven* must have been already established as literary and courtly clichés at the time that Guilhem IX was writing. In this poem Guilhem is burlesquing the genre of the *joc partit*, to which he refers in *Ben vuelh*, and possibly the courtly forerunners of the precious debates on love casuistry which, as we know from Andreas Capellanus, flourished at the court of Poitou in the reign of Guilhem's granddaughter, Eleanor of Aquitaine. That Guilhem was reluctant to accept *amors* as a courtly social convention is apparent from *Pus vezem* (VII, 7–18).

In the second stage of this song Guilhem beguiles his

audience with his apparently serious and obviously affectionate discussion of his 'problem'. Should he choose the refractory horse of the hills or the docile horse of the plains? Abruptly the 'debate' is closed, the 'riddle' solved. The horses are his mistresses, and this second stage is seen to be as bawdily ambiguous in its vocabulary as Guilhem's praise of his skill at gaming in the second stage of *Ben vuelh*.

Guilhem's other two works in this burlesque genre, *Compaigno, non puosc mudar* (II) and *Companho, tant ai agutz* (III), have a different construction and intention. The narrative progression through three stages from *sen* to *foudatz* is replaced by a mingling or *entrebescamen* of the two moods. In each poem Guilhem introduces the topic of the wife who is shut away by her husband, and assumes the role of a zealous and disinterested mentor or *castiador* (II, 10, and III, 13) who pleads in debating style against this social abuse.[18]

The two poems are markedly different in spite of their similarity of theme. In *Compaigno, non puosc mudar* (II), which is by far the less interesting work, Guilhem acts the advocate for a *domna* who has complained of the churlish ways of her *gardadors*. He argues with practical commonplaces, 'every guard must sleep', 'the lady removed from *proessa* will treat with *malvestatz*', 'deprived of a horse she will buy a palfrey', and he sums up his case in the last line with the proverb:

[C]hascus beuri'ans de l'aiga que·s laisses morir de ssei.

Everyone would drink water rather than let himself die of thirst.

Companho, tant ai agutz d'avols conres (III), on the other hand, which is of a quite different calibre, is a key poem for the understanding of Guilhem's burlesque methods. The intention behind this work has been misunderstood because of the thematic use of the word *cons*. A. Jeanroy left the poem untranslated and unexplained: 'La troisième défie l'analyse, même la plus voilée',[19] and H. Spanke condemned it as 'ganz obszön, wohl eigenstes Produkt des Autors'.[20] More recently, L. Pollmann[21] has suggested that *cons* in this context has the secondary meaning of *cunnus* in Horace (*Satires*, I, 2, 36), 'a married woman who is loved adulterously by a young man'. In support of this theory he quotes Gavaudan:

Vils es e cars, e muda trops senhors
Lo cons tafurs, deslials enganaire.

20

The base, disloyal and deceitful wife is cheap and dear and changes lords too often.[22]

Guilhem certainly uses the word with the secondary meaning of 'a married woman' and the poem can be interpreted accordingly on two levels. Marcabru, whom Gavaudan imitates repeatedly, also uses the word with this meaning, although with a different moralising intention, in *Quan l'aura doussana bufa* (XLII) :

> Car qui l'autrui con capusa
> Lo sieu tramet al mazel. (17–18)

For that man who slices the crust off the wife of another man, sends his own to the slaughter house.

Guilhem composed *Tant ai agutz* with a predominance of words ending in -om and -on; *cons, com, c'om, mon, sidons* and euphonically associated words *companho, conres, comte,* in the same way that he built the more elaborately constructed *Farai un vers de dreyt nien* (IV) on a foundation of *nien* and associated negatives.

The text of this poem is found only in MS. E, 114 :

I Companho, tant ai agutz d'avols conres
  Qu'ieu non puesc mudar non chan e que no·m pes,
  Enpero no vueill c'om sapcha mon afar de maintas res.

II E dirai vos m'entendensa de que es :
  No m'azauta cons gardatz ni gorc(s) ses peis,
  Ni gabars de malvatz homes c'om de lor faitz non agues.

III Senher Dieus, quez es del mon capdels e reis,
   Qui anc premiers gardet con, com non esteis?
   C'anc no fo mestiers ni garda c'a sidons estes sordeis.

IV Pero dirai vos de con cals es sa leis,
   Com sel hom que mal n'a fait e peitz n'a pres,
   Si c'autra res en merma qui·n pana, e cons en creis.

V E silh qui no volran creire mos casteis
  Anho vezer pres lo bosc en un deveis :
  Per un albre c'om hi tailla n'i naison [ho] dos ho treis.

VI E quam lo bocx es taillatz nais plus espes,
   E·l senher no·n pert son comte ni sos ses ;
   A revers planh hom la tala si·l dampn...

VII Tortz es cor... dan noi a...[23]

1 Comrades, I have had so much churlish company[24] that I cannot forbear to sing and feel vexed. Yet I do not desire that too much shall be known about my personal affairs.

II And I will tell you what theme I intend to put into my song: I dislike a married woman who is guarded, a mill race without fish and the vain boasting of wicked men from whom deeds are not to be expected.

III Lord God, you who are the guide and king of the world: 'How did it come about that the very first man who imprisoned a wife was not exterminated, for never was there a servant or guard who acted more basely towards his lady?'

IV Yet, as a man who has acted badly in this matter, and has suffered worse because of it, I will tell you about the natural law as it concerns a married woman: 'As other things when they are robbed decrease, so she increases.'

V And let those who will not believe my admonitions go and look in a private thicket, near a wood. For one tree that is cut down there, two or three grow up.

VI And when the wood is cut, it grows more thickly, and the lord who owns it does not lose thereby his capital or his interest; it is wrong to lament destruction if harm [is not sustained thereby].

Guilhem introduces his subject obliquely in this poem. With a paradoxical tilt at a conventional opening, 'I am impelled to sing and feel vexed', he puts his personal affairs to one side in order to introduce a separate theme, which he states in the style of the *enueg* or song about the vexations of life. This theme or *entendensa* of the poem is the topic of contrast between fruitfulness and sterility, and it is within this wider framework that Guilhem begins his case on behalf of the *cons gardatz* whom (and which) he likens to the mill-race without fish and to those men who are rich in vain words but sterile in deeds. Guilhem is using a topic which in a more elaborate form and with a different poetic intention was to dominate Marcabru's moralising poetry, and to provide also a basis for his concept of *Fin'Amors*. Marcabru compares the boastful and unproductive layabouts around him to the elder and the willow tree which promise much but achieve nothing:

> Fuelhs e flors paron de pomier,
> Son al fruchar sautz'e saucs,   (III, 13–14)

They appear to be the leaf and blossom of the apple tree, but when it comes to the fruiting they are the willow and the elder.

and in *Al prim comens de l'ivernaill* (IV):

> Joves homes de bel semblan
> Vei per Malvestat deceubutz;
> Que van gaban

> Dizo, mil essais encogan:
> 'Farem qan lo temps er floritz',
> Mas lai reman lo gabs e·l brutz. (19–24)

I see young men of fair appearance deceived by Wickedness, for they keep boasting and they say, notching up a thousand projects: 'We will act when the time is ripe', but the boasting and the noise goes no further than that.

Whereas Marcabru is serious, Guilhem is writing with a mainly burlesque intention, and Marcabru, who found patronage at Poitiers at the court of Guilhem's successor, may be criticising this light-hearted attitude of *foudatz* in *Al son desviat, chantaire* (v):

> De nien sui chastiaire
> E de foudat sermonaire. (31–2)

I censure the theme of nothingness[25] and I reprove the theme of folly.

The theme which Guilhem chooses to present in this poem is a topic of *sen* and contains within itself the Aristotelian principle of living according to one's needs, abilities and calling in life which, as we shall see with Marcabru (p. 91), is at the basis of the troubadour concept of *mesura*. This topic of contrast between fruitfulness and sterility was a fit subject for sermons, for philosophical argument and for discussion in courtly circles, and Guilhem burlesques this type of debate by his ambiguous use of the theme of the *cons gardatz* and the pseudo-learned level of his argument.

Guilhem is composing in rhetorical style, on a light-hearted note of *foudatz*. As authority for his case he cites himself, his wicked ways, and, with an ironical jest, the suffering his behaviour has caused him (11). With this 'authority' he justifies his presentation of the natural law (*leis*) of his subject which he compares to the trees in a private thicket which grow thickly when cut. As the tree, if it is pruned, reproduces itself, so will the *domna* develop socially and reproduce if she is exposed freely to society. The image of the lord counting the trees in his domain and finding no diminution in number is probably intended as a jest about illegitimate children, a theme which later provoked Marcabru to attacks on the amorality of the nobility. Guilhem concludes his case with proverbial summings-up in line 16, and in mutilated form in line 19.

In these poems, which A. Jeanroy placed in the category of works of 'inspiration sensuelle', Guilhem's main intention was to entertain his audience, and this he accomplished by creating a burlesque effect in which ribaldry marked an abrupt and amusing transition from apparent *sen* to extreme *foudatz*. For a moralist like Marcabru *foudatz* represented sinful and irregular frivolity and in his poetry it has the connotation of wanton behaviour, but in the courtly society of the South in the last part of the twelfth century, *foudatz*, although it was acknowledged as a *joglaresc* quality, was appreciated as an antidote to excessive wisdom or seriousness. The man who was *trop senatz* suffered in reputation. About 1200 Raimon de Miraval gave this advice to Forniers who wanted to become a *joglar*, the minstrel who sang the songs which had been composed and set to music by the troubadour:

> Joglars siatz
> E meitadatz
> Sens ab foudatz;
> C'om trop senatz
> Entre·ls prezatz
> Non val gaire.[26]

Be a *joglar* and mix acts of wisdom with acts of folly, for a man who is too wise has little worth among men of high reputation.

Guiraut de Bornelh, probably under the influence of his patron Raimbaut d'Aurenga, sings about *foudatz*, but as a topic which he treats in a literary fashion. In his song, *Un sonet fatz malvatz e bo* (ed. A. Kolsen, LIII, p. 336), he declares that excess of *sen* and learning has brought upon him a *foudatz* which dislocates his actions and makes him turn the world upside down:

> Detorn me vai e deviro
> Foldatz, que mais sai de Cato.
> Devas la coa·lh vir lo fre,
> S'altre plus fols no m'en rete;
> C'aital sen me fi ensenhar
> Al prim qu'era·m fai foleiar.   (19–24)

Folly goes around and about me, I who know more than Cato. I turn the bridle to its tail if I am not held back by another who is still more foolish, for in the beginning I had myself taught such wisdom that it now makes me act like a fool.

Raimbaut d'Aurenga on the other hand was as serious a

poet as Guilhem IX and also as naturally inclined to light-hearted *foudatz* and to the realisation of the vanity of life, that 'Tot es niens'. At his death in 1173 Guiraut de Bornelh praised his wisdom and learning in the *planh* or funeral lament, *S'anc iorn agui ioi ni solatz*:

> A! bels amics ben essenhatz,
>   nescis als fatz
> e duitz e savis als membratz! (25–7)

Ah! my fair and truly learned friend, ignorant in the eyes of fools, gifted and wise in the view of men of sense.

and Guiraut continues:

> Ar est morta bella foudatz,
>   e iocx de datz
> e dons e domneys oblidatz.[27] (41–3)

Now is fair folly dead, and games of dice, and gifts and wooing forgotten.

Raimbaut had gaily accepted the title of *joglar* which his *foudatz* earned him:

> E soy fols cantayre cortes
> Tan c'om m'en apela ioglar,

And I am a foolish courtly singer so that they call me *joglar*.

and this in a poem, *Escotatz, mas no say que s'es* (ed. W. T. Pattison, XXIV, p. 153), in which he burlesques courtly lyric genres and clichés and throws in for good measure a ribald reference to lady Ayma.

It is in the light of the *foudatz* and mockery in the poetry of Raimbaut d'Aurenga and of the Monk of Montaudon in his dialogues with God,[28] and the mannered bawdiness of Arnaut Daniel, Dante's paragon of love poets, in his *Pois Raimons e·n Trucs Malecs*[29] that Guilhem's burlesque poems should be judged. They are the forerunners of a separate genre in troubadour poetry and their purpose and thematic treatment should not be judged by the standards of his love lyrics. Guilhem is not an isolated precursor writing in a rough and soldierly style,[30] nor is he necessarily the bridge which led the world of knighthood from its jests and manly ways of thought to the phenomenon of love.[31] Guilhem's poems of *foudatz* with their irony and bawdiness exist as a contrast to his own love poetry, as happens also with Raimbaut d'Aurenga and Arnaut

Daniel, and there is no proper evidence of any progression by Guilhem from a burlesque poetry characterised by *foudatz* to a refined form of love lyric.[32] Beneath the jests of the burlesque poetry Guilhem reveals a sophisticated intelligence, acquaintance with Ovid[33] and possibly Martial, and a humorously ironical attitude to themes and rhetorical devices which were to become traditional with later troubadours, and especially with Marcabru, but which must have been already established at the time that he was writing. *Foudatz* in a courtly context is the quality of the court fool or jester who, being part of the court but outside it, is able to startle its conventional attitudes with the unexpected remark or reversal of mood, and, as we have just seen, Raimon de Miraval's advice to Forniers shows that this aptitude was also expected from the successful *joglar*. It was certainly present a hundred years before Miraval in the character and poetry of Guilhem IX, who belongs to a wide vernacular tradition of burlesque writing which was probably of both *joglaresc* and clerical inspiration[34] and which throughout the twelfth century co-existed in the South of France in a minor role with the love lyric, but which in the North provided a main source of inspiration for many poets of the twelfth and thirteenth centuries, among whom may be counted the unknown poet of the *Lai dou lecheor*,[35] the *jongleur* Gautier le Leu,[36] the authors of the early *Renart* stories[37] and the early poets of the 'Confrérie des Ardents' at Arras.

That Guilhem IX and other early troubadours were aware of the existence of a common rhetoric for their poetry is indicated by their use of terms such as *entendensa, razos, colors, lassar, entrebescar, chan esmerar,* and *son afinar*; words can be coloured with several meanings and the levels of meaning in a poem can either be woven together (*entrebescatz*) into the texture of the stanza or disposed in an orderly progression and bound up (*lassatz*), so that the end matches the beginning. In the context of this approach to composition it is possible to discern in their songs three planes of love, a worldly plane of physical desire which may be set within the confines of an embryonic courtly society, a plane of dream-like imagining in which the poet finds an illusory joy, and a 'transcendental' plane which offers him a supreme joy from which good results flow.

Although Guilhem IX uses the topics of *sen* and *foudatz*

extensively in his burlesque poems and either interweaves these contrasts or disposes them in a systematic progression, we may see, if we turn to his love lyrics, that he approaches love essentially on these three levels of experience and that he does not normally combine them but treats each one separately in separate poems.

The physical love which can be desired, hoped for, shared and enjoyed, inspires him in *Ab la dolchor del temps novel* (x).

I Ab la dolchor del temps novel
Foillo li bosc, e li aucel
Chanton chascus en lor lati   3
Segon lo vers del novel chan;
Adonc esta ben c'om s'aisi
D'acho don hom a plus talan.   6

II De lai don plus m'es bon e bel
Non vei mesager ni sagel,
Per que mos cors non dorm ni ri,   9
Ni no m'aus traire adenan,
Tro qe sacha ben de la fi
S'el'es aissi com eu deman.   12

III La nostr'amor vai enaissi
Com la branca de l'albespi
Qu'esta sobre l'arbre tremblan   15
La nuoit, a la ploja ez al gel,
Tro l'endeman, que·l sols s'espan
Per las fueillas verz e·l ramel.   18

IV Enquer me membra d'un mati
Que nos fezem de guerra fi,
E que·m donet un don tan gran,   21
Sa drudari'e son anel:
Enquer me lais Dieus viure tan
C'aja mas manz soz so mantel!   24

V Qu'eu non ai soing d'estraing lati
Que·m parta de mon Bon Vezi,
Qu'eu sai de paraulas com van   27
Ab un breu sermon que s'espel,
Que tal se van d'amor gaban,
Nos n'avem la pessa e·l coutel.   30

With the sweetness of this new season the woods come into leaf and the birds sing, each in its own language according to the verse of the new song. Now is it right that a man should approach that which he most desires.

From there whence comes my greatest joy I see neither messenger nor sealed letter, and so my heart neither sleeps nor laughs. Nor dare I undertake anything until I know truly whether the end [of this quarrel] is as I want it to be.

Our love is like the hawthorn branch which stays trembling on the tree at night, in the rain and frost, until the next day when the sun spreads through the green leaves and the boughs.

I still remember one morning when we put an end to our warring, and she gave me so great a gift, her love and her ring. May God let me still live long enough to have my hands beneath her cloak.

For I do not care about the uncouth talk which may part me from my Good Neighbour, for I know how words go around and start from a short phrase which spreads. For people of that sort boast emptily about love. We have the piece [of bread] and the knife [to cut it with].

In this light and pleasing poem, which attracted Ezra Pound, we have the situation of distant love or *amor de lonh*, which Jaufre Rudel later developed. In this case the lady has accepted her lover but they are separated by physical distance and their quarrel. The imagery of the blossom and the light which scatters the dark is used again by Guilhem in *Mout jauzens* (IX), but with the deeper symbolism of a refining and improving power. In *Ab la dolchor*, the main improvement which the poet desires in his situation is to hold his lady beneath her cloak (24) and enjoy their physical love (30). Let the gossips and vain boasters go their way, he and his lady have the means to enjoy the reality of love, and should do so (25–30). This switch from delicacy of feeling and hope conveyed by the image of the hawthorn to the rough desire of the last lines (24–30) is characteristic of Guilhem, and intentional. It is introduced in the last line of the fourth stanza and amplified in the fifth and last stanza, together with his throw-away jest at those who talk but never do.

Farai chansoneta nueva (VIII) is also concerned with the hope of a shared physical love, but there is some uncertainty, for technical reasons, about the attribution of this poem to Guilhem.[38] In feudal fashion the poet makes submission to his lady. His desire for her – she is whiter than ivory and he adores no other – will kill him if he does not receive a kiss from her. To the distance imposed in courtly fashion by the *domna* ('it appears that you want to become a nun'), the poet opposes the delights of shared love:

Qual pro y auretz, s'ieu m'enclostre
E no·m retenetz per vostre?
Totz lo joys del mon es nostre,
Dompna, s'amduy nos amam.   (25–8)

What will you gain if I shut myself in a cloister and you do not retain me

28

as your servant? All the joy in the world will be ours, my lady, if we both love each other.

Pus vezem (VII) is an important poem, for Guilhem appears to reject the conventional world around him, in doubt and uncertainty. In the spring, he says, each man should enjoy that particular *Jois* which makes him rejoice:

> Ben deu quascus lo joy jauzir
> Don es jauzens. (5–6)

His own happiness from *Amors* is small or non-existent, but he does not deserve more, although Love swiftly gives great joy to those who conform to its orders:

> D'Amor non dey dire mas be.
> Quar no n'ai petit ni re?
> Quar ben leu plus no m'en cove;
> Pero leumens
> Dona gran joy qui be·n mante
> Los aizimens. (7–12)

About Love I should not say anything but good. Why do I not have from it a small happiness or anything at all? Perhaps because anything more does not befit me. Yet swiftly does Love give great joy to the man who upholds its precepts.

Guilhem has too many individual doubts to count himself among the followers of Love:

> A totz jorns m'es pres enaissi
> Qu'anc d'aquo qu'amiey non jauzi,
> Ni o faray ni anc no fi.
> Qu'az esciens
> Fas mantas res que·l cor me di:
> Tot es niens. (13–18)

Always has it befallen me that I never had joy from that which I loved, nor will I do so nor have I ever done so. For with my mind I do many things when my heart says to me: All is vanity.

Guilhem repeats and amplifies his complaint in the next three stanzas:

> Per tal n'ai meyns de bon saber
> Quar vuelh so que no puesc aver. (19–20)

It is because I desire what I cannot have that I have less pleasure.

Guilhem's lack of success in Love is caused by this desire for that which he cannot have and his awareness of the vanity of things, whereas the devotee of Love must be patient and submissive to Love, compliant to society, obedient to many people and courtly in word and deed (21–36). Guilhem appears to reject *Amors* as an embryonic, regulated system of courtly wooing. He is dissatisfied with it and the small amount of *Jois* it affords. He stands to one side and looks for the *Jois* which is the particular reward of each individual man, a *Jois* which may make him forget that 'tot es niens'. It is in the context of Guilhem's disenchantment with *Amors* in this poem, his implicit reluctance to accept its precepts and 'be obedient to many people', and his desire to possess the unattainable, that *Farai un vers de dreyt nien* (IV) must be considered.

Discussion of *Farai un vers* has been largely concerned with whether the poem is a *devinalh* or a burlesque, a *fatrasie* or *gap*, or whether it is a serious love lyric. That Guilhem had the form of the *devinalh* or 'riddle poem' in mind is clear from his enigmatic style of writing and from a comparison between this poem and the anonymous *devinalh*, *Sui e no suy* (P.C. 461, 226), published by C. Appel with its solution *Fuy e no suy senes peccatz* (Chres., 6th edn, pp. 82–3). A *devinalh*, this anonymous poet says, can be interpreted in a definite way, but this should not exclude other meanings:

> Qui aquestz digz estiers enten,
> si mielhs hi dis, non lo·n repren,
> quar s'a trops sens una razos,
> mout m'es mieller quan quecx es bos.
>
> (C. Appel, Chres, LXIIb, 25–8)

If anyone understands these words in another way and speaks of better meanings than I do, I do not blame him for this, for if a theme has many meanings it gives me much more pleasure when each of these meanings is good.

Although this enigmatic quality would appeal to Guilhem, and he must have had the form of the *devinalh* in mind when he called for a *contraclau* or solution to his problem, this poem is much more than a riddle poem. The moods of *sen* and *foudatz* are also intermingled in it, for the first part of each stanza is generally concerned with Guilhem's dilemma and the second part is a form of throw-away jest with a hint of irony such as can be found in the poetry of Villon or Heine, a mockery of self which is implicit in the juxtaposition of the poet's imagined, idealised longing and the rough 'reality' of everyday life. This alternation of mood has been related to the device of the qufl, which in the stanza-structure of the Hispano-Arabic muwaššah and zağal likewise transfers the audience abruptly to a different plane of thought.[39] Such swift transitions, however, are also part of the 'rhetorical' tradition of medieval poetry and much poetry by the earlier troubadours is constructed on a basis of contrast, antithesis and paradox. The foudatz in this poem lies in the reversion from fantasy to worldly reality, and the occasional touch of ribaldry such as the sexually coloured images of the horse (6) and the skeleton key (42). Foudatz sharpens the vanity of Guilhem's attachment to an imagined love and it affirms his freedom from subservience to this love. This ironical use of foudatz, which is a part of Guilhem's uncertain and restless character, in no way dominates the poem, which is not a parody or a jest but a love lyric in a genre entirely different from his poetry of burlesque inspiration.

It is constructed on a foundation of negatives and the idea of superficial negation is fundamental to its theme. The first line, Farai un vers de dreyt nien 'I will compose a poem about just nothing at all', has a paradoxical double meaning, since it is through the negation of himself and the world around him that Guilhem can escape to the reality of his imagination. Guilhem tries to define this reality by the antithetical device of describing what the poem is not about. It is not about himself or other people or Amors or courtly concepts, and here he mixes in the bawdiness of foudatz, for 'it was composed while I slept on a horse' (1–6).

> Farai un vers de dreyt nien :
> Non er de mi ni d'autra gen,
> Non er d'amor ni de joven,
>   Ni de ren au,
> Qu'enans fo trobatz en durmen
>   Sobre chevau.   (1–6)

He exists neither physically nor socially; he has no identity (7), no feelings (8), or courtly relationship with a lady or with society (estrayns ni privatz, 9). His mind is removed from its physical shell and he does not know when he is asleep or awake unless he is told; he hovers between the planes of real life and imagination and dreaming. His explanation of his withdrawn state is the point at which he turns from reality to his imaginary love:

> Per pauc no m'es lo cor partitz
> D'un dol corau   (15–16)

'My heart is almost split by a heartfelt grief', and then the throw-away line 'And by Saint Martial I care not a jot' (17–18). He is sick and fears to die; he will seek a doctor, without knowing what sort of doctor can cure his 'sickness of the heart':

> Bos metges er si·m pot guerir
> Ia non sia mau.[40]   (23–4)

He will be a good doctor if he can cure me although I am not ill.

He escapes to thoughts of his *amigua*:

> Amigu'ai ieu, no sai qui s'es,
> Qu'anc non la vi, si m'ajut fes;
> Ni·m fes que·m plassa ni que·m pes,
>   Ni no m'en cau,
> Qu'anc non ac Norman ni Frances
>   Dins mon ostau.   (25–30)

I have a lady love, I know not who she is, for I never saw her, by my faith, nor did she do anything to please or vex me, nor do I worry about this, for there was never any Norman or Frenchman in my dwelling.

In his contemplation of this ideal and unknown beloved of his imagination, his world of courtly vexation and suspicion about his *domna* is removed. The *ostau*, the dwelling in which he entertains the *amigua*, is his imagination and heart (*ostau* has this extended meaning), and no drunken, gluttonous or sensual Norman or Northern Frenchman is allowed in there.

He continues:

> Anc non la vi et am la fort,
> Anc no n'aic dreyt ni no·m fes tort;
> Quan non la vey, be m'en deport,
>   No·m pretz un jau,
> Qu'ie·n sai gensor et bellazor,
>   E que mais vau.   (31–6)

I have never seen her and I love her greatly. I never had to uphold my rights against her and she never did me a wrong. I am quite happy that I do not see her, and I do not care about this at all, for I know a lady more gracious and more beautiful than she and whose worth is greater.

Not only does his *amigua* cause him no social worries or courtly or feudal disputes about individual rights and wrongs, unlike a real *domna* she causes him no pain when he does not see her. He can enjoy the thought of her at will, for she is always available. In the last three lines of the stanza he switches back from imagined *amigua* to real *domna* and he introduces this change with the line:

No·m pretz un jau (34)

I don't care a jot [marigold] for this,

which is almost identical with the line which precedes the escape to his *amigua* from the *dol corau* inflicted by the real *domna*. This repetition signals the two crises in the poem, the switch into and out of the poet's contemplation of the imagined *amigua*.

The *domna* to whom his thoughts return is addressed in a stanza which occurs in MS. E only and was rejected by A. Jeanroy: 'Ce couplet fort plat, et qui revient sur des idées déjà exprimées, me paraît apocryphe' (ed. p. 33).

> No sai lo luec ves on s'esta
> Si es en pueg ho en pla,
> Non aus dire lo tort que m'a
> Abans m'en cau;
> E peza·m be quar sai reman,
> C[ar] aitan vau.

[MS. remanc aitan]

I do not know the place where she is staying, whether in the hills or on the plain, I do not dare to tell of the wrong she does me – rather do I keep silent about it. And it grieves me to remain here, for such is my lot.

Unlike Jaufre Rudel, Guilhem IX is left with grievous thoughts of the distant *domna* who has wronged him beyond the power of words to express, and possibly inflicted on him the *dol corau* for which he sought solace. If this last stanza is authentic, Guilhem IX is accepting that *tot es niens*, that his release from reality to imagination is temporary and episodic, that imagined happiness, always available, is incomplete and inferior. The *amigua*, whom he can never see, cannot supplant the real *domna* who is *gensor et bellazor*.

This poem has been interpreted in many ways: as a riddle which can be solved by a key-word;[41] a dream and riddle combined;[42] a riddle analogous to the *fatrasie* or *coq-à-l'âne*;[43] a *gap*, *une pure plaisanterie* and a *fatrasie*;[44] a burlesque on a tradition of writing love poetry to an unimaginable lady;[45] a mixture of profane and mystical love aroused by poetical inspiration;[46] a dream vision of the type *vigilans dormire*;[47] a translation to the imagination of an ill-defined passion under the influence of Augustinian thought;[48] a mingling of mystical tension, poetic self-consciousness and knightly thought;[49] a love lyric on the theme of imagined love in which the inspiration can be related to Augustinian thought.[50]

When Guilhem repeats the phrase *no sai* in order to confess his ignorance of his personal, emotional and social identity, and turns for refuge to an imaginary *amigua* who gives him an illusory assurance of contentment because she has no identity and cannot afflict him with the tribulations of love in everyday life, he is following a pattern of religious, philosophical and learned thought, especially the idea of the negation of the physical in favour of the spiritual life, which was already apparent in the soliloquies of St Augustine.[51] The nature of Nothingness was also a subject of medieval discussion, and Fredegisus the pupil and successor of Alcuin had written a speculative treatise on this, *De nihilo et tenebris*, which provoked a counter-attack from Agobard.

It is improbable that Guilhem and his audience were unaware of these philosophical ideas and controversies, in view of the traditional links which had existed between the court at Poitiers and the school of Chartres since the days of Fulbert.[52] In *Companho, tant ai agutz d'avols contres* Guilhem mocks with light irony the formal methods of debating a learned theme. What is his intention with *Farai un vers de dreyt nien*? Is the poem a burlesque of philosophical disputation? Or does it represent a level of self-doubt and self-questioning leading to the knowledge that all is vanity, that one does not know?

The superficial theme is the contrast between the tribulation of love in real life and the transitory joy of imagined love, and this theme is lightened with switches into burlesque *foudatz* which also hint that nothing counts, for life is a riddle. In the same way that he uses irony and *foudatz* to limit and control his imaginings, so he uses words with accepted learned connotations to indicate universal themes of self-questioning and nothingness. The phrases *no sai*, which is used repeatedly, *no sai qui s'es* and *nien* can be related to the *nescio, nescio quid (quis)* and the theme of nothingness of medieval debate. Guilhem's intention in using such words may have been partly humorous, but it was also serious because it provided his theme of frustration in love with the deeper meaning of frustration with life. Guilhem said that his poem was about *dreyt nien*, and this is true in two ways. It describes the nothingness of Guilhem's physical entity as he flies to his imagination from the *dol corau* and his social and physical life, and it expresses the wider theme of *vanitas vanitatum* which he describes with his *Tot es niens* 'everything is nothingness' in *Pus vezem* (VII). If we accept these two levels of meaning, the *dol corau* which afflicts the poet may be caused by the frustration of profane love and also by the vain search for meaning and happiness in life, the search for 'the unattainable beauty, the thought of which was pain'. Jaufre Rudel uses this method to indicate a wider meaning which exists, not in place of but in company with his main theme of a profane love which is either real or imagined.

The lover who loses awareness of his identity through excess of grief or joy becomes a commonplace in courtly poetry and romance. Bernart de Ventadorn sings of the lark which 'forgets itself, and lets itself fall for the sweetness that goes to its heart'. In the lays of Marie de France, Lanval falls into reverie in his sleep immediately before he discovers the beloved, the fairy mistress, and in *Yonec* the disillusioned wife falls into a daydream of romance immediately before the appearance of her new lover. The lover may daydream about his distant lady, like Chrétien's Lancelot who, thinking of Guinevere and oblivious to knightly challenge from his adversary, rides into the river or nearly falls out of the tower, and Perceval who, leaning on his spear and gazing at the three drops of blood in the snow, is oblivious of his everyday identity and of Arthur's messengers. The lover, like Jaufre Rudel, may also find joy 'waking or dreaming' in imagined love with his *domna*.

Raimbaut de Vaqueiras calls this imagined love *per cuda* love, and mocks it in his *Kalenda maya*:

> Con er perduda
> ni m'er renduda
> donna, s'enanz non l'ai aguda?
> Qe drutz ni druda
> non es per cuda.   (ed. J. Linskill, XV, 29–33)

How shall my lady be lost to me or given back to me, if I have not had her already, for a man is not a lover, nor a lady his beloved through imagining it to be so.

Bernart de Ventadorn describes his lady's charms in *A! tantas bonas chansos* (ed. C. Appel, VIII, 36–9) and also uses the phrase *per cuda*:

> que sos cors es bels e bos
> e blancs sotz la vestidura
> (eu non o dic mas per cuda).

For her body is beautiful and pleasing and white beneath her clothes. I say this only on the evidence of my imagination.

The term *cuidars* in connexion with this *per cuda* description of the lady has been equated with the *cogitatio* defined by Alcher of Clairvaux in *De spiritu et anima* (chap. X): 'Facies siquidem hominis et nobis forinsecus nota est, et in memoria nostra habet imaginem suam, incorporalem quidem, sed corpori similem' (Migne, PL, xl, col. 786). Cuidar[53] undoubtedly has the meaning of 'thinking erroneously', and it seems probable that in troubadour poetry it came to be used as a technical term for an imaginary, illusory vision, a form of waking dream.

It is this level of imagined and dream love that Guilhem transcends in *Mout jauzens me prenc en amar* (IX) in which he conjoins the themes of a supreme *Jois* with a supreme *domna*. The *razo* of the poem, *Jois* crystallised in a physical reality, is introduced in the first stanza:

> E pus en joy vuelh revertir
> Ben dey, si puesc, al mielhs anar,
> Quar mielhs orna·m estiers cujar,
> Qu'om puesca vezer ni auzir.   (3–6)

And since I wish to return to joy, I must go to the best, if I can, for the best one whom one can see or hear, adorns me,[54] and not in my imagination.

Mielhs is enigmatic, for it can refer not only to the best joy, the *summum bonum* which he seeks (4), but also to the *domna* as the source of this joy (4 and 5). Longing and reality, which were separate in *Farai un vers* (IV), are now conjoined; his lady is all excellence in *physical* reality (6) and *estiers cujar* implies that no imagination or fantasy has any part in his picture of her.

The construction of the poem offers a progression of ideas. Guilhem describes the supremacy of his *Jois* in stanza II:

> Mas si anc nulhs joys poc florir,
> Aquest deu sobre totz granar
> E part los autres esmerar,
> Si cum sol brus jorns esclarzir. (9–12)

But if ever any joy could blossom, this joy must bear seed more than any others and shine out beyond the others, as the dark day is wont to grow light.

This *Jois* must blossom and bear the seed of a fruitfulness which, as the progressive references to light show – florir 'blossom', *esmerar* 'shine forth' or 'grow more refined', and *esclarzir* – would be free of the imperfection associated with the idea of murky, sombre daylight (*brus jorns*). In this use of nature imagery to indicate fruitfulness and of bright light to show goodness and benefits to the lover, Guilhem is using unobtrusively a descriptive device which Marcabru, among others, was to use effectively, and in the power of this *Jois* to create light, to refine, to perfect and be fruitful, he is anticipating Marcabru's concept of *Fin'Amors*.

But this joy is transcendental. It cannot be formulated by lust or desire, by thoughts or meditation, for Guilhem looks beyond the level of imaginative experience as he does in *Farai un vers de dreyt nien*:

> Anc mais no poc hom faissonar
> Co's, en voler ni en dezir
> Ni en pensar ni en cossir;
> Aitals joys no pot par trobar... (13–16)

Never could a man picture to himself what this joy is, through his longing, his desire, his thoughts or meditation. Such joy can find no equal...

Guilhem describes this ultimate *Jois* by listing its benefits and, in true medieval antithesis, the ill effects which are produced by its opposite, 'the sorrow that his lady may cause':

> Per son joy pot malautz sanar,
> E per sa ira sas morir
> E savis hom enfolezir
> E belhs hom sa beutat mudar
> E·l plus cortes vilanejar
> E totz vilas encortezir. (25–30)

Through the joy she inspires the sick man can be healed, and through the sorrow she may cause the healthy man can die, the wise man can grow foolish and the handsome man lose his looks and the most courtly man become churlish and the churl become courtly.

37

If the lady withholds this joy, the world turns upside-down; if she bestows it she can cure the man who is sick in body and spirit. Guilhem makes explicit with biblical imagery this double meaning of *malautz* which he hints at in *Farai un vers de dreyt nien*.

> Pus hom gensor no·n pot trobar
> Ni huelhs vezer ni boca dir,
> A mos ops la vuelh retenir
> Per lo cor dedins refrescar
> E per la carn renovellar,
> Que no puesca envellezir. (31–6)

Since one cannot find a more gracious lady, nor eyes see, nor lips tell, I desire to retain her for my very own, to refresh the heart within me and renew my flesh so that it may not grow old.

Guilhem had referred to physical renewal earlier in this poem:

> E deu hom mais cent ans durar
> Qui·l joy de s'amor pot sazir. (23–4)

And a man must live on for a hundred years who can gain possession of the joy that comes from loving her.

Now he turns to the healing of the sickness of mind, heart and spirit. In order to win this healing power he will become a courtly lover and obey the conventions of *Amors*:

> Si·m vol mi dons s'amor donar,
> Pres suy del penr'e del grazir
> E del celar e del blandir
> E de sos plazers dir e far
> E de sos pretz tener en car
> E de son laus enavantir. (37–42)

If my lady will give me her love, I am ready to accept it and show my gratitude by concealing it and by wooing with fair words, seeking to please her in words and deeds, cherishing all those things which uphold her reputation and furthering her praise.

In archetypal courtly fashion he is too timid to tell her of his love:

> Ren per autruy non l'aus mandar,
> Tal paor ay qu'ades s'azir,
> Ni ieu mezeys, tan tem falhir,
> No l'aus m'amor fort assemblar;
> Mas elha·m deu mo mielhs triar,
> Pus sap qu'ab lieys ai a guerir. (43–8)

I do not dare to send a message to her by any one else, so much do I fear that she may grow angry forthwith, nor do I myself, so much do I fear that I may fail, dare to bring my love clearly before her. But she must choose what will be my supreme happiness, since she knows that it is with her that I must be healed.

This *mielhs*, the *summum bonum*, is the supreme *Jois* that Guilhem seeks, and *Amors* and courtly service are the means by which he can find it. He seeks rejuvenation, to be *joven* in body and spirit, and to be healed of his self-doubts about himself and love, and the nothingness in life (the *tot es niens*). To gain this he offers a contract, which he sees in feudal terms. He offers courtly service and advancement in courtly society to the *domna*, whose reputation he will cherish and further, and in return he seeks to enter into possession of the joy that she can give, and to retain her and her beneficial effects for his own needs. Guilhem rejects any mood of dream longing (*estiers cujar*, 5) and seeks an ultimate happiness in a shared and fulfilled love which will bring real advantage in everyday life to the *domna* and himself. His reluctant compromise with *Amors* and courtly convention is apparent in the line *A mos ops la vuelh retenir*, for the feudal term *retener* is used as a commonplace by later troubadours in speaking of the lady who retains a suitor in her service, and it also occurs with this meaning in *Farai chansoneta*, which has been attributed to Guilhem.

A courtly society and a doctrine of courtly love undoubtedly existed when Guilhem IX was composing. He was influenced by these and he uses words of courtly terminology in a way that suggests that they were already current: *jois, jovens, solatz, pretz,* and the concept of *valors, connoissensa* and the *lauzengiers*. In *Mout jauzens* Guilhem accepts these ideas, perhaps because of the growing strength of courtly fashion or the insistence of his courtly *domna*. Guilhem hopes to use *Amors* and his *domna* as a bastion against mental doubt and physical decay but he lacks the full and ready submission of the *fis amaire* to his lady. He desires the joys of shared love, and that the lady shall belong to him, and he to her. He also sees the conflict between *Jois*, or the impulse to find one's own individual happiness, and *Amors*, the power which demands submission to a social code of courtly behaviour. This conflict, which is resolved in the poetry of Raimon de Miraval with the triumph of *Amors*, becomes a major theme in troubadour poetry of the twelfth century.

Guilhem has the quality of the great troubadours who keep in view the wider truths beyond the restricted circle of courtly experience and *Amors*. He realises the importance of a balance between *sen* 'sense' and *foudatz* 'apparent folly which mocks conventional response' and he jests at the niceties of learned debate and learned themes such as the conflict between fecundity and sterility. But the underlying *sen* remains. He is aware of philosophical and religious thought on the subject of the identity of the 'self', the 'reality' of nothingness and the rejection of the physical and social state in order to live the life of the spirit. His heart tells him that all is nothingness and vanity, but he continues to search hopefully for the *Jois* that will 'heal' him.

In *Pos de chantar* (xi), which he composed under the fear of death, possibly in 1111 or 1112 when he was lying seriously wounded after the siege of Taillebourg, he describes his personal faith in the life hereafter and his joy in the life he has led. In the first half of the poem he fears that his son is too young to defend his lands against the vassals whom Guilhem has fought for so long. He continues:

Merce quier a mon compagnon
S'anc li fi tort qu'il m'o perdon;
Et ieu prec en Jesu del tron
Et en romans et en lati.   24

De proeza e de joi fui,
Mais ara partem ambedui;
Et eu irai m'en a scellui
On tut peccador troban fi.   28

Mout ai estat cuendes e gais,
Mas nostre Seigner no·l vol mais;
Ar non puesc plus soffrir lo fais,
Tant soi aprochatz de la fi.   32

Tot ai guerpit cant amar sueill,
Cavalaria et orgueill;
E pos Dieu platz, tot o acueill,
E prec li que·m reteng'am si.   36

Toz mos amics prec a la mort
Que vengan tut e m'onren fort,
Qu'eu ai avut joi e deport
Loing e pres et e mon aizi.   40

Aissi guerpisc joi e deport
E vair e gris e sembeli.   (xi, 21–42)

I seek from my comrade the boon of pardon if I ever did him any wrong. And I pray to Jesus in Heaven in romance and in latin.

I have belonged to prowess and joy but now we part from each other; And I will go away to Him with whom all sinners find peace.

I have been greatly joyous and gay, but our Lord does not desire this any more; now I can suffer the burden no longer, so close have I come to the end.

I have given up all that I was wont to love, knighthood and pride; and since this pleases God I welcome it and pray to Him to keep me with Him as his follower.

I pray to all my friends that at my death they may all come and do me great honour, for I have had joy and delight both far and near and in my own home.

So do I give up joy and delight and brightly shimmering furs and grey and sable.

2

Jaufre Rudel and love from afar

THE ROMANTIC LEGEND of Jaufre Rudel's distant love for
a fair princess and his journey to the Holy Land to see her
has inspired poets from Petrarch to Pound. It is largely the
creation of his Provençal biographer:

Jaufres Rudels de Blaia si fo mout gentils hom, princes de Blaia. Et enamo-
ret se de la comtessa de Tripol, ses vezer, per lo ben qu'el n'auzi dire als
pelerins que venguen d'Antiocha. E fez de leis mains vers ab bons sons, ab
paubres motz. E per voluntat de leis vezer, el se croset e se mes en mar, e
pres lo malautia en la nau, e fo condug a Tripol, en un alberc, per mort.
E fo fait saber a la comtessa et ella venc ad el, ad son leit e pres lo antre
sos bratz. E saup qu'ella era la comtessa, e mantenent recobret l'auzir e·l
flairar, e lauzet Dieu, que l'avia la vida sostenguda tro qu'el l'agues vista;
et enaissi el mori entre sos bratz. Et ella lo fez a gran honor sepellir en la
maison del Temple; e pois, en aquel dia, ella se rendet morga, per la dolor
qu'ella n'ac de la mort de lui.[1]

Jaufre Rudel of Blaye was a very noble man, prince of Blaye. And he fell
in love with the countess of Tripoli, without seeing her, for the good that
he heard of her from the pilgrims who came from Antioch. And he composed many songs about her with good tunes and poor words. And
through his desire to see her, he took the cross, and set out to sea; and
sickness came upon him on the ship, and he was brought to Tripoli, into
an inn, as if he were dead. And this was told to the countess and she came
to him, to his bed, and took him in her arms. And he knew that she was
the countess and forthwith he recovered his hearing and sense of smell,
and praised God for having kept him alive until he had seen her. And so he
died in her arms. And she caused him to be buried with great honour in
the house of the Temple; and then, on that same day, she took the veil for
the grief she had at his death.

The house of Blaye began with Jaufre, count of Angoulême
from 1030 to 1048, whose grandson, Guilhem Freland, bear-
ing the title of Prince of Blaye in 1090, was a close acquaintance of Guilhem IX of Aquitaine, and went as a pilgrim to the
Holy Land before the First Crusade. His son Girard, Prince of

Blaye, fought unsuccessfully against Bougrin II, count of Angoulême, and Guilhem IX of Aquitaine, and was succeeded by his son Jaufre Rudel who is named with him in two acts, one of 1125 and the other undated. This Jaufre Rudel, grandson of Guilhem Freland, is almost certainly the troubadour to whom Marcabru sends his song *Cortesamen* to the Holy Land. Jaufre probably took the cross in 1147 with his cousin and suzerain, Guilhem IV Taillefer of Angoulême, who disembarked at St Jean of Acre in April 1148. After this date there is no further trace of the historical Jaufre Rudel, but he was probably the father of the Girard de Blaye who went on a pilgrimage to the Holy Sepulchre in Jerusalem in 1164.[2]

Jaufre Rudel must have known Guilhem IX in person. At an unknown date during the reign of Bougrin II (1120–40), and possibly as retribution for the insurrection of Jaufre's father Girard, Guilhem IX captured the castle of Blaye and destroyed its walls and keep. These were rebuilt by Bougrin, who was the immediate overlord of Blaye, and remain today looking out over the wide sweep of the Gironde towards the open sea.

It may help us to understand the poetry of Jaufre Rudel if we consider him, not as a troubadour in general, but as one of the small group of early troubadours whose themes and poetic inspiration have common features which are not so apparent in later poets such as Bernart de Ventadorn. Bernart composes within an accepted canon of courtly ideas and he acknowledges the supremacy of *Fin'Amors* and the convention according to which the poet, submitting to his *domna* in courtly fashion, may hope for a courtly reward. Earlier troubadours such as Guilhem IX of Aquitaine, Marcabru and Jaufre Rudel have no such rigid thematic framework. The poetry of Guilhem IX and Jaufre Rudel is characterised by the seeking and almost experimental attitude of the poet to the subject of love, and this embryonic state in the evolution of courtly ideas on love is also reflected in the moralising poems in which Marcabru discusses the themes which should concern troubadour poetry and the types of love which should be avoided or aspired to.

Guilhem IX and Jaufre Rudel, unlike Bernart de Ventadorn, are not concerned specifically with their courtly relationship to a particular *domna* or with their position in society. Their independent attitude may be explained by their aristocratic background and the possibility that, like Raimbaut d'Orange, they do not feel obliged to conform to courtly convention. If we consider Marcabru's fierce attacks on promiscuous love among the nobility and his vehement advocacy of *Fin'Amors*, it appears probable, however, that courtly attitudes to love were not as fixed, when he wrote, as they came to be by the time of Bernart de Ventadorn. It is equally possible that Marcabru's ideas were decisive in establishing the pattern of courtly ideas on love which were accepted by later troubadours, and presumably by the audiences for whom they composed.

For Guilhem IX and Jaufre Rudel the search for *Jois* appears to be more important than the experience of *Amors*, which is merely the means by which *Jois* or 'individual happiness' can be found. The degree of *Jois* which can be gained is determined by the quality of the *Amors* which is experienced and hence by the quality of the *domna* to whom the love is addressed. Both poets are searching for a *Jois* which will be supreme, lasting and beneficial and will go beyond the limits of everyday experience. They refer to this greatest happiness as *lo mielhs*, and this *mielhs* or 'supreme happiness' is probably analogous to the *omnium summum bonorum* of Boethius 'which, being the limit of happiness, excludes all other happiness' (*De Consolatione*, III, 2).

Although this *Jois* and 'supreme happiness' can be sought and discovered through *Amors*, *Amors* at this time does not appear to be a defined or codified concept. *Amors* may be praised or blamed, and in so far as it represented an embryonic code of social behaviour may be accepted or rejected, as it was in different situations by Guilhem IX, Jaufre and Marcabru. *Amors* for Guilhem IX and Jaufre Rudel is a phenomenon which can be either sensed or imagined or aspired to and which may provide various degrees of *Jois* and beneficial effects. Three planes of love are apparent in his poetry as in the poetry of Guilhem IX. There is the worldly plane of physical desire which may possibly be expressed within the conventions of courtly society; there is a plane of dreamlike imagining in which the poet puts distance between himself and his earthly love and finds escape in an illusory joy; and there is a 'transcendental' plane which is removed from everyday pleasures and imagined satisfactions and which, because of its excellence, promises a supreme joy from which good results flow. It is interesting, but perhaps coincidental, that these three planes of love coincide with the three types of experience to be found in medieval philosophy, the sensual, the imaginary and the visionary.

The quest for Jois on these three planes is the real inspiration of the love lyrics of Guilhem IX, and if we turn to Jaufre Rudel we see that his main inspiration also lies in the quest for Jois and is marked by the need to escape from a lesser joy to a greater joy which, although it may cause great grief, will be lasting and carry with it the promise of good results and the removal of petty dissatisfaction. Jaufre, in seeking Jois, is experiencing love, as Guilhem had done, through his physical desire, his imagination and his aspiration towards an ultimate and 'secure happiness'. Unlike Guilhem who, in general, remained on one plane of experience in each separate poem, Jaufre intermingles these planes, passing from one level of aspiration to another or seeking Jois on more than one level at the same time. It is this realisation of the different types of Jois which can be won through love, and his aspiration towards them in one and the same poem, which makes uncertain any classification of his poetry into categories of sensual love or of distant aspiring love.[3]

This mingling of the levels on which Jois can be sought is immediately apparent in the poem *Quan lo rossinhols el folhos* (I) in which the levels on which Jaufre seeks Jois progress from the physical, through the imaginary, to the spiritual. Jaufre explains his theme in the first stanza. Like the nightingale who is *jauzent joyos* he seeks a Jois which will allow him to rejoice actively and to remain at the same time in a state of constant happiness.

He begins (stanza II) by expressing this feeling of Jois and this need for Jois in terms of his desire for the *amistat* of a *domna* whose physical reality he describes:

> D'un'amistat suy enveyos,
> Quar no sai joya plus valen,
> C'or e dezir, que bona·m fos
> Si·m fazia d'amor prezen,
> Que·l cors a gras, delgat e gen
> E ses ren que·y descovenha,
> E s'amors bon'ab bon saber.   (8–14)

45

I am desirous of one particular love – for I know no joy that has greater worth – which I pray for and desire, so that she would act nobly if she made me a present of love, for her body is well formed, slim and gracious, and free from unseemly imperfection and the love she inspires is good and pleasingly so.

The phrase *ses ren que·y descovenha* is a commonplace, but the implication is that the joy to be found in this love may be sought within a conventional framework, and in the hope of pleasure.

In stanzas III and IV Jaufre passes to the plane of dream and imagination, when, *cossiros* 'reflecting sadly' about this love, and dreaming while either awake or asleep, he finds wondrous joy:

> Quar lai ay joy meravelhos,
> Per qu'ieu la jau jauzitz jauzen.   (17–18)

Jaufre enjoys this love because, having rejoiced in it, he can still rejoice in it, and this is the theme of his poem. This 'dream love' bestows wondrous joy because it *appears* to be reciprocal and lasting. But as Guilhem IX retreated from his imaginary *amigua* in *Farai un vers* (IV), so Jaufre acknowledges the illusory and intangible quality of his dream love in the image of the lady fleeing from him as he pursues her but nevertheless moves backwards away from her:

> D'aquest'amor suy tan cochos
> Que quant ieu vau ves lieys corren
> Vejaire m'es qu'a reüsos
> M'en torn e qu'ela·s n'an fugen;
> E mos cavals i vai tan len
> Greu er qu'oimais i atenha,
> S'Amors no la·m fa remaner.   (22–8)

I am so full of desire for this love that when I hasten towards her, it seems to me that I turn backwards and that she keeps fleeing from me. And my horse goes towards her so slowly that I shall find it difficult to reach her at all, if Love, acting for me, does not make her stop.

The poet knows that Love will not help him, that the dream of *Jois meravelhos* will not become a reality through physical *Amors*, real or imagined. He emphasises this by picking up the word *Amors* from the last line of this stanza (28) and beginning the next stanza with it:

> Amors, alegre·m part de vos
> Per so quar vau mo mielhs queren   (29–30)

Love, with delight I depart from you because I go to seek my greatest happiness.

The phrase *vau mo mielhs queren* balances the fruitless dream quest *vau ves lieys corren*, which occurs likewise in the second line of the preceding stanza.

In his new state, separated from *Amors*, he is fortunate to have a heart that still rejoices, thanks to his *Bon Guiren* who wants him, calls to him and deigns to think him worthy, and has given him good hope. Although speculation about the identity of *Bon Guiren* ('good witness') may be vain, there is no doubt that this patron, whether God, Christ, a feudal patron or a *domna*, promises him the *Bel Acuelh* or 'fair welcome', which he has not found with *Amors*. The next stanza (VI), which occurs in CEMe only, connects Jaufre's new quest for utmost happiness with the task of following God to Bethlehem. Only by doing this can a man be valiant and come to salvation, and not by remaining behind given over to the pleasure (*deleytos*) of *Amors*. The last lines are significant:

> Qu'ieu sai e crei, mon escien,
> Que selh qui Jhesus ensenha
> Segur'escola pot tener. (40–2)

For I know and consciously believe that the man who is taught by Jesus, can possess assured values [can hold to secure precepts].

With this stanza the theme of the poem in stanza I is *lassatz* or 'bound up'. The poet has both a rejoicing heart (*cor jauzen*, 32) and the anticipation of a happiness (*mielhs*, 30, and *segur'escola*, 42) which will be lasting and will produce good results.

This poem, in the version offered by MSS. CE, is arranged in the type of ordered progression that Guilhem IX used in his burlesque poems. The poem is constructed on the two themes of *Jois* and *Amors*. It is concerned with the quest for *Jois*, and the degrees of *Jois* which the poet finds on the different planes of Love and desire. In stanza v, Jaufre departs with delight from *Amors*, the uncertain and transitory loves of the body and the imagination. The highest joy is to be found in the service of God by which a man becomes *pros*, wins salvation and the assurance that comes from the teachings of Jesus. In this poem, as in *Belhs m'es l'estius* (IV), Jaufre's concept of his highest joy embraces moral worth, spiritual salvation, and the assurance of a *segur'escola* which is denied him by the 'schooling' of profane *Amors* and the sterile illusions of his dream desire, but which he hopes for from the Christian ethic.

In *Quan lo rossinhols* (I), in the version of CE, Jaufre deals distinctly and separately with the different levels of *Jois* and love that he experiences, desires or aspires to. In poems II–V the separate kinds of happiness and Love are no longer kept apart but are evoked by the use of allusive 'coloured'[4] words which would undoubtedly have conveyed different depths of meaning to different members of his audience, as they still do to the present-day reader.

The question arises whether Jaufre uses these evocative words with the poetic purpose of stimulating nuances of extra feeling or whether these words, which are often associated with Christianity and the Holy Land, were so much a part of the common and everyday vocabulary of a knight and Crusader of the mid-twelfth century and of his audience that their use in these poems would not have seemed as provokingly unexpected to his audience as to us. This use of 'coloured' words to evoke enigmatic nuances of meaning is a common device of the early troubadours. Guilhem IX used it for bawdy purposes in his burlesque poetry and may have satirised thereby this poetic usage. Marcabru is explicit about the matter. In *D'aisso laus Dieu*, which is a *gap* against lesser poets, he says: I am filled and taken captive by the most twisted nuances, by a hundred colours so that I may choose the best[5] (see p. 96). In view of this liking by the early troubadours for evocative words and of Jaufre's obvious interest in the precise use of words, it is probable that he is showing poetic intention in using unexpected words to produce overtones of meaning, and to extend the levels on which he is writing. The words he uses in this way are however not subtly poetic, as is sometimes the case with Guilhem IX and Marcabru. They obtain their effect by the unexpectedness of their use in a given context, and it may be this relative lack of rich 'colouring' in his words which led the author of his *vida* to call them 'paubres motz'.

In *Quan lo rossinhols* (I) the levels on which Jaufre is writing are presented clearly and separately and there is little attempt to produce extra nuances of meaning. Jaufre pays close heed to a sequence of 'key' adjectives: *joyos, enveyos, cossiros, meravelhos, cochos, alegre, aventuros, deleytos,* and he uses the various forms of the words *Jois* and *jauzir* to indicate the varying states of happiness that he wishes to describe, but the only words with an obviously double meaning appear to be *jazer* (7) (?) and *cavals* (26), with their overtones of the sexual act, and *Bon Guiren* (33), which has just been mentioned. In poems II–V his use of 'evocative' vocabulary is more apparent, but his central theme remains the same. It is still the desire for a great and assured happiness in a great love, and the renunciation, in order to aspire to this, of frivolous and temporary loves. This distinction between great joy from a lasting love and minor joy from frivolous love bears a marked similarity to the differences between Marcabru's concepts of *Fin'Amors* and *Fals'Amors*. The great joy that Jaufre seeks is invariably linked in poems II–V, as in poem I, with a distant or removed love, which takes from him all petty and minor doubts.

In *Quan lo rius de la fontana* (II) Jaufre longs for distant love, and hints at higher planes of desire. The nightingale sings and the poet's heart grieves:

> Amors de terra lonhdana,
> Per vos totz lo cors mi dol.   (8–9)

This grief, like the *dol corau* from which Guilhem IX sought refuge in his imagination, can be cured only by obeying the summons to love, which by implication is a distant love.

> E no·n puesc trobar mezina
> Si non au vostre reclam
> Ab atraich d'amor doussana
> Dinz vergier o sotz cortina
> Ab dezirada compahna.   (10–14)

And for this I can find no remedy unless I obey your call with its attraction of a sweet and gentle love within the orchard or beneath the curtain with the companion whom I desire.

In stanza III Jaufre burns with desire because he cannot obey this call. 'Never was there a more gracious Christian woman, nor does God desire that there should be, nor a Jewish, nor a Saracen woman. He who gains anything from her love, or from loving her, is well rewarded with manna.'

In stanza IV the poet's heart does not cease to aspire towards his best beloved:

> De dezir mos cors no fina
> Vas selha ren qu'ieu pus am;
> E cre que volers m'enguana
> Si cobezeza la·m tol.   (22–5)

49

Here *dezir* and *volers* are juxtaposed as they are in the *Tristan* of Thomas. Tristan, on his nuptial couch with Ysolt of the White Hands, thinks of the distant queen, Ysolt the Fair:

> Le desir qu'ad vers la reine
> Tolt le voleir vers la meschine;
> Le desir lui tolt le voleir,
> Que nature n'i ad poeir.
> Amur e raisun le destraint,
> E le voleir de sun cors vaint.
> La grant amor qu'ad vers Ysolt
> Tolt ço que la nature volt,
> E vaint icele volonté
> Que senz desir out en pensé.
>
> (ed. J. Bédier, I, 649–58, p. 286)

The desire he has for the queen takes away the physical desire for the girl. This desire takes physical desire from him for nature is powerless in this matter. Love and reason constrain him and overcome the desire of his body. The great love he has for Ysolt takes away what nature desires and overcomes that intention which without [mental] desire he had in his thoughts.

Desir here is the special desire felt by Tristan for the distant Ysolt the Fair, and its allies are *amur* and *raisun* (653). *Voleir* is a more general physical desire, associated with *nature* (652 and 656) and directed towards the unloved wife Ysolt of the White Hands. This *voleir* is devoid of any *desir*, which exists in the thoughts of the lover (658).

If we apply this distinction to the lines quoted from Jaufre Rudel (*Quan lo rius*, 22–5), we see that the meaning may be: 'my heart does not cease to aspire with desire towards that person whom I most love, and I believe that (general) physical desire deceives me if selfish, possessive desire (*cupiditas*) takes her from me'. The word *fina*, although it comes from *finar* 'to finish or cease', evokes the idea of *Fin'Amors*, and what Jaufre is saying in these lines is that he fears that physical desire growing to *cupiditas* may remove from him the joy of the 'distant' aspiring love, represented by *dezir* (22), that he feels.

This idea is supported by the next three lines:

> Que pus es ponhens qu'espina
> La dolors que ab joi sana;
> Don ja non vuelh qu'om m'en planha.   (26–8)

For sharper than a thorn is the grief which is healed by joy; for this reason I do not wish to be pitied by anyone.

This grief and the *Jois* which can assuage it are synonymous with 'distant' love, with the desire of the heart and mind and a love which controls indiscriminate physical desire, and Jaufre seeks no pity for his grief since this type of loving is preferable to the wish for immediate physical possession in the sense of the *voleir* that Tristan felt for Ysolt of the White Hands.

In this poem the main theme of finite, sensual but controlled desire for a distant *domna* is accompanied by religious and Crusading overtones which are associated with individual words. If we accept *dinz vergier o sotz cortina* (13) as a commonplace indication of profane love, nevertheless *dezirada* (14) has associations with Christ.[6] The sequence of adjectives, *crestiana, juzeva, sarrazina*, followed by *mana*, cannot fail to evoke the Holy Land, and in this mood *espina* as an image for the grief that is healed by joy could be associated with the crown of thorns.[7] As has been mentioned, these words, which to us are unexpected in their context, may have been the common currency of Jaufre and his Crusading associates, but it is also probable that he is offering them unexpectedly to his audience to hint at the possibility that the profane joy he aspires to can only be expressed in terms of the happiness that comes from Christian love.

The two poems *Pro ai del chan essenhadors* (III) and *Belhs m'es l'estius* (IV) have a similar theme. The happy progression in *Quan lo rossinhols* (I) from desire for a lesser to desire for a greater joy is replaced by conflict between the dissatisfaction with a lesser, ephemeral joy and the desire for a greater, lasting joy. Both poems, especially *Belhs m'es*, show the possible influence of Marcabru, and both are concerned with the antithetical themes of seriousness/frivolity, fruitfulness/vanity, which inspired Marcabru, and provoked other troubadours such as Bernart Marti to recrimination.

In *Pro ai del chan essenhadors* (III) Jaufre states his *razo* in the first two stanzas. He contrasts the minor joy (*un petit de joy*) that he feels because of the spring, the meadows, orchards and birdsong, with the greater joy for which he yearns. No delight that he may feel in the spring can equal the *solatz d'amor valen* (8), the pleasure of intercourse with a love based on *valors* and producing *valors* (6-8). This contrast of a lesser with a greater joy may be accepted as a *topos* 'topic' or 'commonplace' of introduction,[8] but in stanza II Jaufre is lyrical, succinct and explicit:

> Las pimpas sian als pastors
> Et als enfans burdens petitz,
> E mias sion tals amors
> Don ieu sia jauzens jauzitz! (9–12)

Let piping be the lot of the shepherds, and let petty frolicking belong to the young, and let mine be loves such as I may rejoice in when I have enjoyed them.

Jaufre now amplifies his idea of *solatz d'amor valen* (8) and speaks of the lady to whom he addresses his love:

> Qu'ieu la sai bona tot'aitau
> Ves son amic en greu logau. (13–14)

La (C) in line 13 is a common form of *lai*, and the spelling *lai* is found in the second MS. (*e*), and this gives the translation: 'For I know that a lady exists there who is equally kind towards her suitor when he is in a difficult situation', *greu logau* appearing to be the opposite of *luecs aizitz* (50). Jaufre grieves that he does not have from this distant lady, who is free from inconstancy, what his heart expects (15–16).

The rest of the poem is concerned with the hope that this grief of non-possession, which reminds one of Guilhem IX, may be assuaged by the *Jois* which she can bestow. But 'distant is the castle and the tower where she lies and her husband . . . and if my cause is not helped forward by good counsellors offering their advice – for any other advice is of little use to me, so true and heartfelt is my desire – nothing remains except death, if I do not soon receive some happiness (*alqun joy*, 24)'.

In stanza IV he expresses his devotion in terms of the courtly demeanour he will show to all those who live in the country where she who is his *Jois* was brought up, and once more he stresses the noble desire and inclination that he has towards the love which his lady imprisons in his heart, and he knows she is aware of it.

In stanza V, which occurs in MS. *e* only, his heart is there so completely that nowhere else is there any existence, and when he sleeps, his spirit is there with her. But his love is unheeded, and he will exercise patience.

In stanza VI his *voluntatz* breaks down the barrier of distance between poet and lady.

> Ma voluntatz s'en vai lo cors,
> La nueit et dia esclarzitz,
> Laintz per talant de socors.   (41–3)

My desire goes away in haste, there to her, through the night and the bright day, impelled by the desire for help.

But this, according to Jeanroy's variants, is not what the two MSS. containing the poem say (Ce). Both have per talant de son cors 'through desire for her, her person, or her body' and Jeanroy, in accepting the emendation socors proposed by A. Thomas (ed. Jeanroy, p. 27), has weakened the profane and physical character of this love. This emendation would be bold even if it could be justified by the need to avoid an equivocal rhyme. The reply comes from the lady: 'My love', she says, 'the jealous, uncouth ones have begun such a dispute that it will be difficult to settle it to the point where we may both find joy.'

The last stanza is found only in MS. e and has been heavily emended by Jeanroy. The main emendation occurs in line 50:

> Per so m'en creis plus ma dolors
> Car non ai lieis en luecs aizitz.   (49–50)

For line 50, MS. e, according to Jeanroy's variants, gives:

> Car ieu au lieis en luec[s] aizit[z].

My grief for her increases the more because I hear her in places which are suited to love.

If we accept this stanza as authentic, Jaufre may be referring to the lady's message in the previous stanza. The poet may mean that he is physically en luecs aizitz 'in a situation suited to love' but actually in greu logau (14), since he is devoid of everything except the memory of his domna, a memory that is not 'visual' but is 'heard' by him.

The theme in this poem (Pro ai) is again the search for a Jois which Jaufre may enjoy and which will not be lost (12), a Jois which he seeks from the love of a physically distant domna. As in Quan lo rius, there are enigmatic overtones of a spiritual or religious love. The lady, who is kind to her amic when he is in a dire situation, comes to his spirit in a dream vision (36) and his voluntatz hastens to her presence. Words such as castelhs ('Jerusalem'), tors ('Christ') and sima ni raitz have been interpreted as 'coloured' words[9] and this may possibly represent a poetic purpose on Jaufre's part. But in spite of the brief reference to a dream love and, possibly, hints of a higher spiritual love, Jaufre in this poem is again seeking *Jois* from the profane love for a distant *domna*.

Belhs m'es l'estius (IV) is also concerned with the rejection of a lesser happiness and a lesser love for a greater, but this poem is fuller and richer than *Pro ai* (III), possibly because of the influence of Marcabru. In his opening stanza Jaufre praises winter because more joy has befallen him then:

> Belhs m'es l'estius e·l temps floritz
> Quan l'auzelh chanton sotz la flor,
> Mas ieu tenc l'ivern per gensor
> Quar mais de joy m'i es cobitz.   (1–4)

Pleasing to me is the summer and the blossom-time when the birds sing beneath the blossom, but I consider winter more gracious since more joy has befallen me then.

This is no commonplace seasonal opening. Professor D. Stone Jr has suggested that winter recalls to the lover his victory over himself.[10] 'He has learned to wait: he has learned fidelity.' A further meaning may however be possible. In the opening stanza of *Pois la fuoilla* (XXXVIII) Marcabru prefers winter to summer because it is cleansed of sensual lust, and he also associates *orgoills* 'arrogance' with birdsong and summer. As we may see from later stanzas of his song, Jaufre may be using with personal relevance this 'covered' image of winter as a season free from wantonness, desire and arrogance, and a season in which '*mais de joy*' was accordingly bestowed on him.

In stanza II Jaufre enlarges on his state of winter happiness:

> Er ai ieu joy e suy jauzitz
> E restauratz en ma valor,
> E non iray jamai alhor
> Ni non querrai autrui conquistz.   (8–11)

Now I possess joy and am rejoiced and restored to my state of worth, and I will never go elsewhere, nor seek the things that others have gained.

His previous state deprived him of joy and is associated with seeking in other directions (*alhor*). The word *alhor* in this context can mean other *domnas*, but, as is the case with the word *conquistz*, the meaning is veiled. His present *Jois* is associated with *valor*. Jaufre ends the stanza sententiously by praising the wisdom of patience and the folly of haste and anger. The expression is a proverbial commonplace, but the call he feels is away from the immediacy of response and uncontrolled feelings towards a longer and more detached view of life.

In stanza III Jaufre turns from present joy to past grief which was caused by uncertainty and fear:

> Lonc temps ai estat en dolor
> Et de tot mon afar marritz,
> Qu'anc no fuy tant fort endurmitz
> Que no·m rissides de paor.
> Mas aras vey e pes e sen
> Que passat ai aquelh turmen,
> E non hi vuelh tornar ja mays.   (15–21)

For a long time I have remained grieving and sorrowful about all my affairs, for never have I been so fast asleep that I might not awaken, from fear. But now I see and think and feel that I have passed through this torment and I never wish to return to it.

Endurmitz, with its implication of the 'sleeping' spirit, is as ambiguous here as *alhor* was in the preceding stanza.

In stanza IV Jaufre rejoices in the honour shown him by his counsellors because he has returned to his state of *Jois* (24). This is the amplification of the phrase *restauratz en ma valor* (9). For this good result he says 'I praise her and God and them [MS. *e* gives: 'I praise God and her and them'], for now they have their reward and whatever I might go around saying, there [with this joy] do I remain [MS. *e*: mi *clau* 'enclose myself'] and there do I find my nourishment.'

Stanza V may offer us a key to the meaning of this poem:

> Mas per so m'en sui encharzitz,
> Ja no·n creyrai lauzenjador,
> Qu'anc no fuy tan lunhatz d'amor
> Qu'er no·n sia sals e gueritz.
> Plus savis hom de mi mespren,
> Per qu'ieu sai ben az escien
> Qu'anc fin'amors home non trays.   (29–35)

Since by this means I have improved my standing [my self-respect], I will nevermore believe the slanderer, for never was I so distant from love that now I may not be saved from it and cured of it. A wiser man than I can fall into error, and for this reason I know truly that *Fin'Amors* never betrayed a man.

The implication of the first two lines of this quotation is that his former state of unhappiness is associated with the *lauzenjador* and hence with profane love. This love *amor* (31) which has caused him such uncertainty and torment (stanza III) was never a 'distant' enough love, and for this reason he can be cured of it and saved. In contrast to this earlier 'non-distant' *amors* of l. 31, Jaufre's present love, which has now restored him to *Jois* and *valors*, certainty and peace of mind, is called Fin'*Amors* (35). What Fin'*Amors* is this, and how is it different from *Amors* in l. 31?

Surely it is the Fin'*Amors* of Marcabru, loosely defined but granting a happy, courtly, wise life to the man it chooses (Marcabru, ed., XL, 8–9) and condemning the man it rebuffs to torment and destruction (XL, 10–11), a love which brings with it improvement and good results? Similarly the *amor* which Jaufre is now cured of and saved from (31–2) can be related not only to the *Amors* from which Jaufre takes leave in *Quan lo rossinhols* (l. 29) in order to seek his *mielhs* or greater happiness, but more especially to the earthly, sensual, interested and treacherous *Amors* which Marcabru attacks and removes himself from in *Ans que·l terminis verdei* (VII):

> Amor no vueill ni dezir,
> Tan sap d'engan ab mentir;
> Per aiso vos ho vueill dir
> C'anc d'Amor no·m puec jauzir.
> Tan l'en vueill mal e l'azir
> Can m'en membra·m fai languir.
> Fols fui per Amor servir,
> Mas vengut em al partir.
>
> Per Amor sueill esser guais,
> Mas [eu] no·n serai jamais
> C'una·m n'enguanet e·m trais
> Per que m'en gurp e m'en lais.
> Ben es cargatz de fol fais
> Qui d'Amor es en pantais.
> Senher Deus quan mala nais
> Qui d'aital foudat se pais!   (VII, 9–24)

I do not wish for or desire Love, so much with its lying ways does it know of deceit, and I wish to tell you this because I can never rejoice in Love. I dislike and hate it so much that to think of it makes me languish. I was foolish to serve Love but we have come to the parting.

Because of Love I was wont to be gay but I shall be so no more, for a woman deceived and betrayed me, so that I abandon and renounce it. That man is indeed loaded with a foolish burden who because of Love is confused in his mind. Lord God, how ill-starred is that man who finds nourishment in such foolishness!

The possibility that Jaufre's view of *Amors* in *Belhs m'es l'estiu* (IV) is close to that of Marcabru in *Ans que* (VII) is strengthened by the similarity of theme in the two poems, and the recurrence of a key expression. Marcabru has been gay because of *Amors*, but has been deceived and betrayed, and now abandons and renounces it, in order to avoid the disturbance of mind that it causes him. The phrase:

> Ben es cargatz de fol fais
> Qui d'Amor es en pantais. (21–2)

is so close to Jaufre Rudel's closing lines:

> Qu'ie·m tenc per ric e per manen
> Car soi descargatz de fol fais. (55–6)

that an intentional repetition, probably on the part of Jaufre Rudel, must be considered, and this possibility of a concealed 'dialogue' between the two poets may throw light on the last two stanzas of *Ans que* in which Marcabru reproves the man who is *talantos d'amar* (46) and concludes:

> Drutz que·s fai semblar Baza
> Per Amor que fols i fa.
> Ja el nos senh ab sa ma
> Cui Amors enguanara! (VII, 53–6)

The lover who because of Love causes himself to be compared to Basan, acts like a fool [a sinner][11] in so doing. Never may that man whom Love will deceive make the sign of the cross with his hand.

Basan was killed in the embassy to the Saracens which preceded that of Ganelon in the *Chanson de Roland* (ed. F. Whitehead, ll. 208, 330 and 490) and it may not be too fanciful to see in these Crusading references an allusion to Jaufre's desire in *Lanquan li jorn* (V) to be acclaimed a prisoner for the sake of his love, there in the realm of the Saracens.

The closeness of a poetic relationship between Jaufre and Marcabru, who composed at the court of the counts of Poitou, Jaufre's overlords, is indicated when Marcabru dedicates *Cortesamen vuoill comenssar* (XV) to Jaufre:

> Lo vers e·l son vuoill enviar
> A·n Jaufre Rudel outra mar,
> E vuoill que l'aujon li Frances
> Per lor coratges alegrar. (37–40)

I desire to send this poem and melody to Lord Jaufre Rudel in the Holy

Land, and I want the French to hear it [him?] in order that it [he] may delight their hearts.

This poem by Marcabru also contains the theme of the wisest and most accomplished man who can yet be taught something when the occasion arises (9–12), which Jaufre takes up in *Belhs m'es l'estius* with the line:

Plus savis hom de mi mespren.[12]   (33)

Marcabru's lines in *Cortesamen*:

Aitals amors fai a prezar
Que si meteissa ten en car.   (xv, 31–2)

Such love is to be esteemed which holds itself dear.

are also close to Jaufre's recovery of self-esteem and *valor* when he returns to a state of *Jois* and uses a similar phrase to describe this:

Mas per so m'en sui encharzitz...   (iv, 29)

In the light of the similarities between Jaufre's *Belhs m'es* (iv) and Marcabru's *Ans que* (vii), which are reinforced by a similarity of theme and expression in Jaufre's *Belhs m'es* and Marcabru's *Cortesamen* (xv) and of Marcabru's dedication of *Cortesamen* to Jaufre Rudel in the Holy Land, it is possible to argue that Jaufre's ideas in *Belhs m'es* can be related to those of Marcabru in *Ans que* and *Cortesamen*. Jaufre is rejoicing at freeing himself from a love which he calls *Amors* and which, as he says, was not 'distant' enough and caused him grief and confusion of mind (15–21). He rejoices because he is aware that he has been released from a burden of folly (or sin) when he renounced this *Amors*.

In this context his description of the occasion when he was assailed unclothed at night between the covers, so that others went away laughing and leaving him with his sighs and confusion (*Qu'enquer en sospir e·n pantays*, l. 42), may be considered in its literal sense as a dramatised exemplum of the disturbance (*pantais*) and betrayal into which, according to Marcabru in *Ans que* (19–24), *Amors* can lead the man who is in love. The memory of such a scandalous episode and the *pantais* it causes him would account for Jaufre's joy at being restored to *valor* after abandoning *Amors*; he no longer needs to fear what the *lauzenjador* (30) might say.

Many different meanings have been given to the next stanza (VII) but a more literal interpretation of this may also be possible:

> Mais d'una re soi en error
> E·n estai mos cors esbaïtz
> Que tot can lo fraire·m desditz
> Aug autrejar a la seror;
> E nulhs hom non a tan de sen,
> Que puesc'aver cominalmen,
> Que ves calque part non biais.　　　(43–9)

But I am distressed by one thing and my heart remains in turmoil because of it: namely, that all that the brother forbids me I hear granted by the sister; and no man has so much natural sense that he may not go astray in some direction.

Various interpretations of *fraire* and *seror* in this stanza have been suggested, which like the next stanza (VIII) occurs only in MS. *e*. If the stanza is authentic, Jaufre may be using *fraire* and *seror* with an intentionally enigmatic meaning,[13] but he may also be saying that sensual temptation persists and that all that the male counsellor advises him against, he hears being granted by the female. *Fraire* might refer to another troubadour or to a priest, and the word *seror* can also be used for 'wife'; 'brother' and 'sister' are also used in medieval alchemy as the twin components of the personality.

In stanza VIII, again only in *e*, Jaufre desires that his song should be sung in April and at Easter-time, 'for I consider myself rich and wealthy because I am relieved of the foolish burden'.

> Qu'ie·m tenc per ric e per manen
> Car soi descargatz de fol fais.　　　(55–6)

The theme or *razo* of this poem, with its symbolical winter opening and spring ending, is concerned with the relinquishing of *Amors* in favour of a *Fin'Amors* which, because the poet is more distant (*lunhatz*) from it, restores him to the *valors* he has lost through *Amors*, and to lasting *Jois*. Marcabru cursed the man who nourished himself on the folly (sin) of *Amors*:

> Senher Deus quan mala nais
> Qui d'aital foudat se pais!　　　(*Ans que*, VII, 23–4)

Jaufre, who is now cured and saved from *Amors* (IV, 31–2), speaks of the great *Jois* to which he has returned, and on which he nourishes himself:

Lai mi remanh e lay m'apays. (28)

Distant love in this poem is not the longing for a far country or a far lady. It is Fin'Amors which is to be won by renouncing involvement with the immediate, close, and deceitful love that is Amors. The line:

Qu'anc fin'amors home non trays (35)

is not a casual interjection, but the culminating point to which Jaufre has been leading the poem. Fin'Amors is 'true love', it does not betray a man, as Amors betrayed Marcabru (VII, 19). It causes less immediate sensual involvement than Amors, and it is a love which gives peace of mind (20–1) and a lasting Jois for which Jaufre thanks God and his advisers.

There is undoubtedly the possibility that religious overtones exist in this poem, but in spite of the skilful exegesis of many scholars, there is little evidence of an attempt by Jaufre to add a religious colouring to the Fin'Amors which gives him the promise of lasting Jois. Phrases such as restauratz en ma valor, passat ai aquelh turmen, sals e queritz, vestitz, fraire, seror, pascor, fols fais, can be given a spiritual or Christian interpretation, but twelfth-century poets frequently describe a moment of lyrical or epic intensity in terms of the Christian experience. It is probable that one word, the merest hint, would evoke a Christian or Biblical parallel in receptive members of the audience. Chrétien's Lancelot crosses the sword bridge with hands and feet bleeding (ed. M. Roques, 3100–15), Vivien dies wounded in the side, drinking the salt sea water, but these implied comparisons are not to be over-interpreted. The poet is not showing Lancelot or Vivien as Christ-figures. He is trying to create perspective in the imagination of his audience, to lead them to reach into their profound Christian experience in order to feel the suffering of these profane heroes or lovers. Any religious overtones which may exist in Belhs m'es l'estius (IV) would heighten for a receptive audience the intensity of the personal crisis that Jaufre describes. His temporal victory over Amors would then be related to a wider spiritual victory in which fear (18), torment (20) and the foolish and sinful burden (56) are rejected and the assurance of lasting Jois obtained.

If we ignore for the moment the possible spiritual overtones, the poem Belhs m'es l'estius (IV) appears to be a subjective *exemplum* of a controversy in mid-twelfth-century Southern France between *Amors* and *Fin'Amors*. We find evidence of this controversy in the poems of Marcabru, Peire d'Alvernhe and Bernart Marti, who describes the delights of *Amors*, deceitful as it is, and draws from his hedonist appreciation of them more happiness than can be had from *Fin'Amors*. In the poem *Lancan lo douz temps s'esclaire* (ed. Hoepffner, IX) the lines describing Bernart's sensual love for his lady:

> Qan sui nutz e son repaire
> E sos costatz tenc e mazan,
> Ieu no sai null emperador,
> Vas me puesca gran pres cuillir
> Ne de fin'amor aver mais.   (17–21)

appear to be a rejection of *Fin'Amors* and the demands it imposes. Hoepffner translates: 'Quand je suis nu près d'elle et que je la tiens embrassée et que je la caresse, je ne sais pas d'empereur qui comparé à moi, puisse obtenir plus grand prix ni avoir plus de fin amour.'

The translation of lines 19–21 can be misinterpreted, so that Marti's description of sensual delight is equated with *Fin'Amors*. What he appears to say, however, is that when he is closeted with his lady: 'I know of no emperor who, compared to me, can gather great reputation, or obtain more from *fin'amor*'. Marti is saying that the immediate delights of a 'close' and concealed (l. 15) *Amors* are more rewarding than the pleasures of a presumably more distant *Fin'Amors*. This attitude contrasts with Jaufre's dismay in *Belhs m'es* (IV, 36–42) at being discovered *despolhatz sotz cobertor*, and with his rejection of 'close' love.

All the themes which are apparent in Jaufre's other love lyrics come together in *Lanquan li jorn* (V). These include the longing for utmost *Jois*, the *mielhs*, represented by a love which by its 'distance' will inspire him without involving him in the remorse and uncertainty of 'close' *Amors*, and in addition the colouring of a profane *Fin'Amors*, his *amor de lonh*, with spiritual and religious overtones associated with the Holy Land. This 'colouring' is part of the texture of the poem, which like *Quan lo rossinhols* is essentially a Crusading song. A detailed criticism of this poem would be otiose in view of the brilliant study which Madame R. Lejeune has devoted to it, but confirmation of some points which have been suggested in this chapter may be found in the new critical edition of the poem provided by Madame Lejeune.[14] Her text is based on MS. B and is superior to that in Jeanroy's edition. The main change occurs in the order of stanzas. Stanza II in Jeanroy (*Be tenc lo Senhor per veray*) is interchanged with stanza V (*Ja mais d'amor no·m jauziray*). The new order of stanzas has the merit of keeping references to God until late in the poem, as in *Quan lo rossinhols* (I), and of allowing us to see that the new stanza II can be interpreted as a rejection of *Amors* in favour of *est'amor de loing*. In the context of Marcabru's attack on *Amors* in *Ans que*, when he says:

C'anc d'Amor no·m puec jauzir   (VII, 12)

and of Jaufre's joy at being cured of *Amors* in *Belhs m'es l'estius*, we may see a deeper meaning in the lines:

Ja mais d'amor no·m gauzirai
Si no·m gau d'est'amor de loing. (ed. Lejeune, 8–9)

In *Belhs m'es l'estius* (IV) Jaufre rejected *Amors* in favour of the Jois provided by *Fin'Amors*, and it is possible to see *est'amor de loing* here also as a form of *Fin'Amors*. Jaufre may be saying: 'Never shall I find joy in any form of *Amors* [which I reject], unless I find it in this distant love.' In *Belhs m'es* (IV) the love which Jaufre chose was mentally 'distant'. In *Lanquan li jorn* (V) mental distance is reinforced by physical distance, and this is accomplished by means of the geographical and Crusading references. The distant love (or lady) attracts the poet by its (or her) true worth and reputation, and by the implicit promise that this 'distant' love, when he has seen it and departed from it, will provide his memory and imagination with lasting joy, the *mielhs* or 'supreme joy' which he seeks in *Quan lo rossinhols* (I).

I   Lanqand li jorn son lonc en mai,
    M'es bels douz chans d'auzels de loing,
    E qand me sui partitz de lai
    Remembra·m d'un'amor de loing.   4
    Vauc, de talan enbroncs e clis
    Si que chans ni flors d'albespis
    No·m platz plus que l'inverns gelatz.   7

II   Ja mais d'amor no·m gauzirai
    Si no·m gau d'est'amor de loing,
    Que gensor ni meillor non sai
    Vas nuilla part, ni pres ni loing.   11

Tant es sos pretz verais e fis
Que lai el renc dels Sarrazis
Fos eu, per lieis, chaitius clamatz!   14

III Iratz e gauzens m'en partrai
Qan veirai cest'amor de loing,
Mas non sai coras la·m veirai
Car trop son nostras terras loing.   18
Assatz i a portz e camis!
E, per aisso, non sui devis...
Mas tot sia cum a Dieu platz!   21

IV Be·m parra jois qan li qerrai
Per amor Dieu, l'amor de loing;
E, s'a lieis plai, albergarai
Pres de lieis – si be·m sui de loing!   25
Adoncs, parra·l parlamens fis
Qand, drutz loindas, er tant vezis
C'ab bels [digz] jauzirai solatz.   28

V Ben tenc lo Seignor per verai
Per q'ieu veirai l'amor de loing;
Mas, per un ben que m'en eschai,
N'ai dos mals, car tant m es de loing...   32
Ai! car me fos lai peleris
Si que mos fustz e mos tapis
Fos pelz sieus bels huoills remiratz!   35

VI Dieus, qe fetz tot qant ve ni vai
E fermet cest'amor de loing,
Me don poder – qe·l cor eu n'ai –
Q'en breu veia l'amor de loing,   39
Veraiamen, en locs aizis,
Si qe la cambra e·l jardis
Mi resembles totz temps palatz!   42

VII Ver ditz qui m'apella lechai
Ni desiran d'amor de loing,
Car nuills autre jois tant no·m plai
Cum jauzimens d'amor de loing.   46
Mas so q'eu vuoill m'es tant ahis
Q'enaissi·m fadet mos pairis
Q'ieu ames e non fos amatz!   49

VIII Mas so q'ieu vuoill m'es tant ahis!
Totz sia mauditz lo pairis
Qe·m fadet q'ieu non fos amatz!   52
(ed. Lejeune)

When the days are long in May the sweet song of the birds from afar is
pleasing to me, and when I have departed from there I remember a love
from afar. I wander sad and bowed down with desire so that neither song
nor hawthorn flower pleases me more than the icy winter.

Never shall I rejoice in love unless I rejoice in this love of afar for I know no nobler or better love in any direction, either near or far. Her reputation is so true and perfect that there in the kingdom of the Saracens would I wish, for her sake, to be proclaimed a captive.

Sad and rejoicing will I depart from it when I see this love of afar, but I know not when I shall see her, for our lands are too far. Many are the ports and roads! And for this reason I cannot foretell . . . But may everything be as pleases God.

Joy will indeed appear to me when I seek from her this far love, for love of God, and if it please her I will dwell near her although I am far from her. Then the perfect discourse will become evident when I a distant lover will be so close that with fine words I will enjoy sweet converse.

I consider that Lord as the true one through whom I shall see this far love, but for one happiness that comes to me from it I suffer two ills because she is so far from me. Ah! would that I might be a pilgrim there so that my staff and rug might be seen by her fair eyes.

May God who created all that comes and goes and strengthened this far love, grant me the power – for I have the mind to do it – to see this far love soon, truly, in suitable places, so that chamber and garden might always seem to me to be a palace.

He speaks true who calls me gluttonous and desirous of love of afar, for no other joy pleases me as much as the enjoyment from love from afar. But there are such obstacles to what I desire, for thus did my godfather decree my fate – that I should love and not be loved.

But there are such obstacles to what I desire. May that godfather be cursed absolutely who decreed my fate that I should not be loved.

Jaufre begins this poem sad and bowed down in his physical being (5) and seeing this *amor de loing* in the vision of his imagination as mingled joy and suffering. In *Quan lo rius* (II, 26–7) he calls this suffering 'sharper than a thorn' but knows that it can be cured by Jois. In *Lanquan* he sees this suffering in Crusading terms, and wishes that he were a captive of the Saracens (14) for only through suffering can he understand fully the Jois which is to be won.

In stanzas III and IV (*Iratz e gauzens* and *Be·m parra jois*) Jaufre imagines the Jois which will come from what in another poem *Pro ai* (III) he calls the *solatz d'amor valen*. With *albergarai* (24) he also hints at the serene happiness, shelter and security offered by love, an idea which is found also in Marcabru (V, 49–54) and becomes a commonplace with later troubadours. In stanzas V and VI Jaufre accepts that it is through God that he will see this distant love that God has 'strengthened' (MS. B). When Jaufre asks (38–42) for the power to see this love soon, truly, in suitable places, so that chamber and garden might always seem to him to be a palace, he is asking to see the distant love in reality, and no longer as a vision or dream image. But what Jaufre desires is not so much the physical realisation of *Jois*, the *solatz* which will be *vezis* 'close and temporary', but the memory of this joy, which will be permanent in his imagination when he has left this love, so that the everyday physical reality of chamber and garden will be *totz temps palatz*, an enhanced vision of splendour which will give joy more lasting than anything provided by *Amors*. Jaufre is expanding here the idea implicit in the lines:

> Ja mais d'amor no·m gauzirai
> Si no·m gau d'est'amor de loing.   (8–9)

For Jaufre the only true *Jois* to be had from love lies in the vision of the imagination, in anticipation or recollection. Stanza VII is composed on the two planes of his vision of an incomparable mental *Jois* which he hopes will result from *jauzimens d'amor de loing*, and the physical reality of his recognition of himself as *lechai ni desiran* and of his ill-starred fate in love (47–9). This sudden switch from imagined *Jois* to the plane of physical reality recalls the device used to great effect by Guilhem IX in *Farai un vers de dreyt nien* (IV) in which the mood of Guilhem's escape to a dream longing is switched abruptly in the second part of each stanza to earthly reality, irony and self-mockery. This device appears to have been used by Jaufre in a more or less obscure way throughout *Lanquan li jorn*, but it is particularly clear in the last three lines of the first and last stanzas, both of which describe the reality of the dejection he feels as compared with the *Jois* that he imagines. The poem is *lassatz*, 'bound up', in that Jaufre returns from his dream-vision of longed-for *Jois* to his earlier mood of dejection. Lines 45 and 46 are also *lassatz* with lines 8 and 9. In the *tornada* he emphasises his disappointment by cursing the godfather or *pairis*, whom Madame Lejeune seeks to identify as Guilhem IX.[15]

In the context of his other poems, and of what we know about the poetry of Guilhem IX and Marcabru, Jaufre Rudel's *Lanquan li jorn* would appear to be a poem of aspiration to a profane love, by means of which Jaufre desires to find a moment of transient joy in reality and the hope of a lasting joy for spirit and mind in memory. This is the ultimate expression of what Jaufre has in mind when he says in *Pro ai* (III):

E mias sion tals amors
Don ieu sia jauzens jauzitz.   (11–12)

He knows that, in order to achieve this ideal of a present joy
and a lasting happiness in the recollection of it, his immediate and 'close' contact with his beloved must be temporary
and replaced by distance. He knows that he will be sad at
departure from this Love, when he has found it, but that he
will rejoice at the prospect of the lasting and certain happiness
that this Love will offer to his mind and imagination. This
happiness will displace the actual mood of disconsolate and
unfulfilled longing with which he begins and ends the poem
(5–7 and 48–52). He expresses this idea of imagined sorrow
and joy at departure from his love in the lines:

Iratz e gauzens m'en partrai
Qan veirai cest'amor de loing.   (15–16)

The whole experience of love in this poem is contained in
the poet's imagination and his dream of what might be. In
the edition established by Madame Lejeune Jaufre's ideas and
wishes are arranged in a definite progression. He is sad because of desire for a distant love; he longs to see this in its
reality, he imagines the real and immediate *solatz* of seeing and
speaking to his lady; and he foresees the lasting *Jois* of recollection when he has left her and the ordinary surroundings
and experience of life are enhanced by his memory of her. At
the end, his dream is broken and he returns to his disconsolate mood of unfulfilled longing.

Because the poem is composed in a Crusading framework,
the religious overtones are very apparent. Since this *amor de
lonh* is for Jaufre the highest form of love because it will afford
him the utmost happiness (or *mielhs*), it is natural for him to
express it in terms which associate it with the highest spiritual
happiness, which proceeds, as we see in *Quan lo rossinhols*, from
the pursuit of the highest ideal of knighthood, the Crusade to
the Holy Land, and also from gratitude and submission to
God. Jaufre's profane, 'distant' love in *Lanquan li jorn* is associated with the love of God which he expresses by his purpose
of going to the Holy Land:

Be·m parra jois qan li qerrai
Per amor Dieu, l'amor de loing.[16]

(ed. Lejeune, 22–3)

and:

> Ben tenc lo Seignor per verai
> Per q'ieu veirai l'amor de loing. (ibid., 29–30)

or:

> Dieus, qe fetz tot qant ve ni vai
> E fermet cest'amor de loing. (ibid., 36–7)

There is little doubt that these three references to God in the last three stanzas are a device to strengthen the structure of the poem, and to emphasise the association between Jaufre's profane love and his Crusading zeal and knightly love of God. Because of this association of ideals his profane love is enhanced in his imagination, and so is the prospect of the *Jois* which will proceed from it. But there appears to be in *Lanquan li jorn* no renunciation of a deceiving *Amors*, in order to follow God to Bethlehem, such as may be found in *Quan lo rossinhols* (I). Jaufre's Love in *Lanquan li jorn* is such that he must preserve distance from it, apart from the few moments he may spend in the presence of the beloved. His love is *Fin'Amors* which, as we may see from Marcabru's poetry, is profane but possesses qualities which associate it with Christian love. When Jaufre hopes that the memory of this profane love will turn the ordinariness of his everyday surroundings into a palace, is he not repeating Marcabru's idea?

> Ai! fin'Amors, fons de bontat,
> C'a tot lo mon illuminat. (XL, 36–7)

In their love lyrics Guilhem IX and Jaufre Rudel are concerned primarily with the quest for *Jois*. *Amors* is a phenomenon which can be sensed, or imagined, or aspired to as a source of *Jois*, or of inspiration or goodness. If through *Amors* they discover a person or an ideal who may reveal *Jois* to them, they are concerned with the quality of this *Jois* and they hope that it may be a supreme and lasting happiness, which will also bestow advantages, goodness and reassurance. They experience self-doubt which courtly ideas cannot resolve; they are looking for the highest form of *Jois*, which is not an ephemeral or minor happiness but a lasting sense of harmony and reassurance within themselves and with a higher ideal. Their desire for this 'harmony' leads them to reject, in various degrees, the experience of mundane reality and the 'reality' of transient physical *Amors*.

Guilhem IX seeks happiness on a physical plane of shared

love in *Ab la dolchor* (x) and in the possibly unauthentic *Farai chansoneta nueva* (VIII):

> Totz lo joys del mon es nostre,
> Dompna, s'amduy nos amam. (27–8)

He tries to escape to an ephemeral happiness on the dream plane of his imagination in *Farai un vers de dreyt nien* (IV). He finds in *Mout jauzens* (IX) an incomparable *jois* or happiness (his *mielhs*) in his 'distant' love for a *domna* whom he desires to possess so that he may also possess the *tangible* good results promised by this love (IX, 25, 30, 33–6). In order to win and retain the happiness promised by this embryonic form of *Fin'Amors*, Guilhem is prepared to observe the courtly conventions (38–42) which, together with *Amors*, he appears unable to accept in *Pus vezem* (VII, 7–13 and 25–36). Guilhem IX hopes to achieve this utmost happiness, which will refresh his spirit and renew his flesh, within the world of courtly convention and with a real *domna* who is 'distant' but whom he desires and intends to be 'close'. The lasting quality of this *Jois* is expressed in physical terms:

> E deu hom mais cent ans durar
> Qui·l joy de s'amor pot sazir. (IX, 23–4)

And that man must live on for a hundred years who can possess the happiness which comes from loving her.

Jaufre Rudel's poetry is likewise dominated by a desire for a great *Jois*, for a lasting and assured happiness in love. Jaufre differs from Guilhem IX in that his poetry is influenced by moral considerations, which are apparent also in Marcabru's work, and by religious beliefs and Crusading ideals which, in association with his profane love, remove it to a higher sphere of aspiration than we can find in Guilhem IX. Like Guilhem IX he is seeking the utmost joy, but he associates this with *valor* within himself (IV, 9) and the need on his part to preserve 'distance' between himself and the object loved. If we anticipate the terms which Guillaume de Lorris was to use in his *Roman de la Rose*, *Amor* desires Jaufre to reduce the distance which separates him from his lady, and *Raison* desires him to retain it in order to gain lasting *Jois* which belongs to the spirit and imagination. This love to which Jaufre devotes himself is *Fin'Amors*, which never 'betrayed' a man (IV, 35), and the ultimate happiness, assurance and harmony which

Jaufre hopes for in *Lanquan li jorn* will belong entirely to the spirit, the imagination and the memory. Guilhem's hope of ultimate happiness proceeds from the anticipated pleasure of possessing his lady in worldly and courtly circumstances (IX, 31–42), Jaufre's in the hoped-for contemplation of the *parlamens fis* and the *solatz* or 'conversation' which he will have enjoyed with his 'distant' lady whose *pretz* is *fis e verais*, and for him this memory constitutes the *jauzimens d'amor de lonh*. Jaufre's 'distant' love is the highest form of *Fin'Amors* as we find it described in the poetry of Marcabru. *Fin'Amors* is the means by which a man may live *letz, cortes e sapiens*.[17] It seeks certainty of happiness by removal from the shocks and confusion of the everyday world and it is not separated from Jaufre's religious beliefs. Jaufre's fear that *cobezeza* in Love (II, 25) may destroy love, and his concept in *Lanquan li jorn* of utmost happiness in a sort of spiritual communion with the distant lady whom he will have seen and left, show a resemblance to St Bernard's ideas about the evil of *voluntas propria* and *cupiditas*, and on the value of *caritas* in its highest form as a means of bridging the distance between man and God and of achieving a moment of mystical union with Him.[18] This resemblance should not be over-emphasised but it cannot be ignored. When Jaufre says that 'following God to Bethlehem' is the only way to excellence, salvation and assurance of mind he is, after all, repeating the summons of St Bernard, who preached the Second Crusade.

Unlike Guilhem IX, Jaufre appears to reject the possibility of a great happiness from the senses, and his aspiration to profane love exists side by side with his Crusading ideals and Christian beliefs. In his life he seeks *Jois* on the Crusading and religious plane (I, 29–42) as well as on the plane of profane love, but the higher 'distant' love of which he writes in his poetry,[19] however idealised and enriched by religious overtones, is a profane love and not a religious love.

3

Marcabru and Fin'Amors

THE MOST INVENTIVE and original of all the troubadours, Marcabru, appears to have had the humblest origins. The Provençal vida (MS. K) says:

Marcabruns si fo de Gascoingna ,fils d'una paubra femna que ac nom Marcabruna. . . .Trobaire fo dels premiers c'om se recort. De caitivetz vers e de caitivetz serventes fez, e dis mal de las femnas e d'amor.[1]

Marcabru came from Gascony, the son of a woman who was poor and was called Marcabruna. . . .He was one of the first troubadours that one can remember. He composed wretched songs and wretched sirventes and spoke ill of women and of Love.

Marcabru was probably of Gascon origin,[2] but his mother's name in the vida was taken from a stanza of his Dirai vos (XVIII, 67–72)[3] in which he hints at his illegitimacy.

The vida in MS. A is more colourful:

he was abandoned at the door of a rich man, and no one ever knew who he was or where he came from. And lord Aldric del Vilar saw to his upbringing. Afterwards he was so much in the company of a troubadour called Cercamon that he began to compose. And at that time he had the name Panperdut, but thenceforward he was called Marcabrun. . . .He was very famous and people listened to him throughout the world, and he was feared because of his tongue, for he was so critical that in the end the lords of the castle of Guyenne, of whom he had spoken ill, killed him.

Marcabru probably learnt the art of trobar at the court of Poitou, and if his teacher was Cercamon, he quickly surpassed him in ideas and poetic skill.[4] His patron, the eighth count of Poitou, was the son of the first troubadour, a tall, handsome, well-mannered and impulsive man who was possessed of a gargantuan appetite for food and feudal warfare. His sudden death on a pilgrimage to Compostela in 1137 set Marcabru off on a hunt for patronage, from Aquitaine, where

Eleanor had succeeded as Duchess and Queen of France, to Toulouse and the courts of Barcelona, Portugal and Castille.

Marcabru's difficulties in finding patronage are not unexpected. He does not sing, to please a courtly audience, of the happiness or Jois to be found in love, for he believes in Love as a force which can be used to give moral stability and happiness to the individual and society. His vigorous moralising may have given him no easy success in courtly circles, but it is the true source of the future greatness of troubadour poetry and of the courtly ethic.

Marcabru composed at a time of spiritual and social upheaval, between 1130 and 1150. This was the age of Abelard, William of Saint Thierry and Saint Bernard, and the period when life in the castle was becoming life at court, and the nobility, deprived of its true feudal role as a shield against barbarian invasion, was losing its financial supremacy and many political rights to the increasingly prosperous towns such as Toulouse, Montpellier and Marseille. Abduction, seduction and sexual licence were rife among the noble class for whom marriage was often a business contract for the strengthening of territory or an alliance, or for the provision of heirs. Spiritual lethargy possessed the Church in the South,[5] and heresy was on the increase. In this state of social and moral confusion the nobility needed a new and distinctive code of behaviour by which it could affirm its identity and role in society.

The poetry of Guilhem IX shows that a code of refined behaviour, linked with Amors and using courtly terms such as Jois and Jovens, was in existence in his lifetime, and there is evidence that such a code may have evolved at the court of Poitou in the second half of the eleventh century under the commanding influence of noble ladies, such as Agnes of Burgundy. It is apparent from the poetry of Cercamon that, at the time that Marcabru composed, the domna already possessed in courtly matters the nominal dignity of the feudal lord in feudal matters and could impose forbearance, patience and refinement of manners and speech. The domna was invariably married, for this alone gave social status and power, and the love that was addressed to her was adulterous in intention and achievement. To judge from the poetry of Guilhem IX and Marcabru, the code of Amors in the first half of the twelfth century may have been an Ovidian search for mutual pleasure by both suitor and lady, to the accompaniment of courtly phrases and gestures. Marcabru, it is true, laments the passing of an early courtly age when *Amors* was upheld by *Jovens*, *Jois* and *Proeza* (v, 37–9), but the theme of a golden past was a common medieval device for the castigation of present turpitude. In Marcabru's case it may represent a nostalgic longing for the legendary largesse of the age of Guilhem IX. Marcabru judges the sexual behaviour of the nobility in the light of the Christian ethic and the classical humanism of the great scholars of his day, and condemns it as adulterous, sterile and disruptive, for the individual person and for society. He offers a remedy of rational behaviour which will bring social order and individual happiness. This remedy is *Fin'Amors*.

Marcabru is not a philosopher but a moralist and a poet who has the dual purpose of composing with different levels of meaning and of revealing his meaning clearly. Schooled in the arts of rhetoric of Cicero and Quintilian, he abhors the misuse of eloquence and the empty gilded phrases (*la falsa razo daurada* [xxv, 24]) that are spun in order to deceive.[6] He believes that eloquence must express a moral truth clearly, and admits, in what is probably not a modesty *topos*, his own difficulties in avoiding obscurity:

> Per savi·l tenc ses doptanssa
> Cel qui de mon chant devina
> So que chascus motz declina,
> Si cum la razos despleia,
> Qu'ieu mezeis sui en erranssa
> D'esclarzir paraul'escura. (xxxvii, 1–6)

I consider that man indisputably wise who, hearing my song, understands what each word says and the way in which the theme unfolds, for I am troubled myself by the task of making the obscure word clear.

Troubadours who distort what is granted by truth are anathema to him. They have the wits of a child, and sin through the incomplete meaning which they weave into their verse:

> Trobador, ab sen d'enfanssa,
> Movon als pros atahina,
> E tornon en disciplina
> So que veritatz autreia,
> E fant los motz, per esmanssa,
> Entrebeschatz de fraichura. (xxxvii, 7–12)

Ia. Jaufre Rudel (Bibl. Nat. MS. fr. 12473)

Ib. Marcabru (Bibl. Nat. MS. fr. 12473)

II. Troubadour musician; end of twelfth century
(Vanne (Cath.) - Coffret de Mariage bois peint, 003. P. 426)

IIIa. Jaufre Rudel and the Countess of Tripoli
(Bibl. Nat. MS. fr. 854)

IIIb. Bernart de Ventadorn
(Bibl. Nat. MS. fr. 12473)

IIIc. Raimbaut d'Aurenga
(Bibl. Nat. MS. fr. 12473)

IV*a*. Arnaut Daniel (Bibl. Nat. MS. fr. 12473)

IV*b*. Raimon de Miraval
(Bibl. Nat. MS. fr. 12473)

IV*c*.
Guilhem de Montanhagol
(Bibl. Nat. MS. fr. 854)

Troubadours with the mentality of a child make trouble for men of excellence. They turn into torment what is granted by truth. They compose words intentionally interlaced with fragmented meaning.

Writing with fraichura, they cannot distinguish between Fin'Amors and Fals'Amors (XXXVII, 13–14).

The main problem that a man faces in life is the choice between the way of thinking that is fragmented (frait) and the way that is integrated or whole (entiers). To discover the right way of thinking is man's great challenge:

> En dos cuidars ai conssirier
> A triar lo frait de l'entier,
> Be·l teing per deum naturau
> Qui de cuit conoisser es guitz. (XIX, 10–13)

Faced with two ways of thinking I am deeply concerned to separate the fragmented way from the whole way. I consider that man indeed to be, through God,[7] at one with nature who can be a guide in discriminating between ways of thinking.

Peire d'Alvernhe later praised Marcabru for his ability to recognise the meaning of natura and to realise why he was born:

> Marcabrus per gran dreitura
> trobet d'altretal semblansa,
> e tengon lo tug per fol
> qui no conois sa natura[8]
> e no·ill membre per que·s nais. (XIII, 38–42)

Marcabru through his great sense of what was right composed in this very fashion, and they all think of him as a fool who does not understand his own nature or realise why he is born.

This reference to Marcabru's interest in natura and salvation comes immediately after the difficult lines in which Peire speaks with irony of men who are preoccupied with the loves of the flesh: 'No man is capable of feeling secure [within himself] if he does not desire carnal living, for I see that the body is mindful of nothing except to fatten its lord.' Peire is praising Marcabru for his dreitura, his upright, natural and religious way of thinking, in contrast to the amor carnalis of those who despise him for a fool (see p. 180).

Marcabru was aware that his art of 'natural' composing was an innovation and exposed him to mockery:

> E segon trobar naturau[9]
> Port la peir'e l'esc'e·l fozill,

> Mas menut trobador bergau
> Entrebesquill,
> Mi tornon mon chant en badau
> E·n fant gratill. (XXXIII, 7–12)

And in following the art of natural composing I bear the flint and the tinder and the steel, but paltry troubadours, like muddle-headed hornets, turn my song into an empty yawn and make mock of it.

Integrated thinking (*entiers cuidars*) means thinking according to the ways of nature, and of what is beyond nature, and it gives understanding of the ways of man:

> Pus s'enfulleyson li verjan
> E·l glaujol de lonc lo riu blan,
> Qui que paus, ieu pes e cossir
> De moutas cauzas a sobriers,
> Segon natura et estiers,
> De qu'auzem lo poble brugir. (XLI, 1–6)

Since the branches are coming into leaf, and the iris along the white stream, whoever else may be at rest, I think and meditate immoderately long, according to the laws of nature and to other laws beyond, about many matters concerning which we hear the people grumble.

The first line of this poem is based on MS. C but the other three MSS. *AIK* give *Mos sens foilla soz* [*sul A*] *lo verjan* 'my wisdom comes into leaf beneath [on *A*] the bough', and the reading from these three usually trustworthy MSS. strengthens the implicit theme of nature as a guide to wisdom.

Marcabru sees the world as God's creation and finds a moral truth in the order of things which God has established in nature. This truth can be discerned by the 'natural' man who through his belief in God is in harmony with nature (*per Deum naturau*, XIX, 12) and who is not sidetracked by vain and purposeless ways of thought and living. The order and truth which a man can discover in nature will allow him to come to a right opinion on matters of everyday concern.

The knowledge that Marcabru possesses and which makes him rejoice, leads him to a serene attitude to life, praising nature and avoiding tiresome and feckless behaviour and thought:

> Qe scienza jauzionda
> M'apres c'al soleilh declin
> Laus lo jorn, e l'ost'al matin,
> Et a qec fol non responda
> Ni contra musar[t] no mus. (XII bis, 6–10)

74

For the knowledge which makes me rejoice, has taught me to praise the day at sunset and my host in the morning, and not to reply to each and every fool and not to gawp at the gawper.

Medieval exegesis of the Bible and of works of classical Latin, including Ovid, made use of meanings and moral truths which could be discerned in nature. The purpose of this exegesis was to reveal the outer shell of the natural object and its inner significance and place in the natural, and hence divine order. Marcabru also seeks to express 'what is granted by truth' through the moral symbolism of colours and of natural objects, trees, plants, animals, insects and birds.

Because of this, his seasonal openings are not commonplace, but introduce the moral and the theme of his song. In the first stanza of *Al departir*, the sap rises, and the broom, heather and peach tree flower. But promise goes with uncertainty and beauty with ugliness, and the smooth line *E floreysson li presseguier* contrasts with rough, *braus*, word-endings in *-aucs* and *-ucs*. After *presseguier* 'the peach tree' comes the abrupt *rana* 'the frog', symbol of empty and garrulous speech, followed by the budding willow and elder, *sauzes e saucx*, harsh in sound and symbols of the sterile promise which bears no fruit, and the dry season, *yssucs*, which is harsh again and balances the first promise of the rising sap.

> Al departir del brau tempier,
> Quan per la branca pueja·l sucs
> Don reviu la genest'e·l brucx
> E floreysson li presseguier
> E la rana chant'el vivier
> E brota·l sauzes e·l saucx,
> Contra·l termini qu'es yssucs
> Suy d'un vers far en cossirier. (III, 1–8)

As the rough season of tempest departs and the sap rises along the branch so that the broom and heather come to life again, and the peach trees bloom, and the frog croaks in the pond, and the willow and elder bud, now that I see the season of dryness at hand I think deeply about composing a song.

This theme of fruitfulness and sterility, which Guilhem IX had mocked at in his burlesque poem *Companho, tant ai agutz*, is now amplified by Marcabru who describes a great orchard with shrubs, trees and good grafts. In leaf and blossom they are like apple trees, in their fruiting they are willow and elder:

> Fuelhs e flors paron de pomier,
> Son al fruchar sautz'e saucs.   (III, 13–14)

The orchard is the world of men: the fine old trees are dead and those now alive are lopped branches and wisps of straw, full of promises which they fail to keep, given to empty noise and gambling through the night:

> De promessas son bobansier(s)
> Al rendre sauzes e saucx.   (21–2)

They are prodigal with promises but are like willow and elder in keeping them.

The greatest of living men are true elder trees; happy the man who can find among them a laurel or an olive tree, symbols of fruitful and serene wisdom.

In his remarkable *Pois la fuoilla revirola* (XXXVIII) Marcabru uses the symbolism of the seasons and the birds to contrast the ways of nature and man:

I   Pois la fuoilla revirola
   Que vei d'entre·ls cims cazer,
   Que·l vens deromp e degola,
   Que no·is pot mais sostener,
   Mais pretz lo freich temporau
   Que l'estiu plen de gandill
   Don nais puti'et enveia.

II   Lo pics e la rossignola
   Tornon lor chant en tazer,
   Si·s fa·l gais e l'auriola,
   Don l'inverns fai son plazer;
   E l'orgoills torn'en canau
   Per garssos plens de grondill,
   Qu'en estiu contradenteia.

III   Graissans ni serps que s'amola
   No·m fant espaven ni mau,
   Mosca ni tavans que vola,
   Escaravait ni bertau,
   Aquist malvatz volatill
   Non sent bruir ni oler,
   Don francs inverns nos neteia.[10]

IV   Ges l'afilatz bec d'aissola
   Non pert son loc al fogau,
   Anz porta pic e massola
   Don son gran li dui mau.
   Cest tol si donz al jazer
   La dolor del penchinill,
   Pel feminiu don se breia.

v Cest trai del mieill la briola
  Plen'al maitin et al ser,
  E sobre·l faire faissola,
  Car pot la coa mover;
  Cest fai la nuoich son jornau,
  Don engenrra un bel fill,
  Per que sobreseignoreia.

vi Cazen levan trobaiola
  Va·l segles, e no m'en chau,
  Aissi cum la seguignola
  Poi'amon e chai avau.

Since the leaf twists as I see it fall from the tree tops, as the wind tears and parts it so that it can no longer hold fast, so do I value more the cold of this season than the summer full of resources from which are born wantonness and desire.

Woodpecker and nightingale turn their song to silence, and so do the jay and the oriole with which winter does its pleasure; and pride, which in summer bares its teeth, is knocked into the gutter by ruffians who are full of complaints.

Toad or snake with whetted tongue cause me no fear or harm; fly and gadfly in flight, beetle and gnat, my sense is not touched by the buzzing and the smell of these wretched flying insects which noble winter cleans away for us.

The man with the adze-sharp beak does not lose his place at the hearth. On the contrary, he carries a pike and a club which cause great and two-fold hurt. He lies with and takes from his lady the pain of her pubic hill, in exchange for the feminine gift by which he is shortened.

Another takes an armful of the best, morning and evening, and with a tight embrace as he does it, for he knows how to stir the tail. Another does his day's work at night, and so will sire a fine son through whom he lords it over everyone.

The world of men heaves down and up in turmoil (and I care not), just as the swan rises up and falls down.

Winter is clean and chaste. It has its pleasure with the birds which it silences, the woodpecker and nightingale, jay and oriole, the symbols of vain loquacity and passing summer love, of harsh calls and blatant plumage. Pride loses its gleaming summer smile and is whirled into the gutter by winter's grumbling minions. Arrogance (*graissans*) and temptation (*serps*) and the pinpricks of annoyance (*mosca, tavans, escaravait, bertau*) are swept away as the world of nature is purified.

But man has no pure season and continues in carnal lust. The serpent and the insects are swept away, but man still plies his adze-sharp beak, his pike and club with which to belabour his lady and sire an illegitimate son.

The song is 'bound up' in the tornada in which the world of man, in its moral and social confusion, is contrasted with the ordered and purified life of nature in winter, the placid rise and fall of the swan, white symbol of constancy.

In Bel m'es quan la fuelh'ufana (XXI) Marcabru compares the straightforward ways of nature in its sensual summer mood with the crooked ways of man. In nature's summer profusion, bird, frog and owl give voice:

> Quecx auzel[s] quez a votz sana
> De chantar s'atilha,
> E s'esforsa si la rana
> Lonc la fontanilha,
> E·l chauans ab sa chauana,
> S'als non pot, grondilha. (7–12)

Each bird that has a healthy song voice prepares to sing, and the frog strains to do the same beside the spring, and the owl with its mate, if it can do nothing else, grumbles away.

To this natural world love brings order and joy, but man is so driven by deceit that he achieves nothing and his joy is inconstant:

> Sesta creatura vana
> D'amor s'aparilha,
> Lur joys sec la via plana
> E·l nostre bruzilha;
> Quar nos, qui plus pot enguana,
> Per qu'usquecx buzilha. (13–18)

These simple creatures come together through love. Their joy follows the smooth path and ours wavers, for each one of us deceives as much as possible and so achieves nothing worthwhile.

In the world of man, the slandering coward (lauzengier) with crooked tongue advises and overturns and destroys with deceit and lies, so that Marcabru, in an image which Raimbaut d'Aurenga used later (see p. 139), can find no love which may inspire confidence or be free from rust:

> So per qu'amor segurana
> Non truep ses ruylha. (23–4)

Malvestatz triumphs over the courtly virtues; Jovens betrays, Donars perishes and Valors wavers (25–30).

Amors, which brought joy to the simple creatures of nature, brings pain, burning and sickness to man:

Pieger es que gualiana
Amors que guespilha,
Cruzels cozens e baiana
Calens e frezilha,
Quar molt tratz mal e safrana
Selhuy cui estrilha.   (31–6)

Worse still is the love that deceives, that stings like a wasp, cruel, burning
and treacherous, hot and freezing, for the man who is scourged by this
love suffers great ill and turns yellow [with jaundice].

Such tyrannical and uncontrollable love destroys courtly
and Christian values and the physical and spiritual well-being
of the individual; 'these false Christians who tremble in
senseless crime turn the refuse [of their virtue] towards
Khorassan, for the baptism of Jordan brings them harm and
danger' (37–42).

Malvestatz triumphs when, a century before Jean de Meung's
continuation of the Rose, allegorical battle between vice and
virtue is joined in the style of the Psychomachia of Prudentius.
The army of Malvestatz has captured the castle and the hall of
Jois, Jovens and Proesa. The courtly virtues are hard pressed in
their keep:

Qu'usquecs crida 'fuec e flama!
Via dinz e sia prisa!
Degolem Joi e Joven
E Proeza si'aucisa.'   (XI, 21–4)

For each man shouts: 'Fire and flame! Let us get in and take the tower!
Let us slit the throats of Joy and Youth, and let Prowess be put to
death.'

Malvestatz is no empty allegory; it is manifest in dukes and
kings who are untrue to their estate, and in the husbands and
wives who are engaged in a chain-reaction of adultery:

Maritz qui l'autrui con grata
Ben pot saber que·l sieus pescha...   (XI, 49–50)

The husband who scratches the wife of another man knows well that his
own wife sins...

Married men with goat-like mentality destroy their peace
of mind and weaken society with illegitimate children (XVII,
31–6).

Amors inflames uncontrollable desires:

> Amors vai com la belluja
> Que coa·l fuec en la suja
> Art lo fust e la festuja,[11]
>   — Escoutatz! —
> E non sap vas qual part fuja
> Cel qui del fuec es gastatz.   (XVIII, 13–18)

Love acts like the spark which makes the fire smoulder in the sooty cinder and burns up the wood and the straw – Hear me! – and the man who is devoured by this fire does not know in which direction to flee.

Marcabru vituperates against carnal love in the style of the *genus demonstrativum*:[12] its tyranny is all powerful because *Jovens* is in decline, broken and smashed (XVIII, 7–12); *Amors* was once morally straight, now it is bent and clipped (25–7); the man who joins *Fals'Amors* (*Amors* in *ADIK*) is trading with the devil (37–8); Love behaves like the mare who wants to be followed all day and refuses to give a truce (49–51); Love smooths and polishes its words, it stings more gently than a fly, but the cure is more difficult (55–60); the Scriptures tell us that a man justly suffers harm who acts in accordance with a woman's ideas (61–3). Marcabru ends with the hint of his illegitimacy which is quoted in the *vida* in *A*:

> Marcabrus, fills Marcabruna,
> Fo engenratz en tal luna
> Qu'el sap d'Amor cum degruna,
>   — Escoutatz! —
> Quez anc non amet neguna
> Ni d'autra non fo amatz.   (XVIII, 67–72)

Marcabru, son of Marcabruna, was sired under such auspices that he knows how Love casts its seed – Hear me! – so that he never loved any woman, nor was he loved by another woman.

Proeza and *Jovens*, the knightly and courtly virtues which were once the buttress of *Amors* have been ousted by money, and *Amors*, no longer tied to personal virtue, has become venal:

> C'Amors es plena d'enguan,
> Per aver se vai camjan,
> E·ls plus pros torn'e soan,
> Que·l malvatz l'aura enan.   (VII, 25–8)

For love is full of deceit; it keeps changing for the sake of money and scorns the men of highest virtue, so that the wicked man will have it first.

Marcabru contrasts such venal love or *amars* with *Bon'Amors*, which is love related to personal *Honors*, *Valors* and *Pretz* (XXXI, 64–7).

Bon'Amors porta meizina
Per garir son compaigno,
Amars lo sieu disciplina
E·l met en perdicio;
Ai!
Tant cant l'avers dura, sai,
Al fol semblan d'amor fai,
Hoc,
E quan l'avers faill buzina.   (XXXI, 28–36)

Good Love brings a remedy to heal its disciple. Venal love destroys its follower and consigns him to perdition. Alas! – As long as the money lasts, venal love does I know, make a pretence of love to the fool – Yes, indeed! – and when the money fails, it shouts its complaints.

The man who follows *Amars* destroys himself in body and mind:

Qu'ieu dic que d'Amar s'aizina
Ab si mezesme guerreia;
C'apres la borsa voianssa
Fai fols captenenssa dura.   (XXXVII, 15–18)

For I say that the man who consorts with venal love is warring with himself, for the fool, once his purse is emptied, conducts himself in a harsh, dry way.

Marcabru laments the deceits he has suffered in love and in a line which Conon de Béthune may have imitated (ed. A. Wallensköld, VII, 17) curses pie-coloured love and its values:

Dieus maldiga amor piga e sa valor.   (XXIV, 10)

The queue of men rushing carnally at his *amia* turns love to blackness and degradation:

Denan mei n'i passon trei al passador,
Non sai mot tro·l quartz la fot e·l quinz lai cor.
Enaissi torn'a decli l'amors e torn'en negror.
                              (XXIV, 19–21)

Although these ferocious lines may be a vituperative device to dramatise his hatred of sexual promiscuousness, Marcabru describes what appears to have been a personal crisis when in *Ans que*[13] he takes leave of the foolish burden of Love which has left him for money and mocks men of virtue: 'Do not go wooing without *deniers* and, however great your courtly virtue, do not put on courtly airs after your money is spent' (VII, 25–40).

Love and its attendant virtues had a golden past:

81

> Tant cant bos Jovens fon paire
> Del segle e fin'Amors maire,
> Fon Proeza mantenguda
> A celat et a saubuda. (v, 37–40)

As long as noble Youth was father of the world and True Love the mother, Prowess was upheld in private and in public.

but now that *Amors* is ruined:

> Qu'ieu sui assatz esprovaire,
> Deffendens et enquistaire,
> E vei cum Jovens se tuda,
> Per que Amors es perduda
> E de Joi deseretada
> E cum Amors es cujaire. (43–8)

For I am very much the examiner of proof, the defender and inquisitor, and I see how Youth is extinguished so that Love is ruined and deprived of its heritage of Joy, and I see how Love is prone to illusion.

he hopes for a higher and more secure love:

> L'amors don ieu sui mostraire
> Nasquet en un gentil aire,
> E·l luoc[s] on ill es creguda
> Es claus de rama branchuda
> E de chaut e de gelada,
> Qu'estrains no l'en puosca traire. (49–54)

The love which I am professing was born in a noble dwelling, and the place where it grew up is enclosed by an arbour of boughs and protected from heat and ice so that no person foreign to it can take it away from there.

Coming from an allusive poet such as Marcabru, these lines must have aroused ideas in a medieval audience about the *hortus conclusus* as a symbol of the Virgin Mary, and this additional level of meaning is strengthened by the *envoi* or *tornada* of the poem in which *Desirat* 'the desired one' may be taken as a reference to Christ.[14]

In this poem, *Al son desviat*, Marcabru rejects *Amors* which is based on *nien* and *foudat*, the qualities of nothingness and folly which had attracted Guilhem IX but which Marcabru castigates as frivolous and self-gratifying (v, 31–2). He condemns those people who see a flame of love kindled between two foolish lovers, and then cause it to burn brightly (v, 31–6), and in place of such *Amors* he professes a higher love which is as true, assured and protected as the love which one may have

82

for the Virgin Mary. Marcabru may be speaking directly of love for the Virgin Mary, but it is more likely that he is using this image of exalted Christian love to convey the idea of the exalted profane love to which he aspires.

This ideal of perfect, true and complete love, Fin'Amors, is rarely found, for love takes its quality from the qualities of those who practise it: 'my heart is dismayed and I will not hide this; it is difficult now to find genuine love [Amors veraia] and true love [Amors fina] which does not have within it some trait of falseness. Towards the wicked man Love is soon wicked and for the good man, it is good' (XXXII, 37–45).

Fin'Amors excludes uncontrolled carnal desire:

> Dompna non sap d'amor fina
> C'ama girbaut de maiso;
> Sa voluntatz la mastina
> Cum fai lebrieir'ab gosso.   (XXXI, 46–9)

That lady knows nothing of true love who loves a household scullion; she is covered by her desire as the greyhound bitch is covered by the cur.

The distinction between Fin'Amors and Fals'Amors must be made clear and the witless troubadours who think in a fragmented way must be condemned. Marcabru sets himself to this task in Per savi (XXXVII), and after the introduction of his theme in lines 14–15 proceeds to use Amors in the sense of Fin'Amors and Amars in the sense of Fals'Amors.

'I suffer sorrow and grief when I hear those tramps, the trobador ab sen d'enfanssa say that Amors [Fin'Amors] deceives and betrays the man whom Amars rejects. They lie, for the benefits [of Fin'Amors] are Jois, Sofrirs e Mesura' (19–24). Jois for Marcabru is the assured happiness of a love which does not deceive, Sofrirs is patience and humility and Mesura is the rational control by which a man can choose to think and act in the way that will bring him happiness.

There is no inconsistency in Marcabru's use of Amors as praiseworthy love, synonymous with Fin'Amors in this song, and his attacks on Amors as carnal love in other poems. Amors is love in its widest meaning, in all its manifestations, in theory or in practice, loyal or deceitful, spiritual or carnal. Fin'Amors and Bon'Amors, and Fals'Amors and Amars are the subtypes of this main genus which is Amors. Contemporary philosophers such as William of Saint Thierry use Amors with this width of meaning, and so does Jean de Meung in the *Roman de la Rose*.

The quality of true/perfect/good love comes from its trustworthiness and constancy. Marcabru speaks of the lovers who win this reward of *Jois, Sofrirs e Mesura*:

> Aitals pareills fai mostranssa,
> S'en doas partz non camina,
> Pois Bon'Amors n'es vezina,
> Ab dos desirs d'un'enveia
> Ab segurana fianssa
> Blanca cara ver'e pura. (XXXVII, 25–30)

Such a pair of suited lovers who do not travel in separate directions, since *Bon'Amors* stays by their side, are clear proof of one wish born of two desires and a trust that is secure, white, precious, true and pure.

Love in the sense of *Fin'Amors* (XIII, 7) is without deceit and cannot be degraded: 'False friends, false lovers, debase Love and exalt evil deeds. Do not imagine that Love can become bad; it has the same qualities that it had in the beginning. It always had a perfect colour [*Totz temps fon de fina color*] and always the same appearance. No man can know the beginning or the end of its qualities' (XIII, 9–16).

In *Pus mos coratges* (XL) Marcabru defines *Fin'Amors* by its rewards and punishments:

> Aicel cui fin'Amors causitz
> Viu letz, cortes e sapiens,
> E selh cui refuda delis
> E met a totz destruzemens;
> Car qui fin'Amor vol blasmar
> Elha·l fai si en folh muzar
> Que per autra cuid'es peritz.[15] (8–14)

The man who is the chosen one of *Fin'Amors* lives happy, courtly and wise, and the one whom it rejects, it destroys and consigns to complete destruction, for if a man speaks against *Fin'Amors*, it turns him into a fool gaping at illusion, misled and destroyed by his different way of thinking.

In attempting to define the qualities of *Fin'Amors* in this poem, Marcabru contrasts two ways of thought and life. The one way gives happiness through a wise mind, and controlled and praiseworthy conduct, the other way (*autra cuida*) comes from folly, is adrift from the secure values which give happiness, and leads to destruction. Those who do not follow the thought and conduct associated with *Fin'Amors* are like the damned, and with fierce words Marcabru prophesies the burning fire and the Hell which await wanton, false, hypocritical men and women. He ends his peroration:

> Ebriaic et escogossat,
> Fals preveire e fals abat,
> Falsas recluzas, fals reclus,
> Lai penaran, ditz Marcabrus,
> Que tuit li fals y an luec pres,
> Car fin'Amors o a promes,
> Lai er dols dels dezesperatz. (29–35)

Drunkards and seducers, false priests and false abbots, false recluses, male and female, will be tortured there – thus speaks Marcabru – for all these false people have a place reserved there and Fin'Amors has promised that there [in Hell] will be the lamentation of the despairing.

This catalogue of sinners who speak against Fin'Amors (12) is so close to St Paul's list of sinners who will not possess the kingdom of God (Galatians, v, 19–21) that Marcabru has obviously gone to the Christian ethic with its ideas of Hell-fire and peace eternal for a system of rewards and punishments with which to illustrate the power and virtue of Fin'Amors. Although the two planes of profane and religious love are brought so close, Fin'Amors is not Christian love of God. The religious connotations of Marcabru's attack on the enemies of Fin'Amors would deeply impress a twelfth-century audience. Marcabru is saying that the virtues required by Fin'Amors exclude uncontrolled behaviour which is dominated by deceitful self-interest and carnal desire, and which is as offensive to the Christian ethic as it is to the concept of *mesura* and the 'natural' order of life in society. This idea is repeated later by Guiraut de Bornelh in his *Per solatz*:

> Chavalers si'aunitz
> Que·s met en domneiar,
> Pos que tocha dels mas moltos belans
> Ni que rauba gleizas ni viandans!
> (ed. Kolsen, LXV, 27–30)

Let that knight be shamed who goes wooing in courtly fashion after laying hands on bleating sheep and robbing churches and travellers.

The partition between the courtly and Christian ethic becomes tenuous when Marcabru moves from the punishments of those whom Fin'Amors rejects, and praises the rewards it offers its disciples with the traditional Christian imagery of the *fons bonitatis* of St Augustine and the *lux mundi . . . , lux vera quae illuminat omnem hominem . . .* (St John, viii, 12, and i, 9).[16]

Ai! fin'Amors, fons de bontat,
C'a tot lo mon illuminat,[17]
Merce ti clam, d'aquel grahus
E·m defendas qu'ieu lai no mus;
Qu'en totz luecx me tenh per ton pres,
Per confortat en totas res,
Per tu esper estre guidatz.   (XL, 36–42)

Ah! True Love, fount of goodness which has given light to the whole world, I ask that of your mercy you may protect me so that I may not join the cries of the tormented or cast idle thoughts towards them. For at all times I consider myself as your prisoner and you as my consolation in all things; by you do I hope to be guided.

St Paul said: Dico autem: Spiritu ambulate, et desideria carnis non perficietis, and listed the works of the flesh. Marcabru says (ditz Marcabrus, 32): Walk in the ways of True Love, avoid the tormenting confusion of mind and spirit which is the lot of its adversaries and find the secure peace, comfort and guidance of Fin'Amors so that you may live happy, courtly and wise, with a sure confidence (XXXVII, 29) and with Joy, Patience and Mesura (XXXVII, 24). The follower of Fin'Amors will thus possess qualities comparable to those which in St Paul's Epistle are the fruit of the Spirit: Fructus autem Spiritus est: charitas, gaudium, pax, patientia, benignitas, bonitas, longanimitas, Mansuetudo, fides, modestia, continentia, castitas. Adversus huiusmodi non est lex (Galatinas, v, 22–3).

The courtly code is less disinterested and more narrowly self-seeking than the Christian. Courtly man seeks happiness here on earth, within himself and in society. The courtly counterparts of many of the Christian virtues are controlled by the rational and moderating quality of mesura which enables a man to live a wise and happy life in harmony with himself and his surroundings. The man without mesura or any sense of personal order and courtly virtue is the equal of a base animal or a thief:

Qui per aver pert vergonh'e mezura
E giet'honor e valor a non cura
Segon faisson es del semblan confraire
A l'erisson et al gos et al laire.   (IX, 17–20)

If a man for the sake of money loses his sense of proper shame and of the fitness of things, and casts away honour and personal virtue and is indifferent to them, he appears by these actions to be the equal of the hedgehog, the cur, and the thief.

T he man with mesura and valors must improve through
Fin'Amors. The fool, who because of his desmesura does not
understand his role in life, cannot escape from folly; without
hope of Jois he must go from bad to worse, and so must the
foolish woman:

> Ja non creirai, qui que m'o jur,
> Que vins non iesca de razim,
> Et hom per Amor no meillur;
> C'anc un pejurar non auzim,
> Qu'ieu vaill lo mais per la meillor,
> Empero si·m n'ai doptansa,
> Qu'ieu no·m n'aus vanar, de paor
> De so don ai m'esperansa.
>
> Greu er ja que fols desnatur,
> Et a follejar non recim
> E folla que no·is desmesur;
> E mals albres de mal noirim,
> De mala brancha mala flor
> E fruitz de mala pesansa
> Revert al mal outra·l pejor,
> Lai on Jois non a sobransa.   (XIII, 25–40)

I will never believe, whoever may swear it to me, that wine does not come
from the grape and that a man does not improve because of love; for we
never heard of any man growing worse [because of Love], for my personal
worth is as great as it can be thanks to the best domna. Yet I am fearful and
dare not speak openly of this, for fear of losing that on which I have set
my hopes.

  It will be hard for the fool to be untrue to his nature, on any occasion,
and not to relapse into folly, and for the foolish woman not to act in an
unseemly, wilful way. A bad tree comes from a bad shoot, and bad
blossom from a bad branch, and the fruit of bad thoughts reverts to evil,
and passes beyond the worst limits in that person over whom Joy holds
no sway.

Mesura is the quality of the man who controls his thoughts
in order to be wise and courtly in word and deed. It is the
foundation of cortesia, which is the quality of the man who
possesses all the courtly virtues and who acts accordingly:

> De Cortesia·is pot vanar
> Qui ben sap Mesur'esgardar;
> E qui tot vol auzir quant es,
> Ni tot cant ve cuid'amassar,
> Del tot l'es ops a mesurar,
> O ja non sera trop cortes.
>
> Mesura es de gen parlar,
> E cortesia es d'amar;

E qui non vol esser mespres
De tota vilania·is gar,
D'escarnir e de folleiar,
Puois sera savis ab qu'el pes.

C'aissi pot savis hom reignar,
E bona dompna meillurar . . .   (xv, 13–26)

That man can boast of being courtly who knows well how to heed his
sense of what is fitting, and the man who wants to hear everything that
can be heard, and who thinks he can gather up all he sees, needs above all
to act with a moderating power of judgment or he will never be very
courtly.

Good judgment is shown through decorous speech, and courtliness
through the way one loves, and let that man who does not wish to be
blamed, refrain from all churlish deeds, from mockery and acting the
fool. Then he will be wise, provided that he thinks.

For in this way he can behave like a wise man, and a noble lady can
improve . . .

Marcabru's delightfully humorous *pastorela*, *L'autrier jost'una
sebissa*, the first and the best of this genre, also has its serious
side, for its theme is the importance of *mesura* for human
behaviour. The poet, in the role of the knight, meets the lonely
shepherdess:

L'autrier jost'una sebissa
Trobei pastora mestissa,
De joi e de sen massissa;
Si cum filla de vilana,
Cap'e gonel'e pelissa
Vest e camiza treslissa,
Sotlars e caussas de lana.   (xxx, 1–7)

The other day beside a hedge I discovered a shepherdess of low birth,
abounding with joy and good sense. Like the daughter of a peasant woman
she is wearing a hooded cape, a skirt and fur lined coat and an open-weave
blouse, shoes and woollen stockings.

The poet begins his wooing:

Toza, fi·m ieu, res faitissa,
Dol ai car lo freitz vos fissa.   (9–10)

Damsel, I said, fairest one, I grieve because the cold pierces you.

Rebuffed for this bribe of clothing, he offers the joys of
companionship:

Quar aitals toza vilana
No deu ses pareill paria
Pastorgar tanta bestia
En aital terra, soldana.   (18–21)

For such an attractive peasant girl ought not to pasture so many cattle in such a lonely place without suitable company.

The damsel answers with sharp irony:

> Don, fetz ela, qui que·m sia,
> Ben conosc sen e folia;
> La vostra pareillaria,
> Seigner, so·m dis la vilana,
> Lai on se tang si s'estia,
> Que tals la cuid'en bailia
> Tener, no·n a mas l'ufana!   (22–8)

Sir, she said, whoever I may be, I know well the difference between sense and folly. Let your [noble] companionship, my lord, the peasant girl said to me, remain where it is suited, for there are people who imagine that they possess this quality but have no more than the illusion of it.

The knight, at this hint of his spurious nobility – which would be doubly humorous if Marcabru played the part – exceeds himself in courtly flattery: 'Damsel of noble condition, your father was a knight who begot you on your mother, for she was a courtly peasant woman. The more I look at you, the more pleased I am and happy in the thought of the joy you can give – if only you acted in a human way towards me!' (29–35).

The damsel rejects the flattery:

> Don, tot mon ling e mon aire
> Vei revertir e retraire
> Al vezoig et a l'araire,
> Seigner, so·m dis la vilana;
> Mas tals se fai cavalgaire
> C'atrestal deuria faire
> Los seis jorns de la setmana.   (36–42)

Sir, all my lineage and my kin do I see going back and returning to the sickle and the plough, my lord, the peasant girl said to me, but there are people who pretend to be knights who should be doing this same [work] the six days of the week.

If your beauty does not come from a knightly father, it must have been bestowed by a noble fairy when you were born. And this beauty would be doubled if you would lie beneath me (43–9).

> Seigner, tan m'avetz lauzada,
> Que tota·n sui enojada;
> Pois en pretz m'avetz levada,
> Seigner, so·m dis la vilana,
> Per so n'auretz per soudada
> Al partir: bada, fols, bada,
> E la muz'a meliana.   (50–6)

My lord, you have praised me so much that I am quite vexed by it. Since you have increased my reputation, my lord, the peasant girl said tò me, you shall have as payment when you leave: 'Gape, fool, gape, and the foolish hope at midday.'

The shepherdess mocks the knight's lust by affecting the courtly *domna* who chides her suitor for his excessive praise and yet offers him a reward for it. As the song was sung, a pause before the word *bada* and the proverb about foolish dreamers in the midday sun would heighten the humour of the abrupt switch from the knight's illusory expectations to the earthly reality of the shepherdess. She rejects his offer of sincere friendship (*amistat de coratge*) which will be free from deception (61–3): 'Sir, a man impelled by folly, swears and vows and promises a pledge, and so would you do me homage... but I, for a small entrance fee, am not willing to change my maidenhood for the name of a wanton.'

Marcabru sums up the dispute in the last two stanzas and in the two *tornadas* or *envois*:

> Toza, tota creatura
> Revertis a sa natura:
> Pareillar pareilladura   73
> Devem, ieu e vos, vilana,
> A l'abric lonc la pastura,
> Car plus n'estaretz segura
> Per far la cauza doussana.   77

> Don, oc; mas segon dreitura
> Cerca fols sa follatura,
> Cortes cortez'aventura,   80
> E·il vilans ab la vilana;
> En tal loc fai sens fraitura
> On hom non garda mezura,
> So ditz la gens anciana.   84

> Toza, de vostra figura
> Non vi autra plus tafura
> Ni de son cor plus trefana.   87

> Don, lo cavecs vos ahura,
> Que tals bad'en la peintura
> Qu'autre n'espera la mana.   90

Damsel, every creature reverts to its nature. You and I, my peasant love, should make a pair by pairing, in the shade beside the pasture, for you will be more secure to do the sweet thing.

Sir, yes, – but according to what is right, the fool seeks his folly and the courtly man courtly adventure, and the peasant man goes with the peasant woman. Good sense is lacking on those occasions when one pays no heed to one's sense of what is fitting, and this is what the Ancients say.

Damsel, I never saw another woman who had your looks and was more mischievous than you, and more treacherous in her heart.

Sir, the owl is an augury for you, for one man gapes at the picture while another hopes for the reward.

The shepherdess is the protagonist of Marcabru's ideas and the knight speaks from a carnal desire which is concealed by *ufana* or outward show of courtly hypocrisy. They have different ideas about *natura*. The knight sees it as the animal mating to which each creature reverts (71–7). The shepherdess sees *natura* as the essential quality of each individual which, according to *mesura*, he or she must express in life; the fool must act like a fool, and the courtly man behave in a courtly way. Good sense is lacking when *mesura* is not observed, and when people act out of keeping with their abilities, ideas and station in life. In this way, this remarkable poem is not only a *pastorela* but an imaginary *tenso* or a debate between the courtly artifice which conceals deceit and the good sense of thinking and acting according to *mesura* and *natura*, the natural order of things in which each individual can choose, by virtue of *mesura*, to act according to the qualities of his or her nature, and can see and reject the illusion of pleasures which betray this principle.

In the *tornadas*, the knight, frustrated, sheds the veneer that Raimon de Miraval calls *cortez'ufana*, and turns to churlishly outspoken truth, and the shepherdess mocks him in his defeat for his foolish gaping at the illusion of appearance (*peintura*), which, in Marcabru's eyes, was the sign of the irrational and uncourtly nature.

Amors is estimable when it cherishes its own values (xv, 31–2), and so is *cortesia* when it is directed by thought and *mesura*, and tied to the ideal of Fin'Amors. Marcabru attacks the courtly way of life only when it is untrue to its values of *cortesia* and becomes a mask for the seducer and an excuse for wantonness on the part of the *domna*. The lady who takes two or three suitors and will not choose one and place her trust in him, degrades herself, her reputation and her courtly quality (xv, 25–30).

In his two starling poems Marcabru again mocks courtly forms which disguise carnal desire. In *Estornel* he sends as a messenger to his lady the common starling which, having no song of its own, imitates with harsh cries the songs of other birds. The poet's thoughts of his lady, in a parody of the *Farai un vers* of Guilhem IX, change abruptly from courtly fantasy to earthly reality:

> No sai s'aissi·s fo fadada
> Que no m'am e si'amada;
> C'ab una sola vegada
> Fora grans la matinia,
> Si·ll plagues
> Ni volgues
> Qu'o fezes.   (xxv, 12–18)

I know not if a fairy laid a spell on her so that she may not love me and may still be loved; for with one single go the morning would be great, if this pleased her and she wanted me to do it.

He leaves the *mana* of hoped-for reality and attacks the *peintura*, the illusion of courtly deceptions and especially the words of false suitors:

Ah! how false and gilded speech is esteemed as excellent: it walks as a chosen one foremost in the presence of all the ladies. Away with it! He is a very fool who trusts it; beware of its dice that it has loaded...[18] (xxv, 23–9)

The lady whom he desires with *Fin'Amors* is, he declares, dissolute:

> De fin'amor dezirada
> Az una flor pic vairada
> Plus que d'autruna pauzada;
> Paucs fols fai tost gran folia.   (xxv, 67–70)

Desired with true love, she has a pie-coloured flower, and more so than any other prostitute; the small fool soon commits a great folly.

The mingling of mock courtliness and ribald carnality continues into the last stanza:

> Del deslei
> Que me fei
> Li fauc drei,
> E·il m'autrei,
> Mas sotz mei
> Aplat sei,
> Qu'ela·m lass'e·m lia.   (xxv, 78–84)

For the faith which she owed me and broke I give her pardon, and grant myself to her; but let her lie flat beneath me and entwine and bind me.

Ges l'estornels non s'oblida, the sequel, has a lighter humour. The bird does not 'lose itself' in courtly thoughts of the

beloved, but hastens to fly straight, a lofty undertaking in the
light of Marcabru's ideas on the 'straight path' or *dreita carrau*.

In the rhetoric of courtly poetry (*esclarzir* and *entensa*) the
'noble' bird clears its voice:

> Sobr'una branca florida
> Lo francx auzels brai e crida;
> Tant ha sa votz esclarzida,
> Qu'ela n'a auzit l'entensa.
>   L'us declui,
>   Lai s'esdui
>   Truesc'a lui.
>   'Auzels sui,'
>   Ditz:– 'Per cui
>   Fas tal brui
> Ho cal[s] amor[s] tensa?'   (XXVI, 12–22)

On a branch in blossom the noble bird clamours and cries; it has cleared
its voice so well that she has understood what it is trying to say. She opens
the door, it backs, dances towards her: 'I am a bird' it says. – 'On whose
behalf do you make such a noise, or what love torments you?'

The lady denies that she has fought with a thousand loves
beyond Lerida: 'Go and tell him to be here in the morning so
that beneath a pine, with me beneath him, we may put an end
to this misunderstanding.'

Humour lies in the grotesque of the courtly lover hard
pressed by lust, in the symbol of the starling which sings so
badly that it has to declare itself a bird, and in the *domna*,
desired with Fin'Amors, who denies her dissolute reputation
but is as sensually urgent as her suitor, or any heroine of the
chanson de toile. Marcabru's purpose is to satirise the deceit and
pretence of an empty courtliness. In the *pastorela* he did this
through the rational good sense of the shepherdess, but in the
starling poems he uses the ironical methods of Guilhem IX to
provide a burlesque of the courtly lover, the bird messenger
and the *domna*.

The influence of Guilhem IX is also apparent in Marcabru's
D'aisso laus Dieu.[19] In *Ben vuelh* Guilhem IX had sung his own
praise as poet, gambler and lover, with good humour and
ribaldry. Marcabru is more thoughtful; he thanks God and
St Andrew for the supreme gift of reflection and judgment
which are essential in any debate (XVI, 1–12):

> De gignos sens
> Sui si manens
> Que mout sui greus ad escarnir;

Lo pan del fol
· Caudet e mol
Manduc, e lais lo mieu frezir. (XVI, 13–18)

In cunning meanings I am so rich that it is very hard to mock me. I eat
the bread of the fool that is warm and soft and let my own cool off.

He continues: As long as the fool's bread lasts, I swear I
will not leave him; when it runs out, let him gape, adrift in
his mind, and acquire a desire for my bread [19–24]. It is
right for the fool to act as a fool and for the wise man not to
be won over to folly [25–30]. I excel with Breton staff or
stick, and at fencing, and when I strike another and take
guard, he cannot cover himself against my blow [31–6]. In
my neighbour's thicket I hunt when I will, and make my two
little dogs bark, and the third bloodhound rushes forward,
joyous and intent, and there is no lying about that [37–42].
He continues:

Mos alos es
En tal deves
Res mas ieu non s'en pot jauzir,
Aissi l'ai claus
De pens navaus
Que nuills no lo·m pot envazir.

Dels plus tors sens[20]
Sui ples e prens
De cent colors per mieills chauzir;
Fog porti sai
Et aigua lai,
Ab que sai la flam'escantir.

Cascuns si gart
C'ab aital art
M'er a viure o a morir;
Qu'ieu sui l'auzels
C'als estornels
Fatz los mieus auzellos noirir. (XVI, 43–60)

My fief is in such an enclosure that no one but I can enjoy it; I have shut
it up in such a way, with dissimulating thoughts, that no one can invade
what is mine.

I am filled and taken captive by the most twisted meanings, by a hundred colours so that I may choose the best. I carry fire here and water
there with which I know how to quench the flame.

Let every man beware, for with skill such as this will I have to live or
die, for I am the bird that causes its fledglings to be brought up by the
starlings.

Marcabru states the theme of this poem, which is anti-

Guilhem IX, in the first stanza, when he thanks God for the gift of his pre-eminent power of judgment and decision (albir, 3). He knows that, unlike Guilhem IX, he is a reflective poet who not only recognises folly and wisdom in love, life and poetry, but determines his actions accordingly. The world that he sees is divided between the fool and the wise man; each has his bread and his thicket, and Marcabru admits that he shares the bread of the fool and hunts in his thicket. With Guilhem IX bread had the meaning of sexual reward, and the private thicket was a sexual symbol of the domna (III, 14). It is probable that 'eating the fool's bread' here means self-indulgence in carnal pleasure; this pleasure is ephemeral and the wise man, when the fool's bread fails, must return to his own way of life, and perhaps carry the fool, adrift and inconstant (23), along with him.

In contrast to the thickets of other men, which offer enticement to lust, Marcabru's own refuge is enclosed and inviolable. In another poem, Al son desviat, he turns his thoughts from the turmoil of adulterous love around him to a love which grew, sheltered from intrusion, in a noble place claus de rama branchuda (V, 49–54). In D'aisso laus Marcabru's refuge (deves, 44) may be a form of higher love comparable to love of the Virgin Mary, or it may be the ostaus, the dwelling of his own heart.

Marcabru is saying that he can be tempted to try the ways of thought and life of the fool, but he thanks God for the rational control which returns him to his own bread and thicket. This theme of weakness overcome occurs in Ans que when he rids himself of the fols fais 'the foolish burden' of Amors (VII, 21–4), and in Doas cuidas: 'Through noble thoughts I rejoice and through base thoughts I am made brutish' (see p. 97).

But the temptation of fol cuidar is strong:

> De fol cuidar
> No·m sai gardar,
> Que s'ieu cuich esser de bon fiz
> E·l fols m'en bruig long los auzitz,
> E·m tornara d'amon d'avau.   (XIX, 14–18)

I cannot protect myself from foolish [sinful] ways of thinking, for if I think that I am acting in truth and goodness, the fool comes roaring round my ears and throws me down from on high.

The last two stanzas of *D'aisso laus* emphasise the importance for the poet of moral reflection (*albir*) and judgment (*dreitura*), the quality that Dante was to esteem as *rectitudo*. The poet must know how to quench the flame he has lit, and in *Al son desviat* he amplifies this theme: 'For after the flame is born between the foolish lover and beloved, if the fool then burns on account of the lady who is scorching with passion, I am not guilty and I am no criminal' (v, 33–6). Men who excite foolish lovers to folly are the poets of the *nien* and *foudatz* that Marcabru castigates and condemns (v, 31–2). This ideal of a moral sense which can reject the vanity of superficial and transitory folly is the theme which Marcabru is unfolding in the coloured imagery of *D'aisso laus Dieu*. Guilhem IX's boast of poetic and amatory skill is vanity, he implies, since any foolish person can commit such folly. Wisdom lies in the power of judgment (*albir*) which can recognise and reject such *fol cuidar*. Marcabru exercises his power of moral judgment when, from among the twisted meanings and hundred colours by which his mind is filled and held captive, he chooses the best (*mieills*). There can be little doubt that the secondary meanings that he gives to 'bread' and 'thicket', folly and wisdom, would be readily grasped by a twelfth-century courtly audience, which would also realise that this poem, composed in a highly allusive but not in an obscure style, is an attempt to treat the theme of literary and amatory prowess, which Guilhem used in *Ben vuelh* (VI) for humorous effect, as a *plait* (8) or dispute between the ways of the fool and the wise man in love, life, poetry and thought. When Marcabru rejects the path of *fol cuidar* in poetry, he praises his own skill in quenching the flame of folly:

> C'ab aital art
> M'er a viure o a morir. (XVI, 56–7)

For by means of skill such as this I must live or die.

'Living' (*viure*) here can have the extended meaning of 'life eternal', and, on a lower plane, Marcabru has posterity in mind when in the last two lines of the poem he gives his songs and ideas (his 'fledgelings') to the lesser poets and *joglars* (the 'starlings') to sing and spread abroad (XVI, 58–60).

The duality of thought and life which is revealed in the allusive poetry of *D'aisso laus Dieu* is discussed explicitly in *Doas cuidas*:

> Doas cuidas ai compaignier
> Que·m donon joi e destorbier,
> Per la bona cuida m'esjau
> E per l'avol sui aburzitz;
> D'aital cuidar
> Doutz et amar
> Es totz lo segles replenitz,
> Si qu'ieu for'ab los esmaïtz
> Si tant no saubes ben e mau. (XIX, 1–9)

I have two companion ways of thinking which give me joy and confusion. Through noble thoughts I rejoice, and through lowly thoughts I am made brutish. With ways of thinking like these, sweet and bitter, is the whole world filled, so that if I did not know so well what is good and what is evil, I should be among those who are in turmoil.

These two ways of thinking are *frait cuidar* and *entier cuidar*:

> En dos cuidars ai conssirier
> A triar lo frait de l'entier. (XIX, 10–11)

With two ways of thinking I am deeply concerned, in order to separate the fragmented way from the whole way.

He considers that man as *naturaus* 'natural' who, through (the gift of) God, is a guide in discriminating between different ways of thinking (XIX, 12–13). He sees himself as a poet of the natural order of life (see p. 74), and also as a weak individual who is beset by the temptation of *fol cuidar*, at the moment when he thinks that he is on the path of truth and goodness (XIX, 14–18).

The difference between thinking that is *frait* and *entier* has been explained in various ways, such as the contrast in Augustinian terms between carnal and spiritual love or between life seen with the outward eye of reality and the inward eye of vision. It is possible, however, that these terms mean what they say and that one way of thinking is broken or fragmented (*frait*) and the other is whole or integrated (*entier*).

Marcabru looks at the world around him for examples of fragmented thinking. He turns to the mercenaries whose outward eye chooses to see the flashing gold and bejewelled armbands of King Gaifier (Waïfarius) of Aquitaine which were seized after his assassination by the hirelings of Pepin the Short in 768 and hung as a trophy of war in St Denis. But the inward eye of the mind sees the joyless spectral dance of the way of thinking and the failed promise of the dead king.

La vostra cuida, soudadier,
fai elhausar los baus Gaifier
qu'en vis si balon, sem en gau,
la cuid'e·l prometres faillitz.[21]   (XIX, 19–22)

Hired warriors, the way in which you think makes Gaifier's bracelets
flash so that within the eye there dance, devoid of joy, the [vain] thoughts
and failed promise of the king.

Marcabru attacks men who are tamed by the 'single' way of
thought which they reveal in their illusory dreams of inconstant love:

Cuiador d'amor volatgier
Son de sola[22] cuida mainier,
Qu'en mil no·n trob una corau
D'aqestas amors cuidairitz.   (XIX, 37–40)

Men who are given to dreams of inconstant love are tamed in their single
way of thinking, for among a thousand of these dream loves I find not one
that is heartfelt.

Marcabru does not blame all thoughts and dreams of love,
for this would shame *Jovens* and debase *Jois* (XIX, 41–5); it is
the fragmented, 'single' way of thinking and dreaming about
inconstant, ephemeral loves that he condemns, and the lack
of true and higher aspiration.

He turns to the limited and illusory ways of thought and
life of noble ladies and lords: 'ladies through their way of
thinking, act foolishly in their foolish pursuits, and knights
through their way of thinking, are foolish, poor, arrogant and
untamed. May God sustain these wretched people! For never
through imagining it to be so have we seen the head of the
plant bring forth any more seed than the root, and a man
perishes among his noble thoughts if an achievement which
may surpass his thought does not result from it' (XIX, 55–63).

Soldiers, lovers, ladies and knights are led by a narrow,
'fragmented' way of thinking which is unrelated to any wider
system of values. Just as, according to St Bernard, *voluntas propria*, unless it is overcome, bends a man's nature so that it cannot be upright in the likeness of God, so for Marcabru *frait
cuidar* shows a man the bent path (*lo tort sentier*) in life so that
he mistakes illusion for reality. The ladies and knights who
are intent on their particular pursuits 'go off along the
crooked path, whistling at the gadfly as if it were a hawk, and
they abandon the straight road [*la dreita carrau*]' (XIX, 64–6).
Youth withers and Joy fails.

If we look back at the *pastorela*, *L'autrier jost'una sebissa*, we see that the knight is given to *frait cuidar* and is arrogant and *braus*, literally 'untamed', because he has not accepted the higher code of knightly and courtly behaviour which he affects. The shepherdess, abounding with *joi* and *sen*, wins the 'debate' because her sense of *conoissensa* 'discrimination' (23) and *mesura* (83) allows her to think with *entier cuidar* and to see that the knight is gaping at an illusion of reality (*Que tals bad'en la peintura*, 89). She tries to show the knight the qualities which should be a part of his way of thinking. She is *naturaus*, and can choose between the false and the real in order to lead her life according to *mesura* 'as the Ancients tell us' (XXX, 84).

It is possible to interpret the difficult poem *Contra l'ivern* as an example of the mind controlling desire:

> Mos talans e sa semblansa
> So e no so d'un entalh,
> Pueys del talent nays semblans
> E pueys ab son dig l'entalha,
> Quar si l'us trai ab mal vesc
> Lo brico, l'autre l'envesca.   (XIV, 13–18)

My desire and the appearance of it to my mind are and are not of the same sculpted shape, since the appearance [in my mind] is born from desire and then shapes it with what it says, for if the one [the desire] attracts the simpleton with its evil bird-lime, the other [the appearance of it to the mind] fixes him fast in it.

Desire is related to the immediate reality of the physical *domna*, but once this desire appears in his mind, it is absorbed and changed by his idea of love so that his desire now goes beyond immediate childish (*tozetz*, 24) reward:

> Per cujatz n'ai esperansa
> Qu'enquer ab mi s'enguasalh,
> Mas tan n'ay bons esperans
> Estranhs de corta guasalha
> Qu'en mieg mon afar folesc
> Non dic paraula folesca.   (XIV, 25–30)

In my thoughts I have the hope that she may yet be a companion to match [my ideal], but I have so many fine hopes that are alien to a short-lived, sensual profit that in the middle of behaving foolishly I do not speak foolish words.

If this interpretation is admissible, Marcabru is saying that his inner vision of happiness (*Fin'Amors*) allows him to judge his everyday behaviour as folly committed under the impulse of desire for the *domna*. When he refuses to use foolish words to win short-term sensual rewards from Love (*guasalha*, 28, taking its colour from *gazal* 'a prostitute'), he is defending himself against the tyranny of treacherous desire inflicted by *Amors* (XIV, 37–42). Love takes its quality from the quality of the lover who may succumb to sensual desire and allow his mind to speak foolish words or who may use his mind to disentangle himself from the sensual web (XIV, 35–6) and shape desire into a form comparable to a higher ideal of Love, such as Fin'*Amors*. The man who can shape self-interested desire so that it forms part of a higher ideal is thinking in a 'whole' or integrated way, and when Marcabru says that he never loved, nor was loved, he may mean that he never loved in this ideal way.

This interpretation of *entiers cuidars* as thinking in a 'whole' way may explain why Marcabru, unlike later troubadours, felt no conflict between his ideal of profane love, Fin'*Amors*, and his Christian belief and hope of salvation. In his Crusading song *Pax in nomine Domini!* he describes the *lavador* or cleansing place which God has provided in Spain where the defenders of Christianity 'are suffering the burden of pagan pride!'. Those people who do not go to this Christian *lavador* are the very opponents of Fin'*Amors*, they are guilty of *Escarsedatz* 'niggardliness' and *No-fes*, 'non-faith', 'which separates Joven from its companion'. They are the vain layabouts, ruled by carnal desire:

> E·il luxurios corna-vi,
> Coita-disnar, bufa-tizo,
> Crup-en-cami
> Remanran inz el felpidor;
> Dieus vol los arditz e·ls suaus
> Assajar a son lavador;
> E cil gaitaran los ostaus;
> E trobaran fort contrafort,
> So per qu'ieu a lor anta·ls chas.   (XXXV, 46–54)

And the licentious wine-blowers, food-bolters, ember-blowers, road-squatters will remain inside the place of torment. God wishes to test the bold and the gentle in his cleansing place, and the others will watch over their own dwellings and will find strong opposition [in Death], and for this I chase them away to their shame.

Those people who fail the Christian call lead self-centred, carnal lives, rooted in their dwellings and their hearts (*ostau*) by *sola cuida* and 'fragmented' thought. The Crusade, like

Fin'Amors, demands the bold, the serene (*suaus*) and the generous, and 'the French go against their nature, and the natural
order of life, if they say no in this matter concerning God'
(xxxv, 64–5).

The rewards of the *lavador* are wordly and spiritual:

> Que·l Seigner que sap tot quant es
> E sap tot quant er e c'anc fo,
> Nos i promes
> Honor e nom d'emperador.
> E·il beutatz sera – sabetz caus –
> De cels qu'iran al lavador?
> Plus que l'estela *gauzignaus*.   (xxxv, 28–34)

For the Lord who knows all that is, and knows all that will be and that
ever was, promised us in this matter honour and the name of Emperor.
And do you know what beauty will belong to those people who go to the
cleansing place? More than that of the morning star.

and:

> C'ab la vertut del lavador
> Nos sera Jhesus comunaus.   (xxxv, 42–3)

For through the virtue of this cleansing place Jesus will be united with us.

The early troubadours were faced with the need to invent
ways of describing profane love. Marcabru uses the imagery
of the New Testament: his refuge from the deceit of *Amors* is
an arbour closed with branches, symbol of the Virgin Mary;
the followers of *Fals'Amors* are like the carnal sinners in the
Epistle to the Galatians; and the rewards of *Fin'Amors* are described in terms used by St Paul and St Augustine for the fruits
of Christian love. The courtly virtues required for *Fin'Amors*
are those which also impel men to go on the Crusade. Marcabru's mind moves easily between the co-existent but separate planes of profane *Fin'Amors* and Christian love of God.
The Christian associations of the rewards and qualities of
Fin'Amors, as he describes them, would win a deep response
from his twelfth-century audience, but Christian influence
extends beyond his imagery to his radical division of profane
love into self-indulgent carnality and a higher love which is
accepted by the mind, nourished by courtly virtue and fruitful in good results.

The conflict between the carnal and the spiritual, which
must be as old as thinking man, dominated the thought of
twelfth-century France. St Augustine had said that man loves
because he is searching for happiness; *unde se fieri putat beatum,*

hoc amat (PL, xl, col. 672), and that the desire to love and to be happy determines a man's striving, and makes him worthy or unworthy. Man is raised by his spirit to *caritas*, love of God and neighbour, or is dragged down by the weakness and burden of his flesh to *cupiditas*, love of the world and worldly things. Love is the force which drives a man in all he does, to the Good or the Bad, and all loving in the last resort is directed towards God.

Classical humanist thinking in the twelfth century gave new importance to reason as a bridge between the carnal and the spiritual. In reason lies man's true dignity, and he must use reason to order his whole way of life so that he may aspire to the Highest Good. Reason reveals the virtues of the body as well as the soul, of the world and of God, and reconciles the differences between them.

The ideal of a life led according to reason (*modus secundum rationem vivendi*) was put forward strongly by William of Saint Thierry, the close friend and companion of St Bernard. In his *De natura corporis et animae*, which he wrote between 1130 and 1138, he defines the three steps on the way to perfection as the organic life of natural man, the life of reason and the spiritual or divine life. That man alone is perfect who lives all three lives together. The debauched man stamps on his dignity and neglects soul and spirit, the thinker, bound up with knowledge, forgets his concern with God. Only the Christian achieves the fullness of life in which body, soul and spirit retain their own activity and help one another; nature in such a man reaches its full flowering. God created Heaven and earth, and man rejoices in God by using the things of this world. Reason serves the spirit by dominating the body and controlling the passions, and nurses the lower life of the senses towards the happiness of life in God.[23]

In his *De natura et dignitate amoris*, which he wrote between 1119 and 1120, and which in many MSS. is wrongly attributed to St Bernard, William contrasts natural love in which *voluntas* becomes *amor*, *amor* becomes *caritas* and *caritas* becomes *sapientia*, with the unnatural love advocated by Ovid. In the section *On false love and its teachers* he says:

Love has been placed naturally in the soul by the creator of nature. But this love, since it has lost the rule of God, needs to be educated and taught by man. Not of course in the manner of something which does not exist and must be brought into being, but like something which must be purified, developed and strengthened. What the soul must learn is the way to purify, to increase and consolidate the love which is natural to it. In former days, carnal, offensive love had its masters, teachers who were so consummate in the act of transmitting to others the corruption which soiled them, that the 'Doctor of the Art of Love' was compelled by libertines and his companions in debauch to renew in his songs what he had recently praised with too little restraint...he taught men to turn the natural virtue of love to libertinage, by their undisciplined morals, and to pursue this love by the useless excitement of sensuality until it reached a kind of madness. In such individuals, wretched, depraved, submerged by the waves of carnal concupiscence, the whole order of nature has foundered in death. In accordance with this order, indeed, their spirit should have risen, born by the wings of love, to the God who created it. Debased by the temptations of the flesh, man has understood no more than this, he has compared himself to the animals who have no reason, and has made himself like them... (PL, clxxxiv, col. 381)

The whole of man is the creation of God and William of Saint Thierry praises the man who recognises this wholeness and uses his reason to reconcile his natural carnal side and his aspiration to the spiritual and divine life. The love that Ovid praises is one-sided concupiscence which indulges the carnal side of man, but ignores his rational and spiritual self. Such love defies the concept of the whole natural man created by God, and thereby flouts nature.

These ideas of William of Saint Thierry are very like those of Marcabru, who was his contemporary. Behind Marcabru's Fin'Amors there is also the idea of man as part of the nature which was created by God, and able to respond entirely to this nature that has been given to him, by bringing into harmony the desires and demands of his body, reason and spirit. This man's attitude to life is whole (entiers) and not fragmented. His merit is that he thinks, and can assimilate his carnal desire, which is his God-given natura, to a higher concept of Love, Fin'Amors, which is constant and free from deceit. Such a man must possess mesura which will allow him to live according to his qualities and natura. The natural man, through God, is blessed with the power to show others the path to choose in life and love. To be aware of the higher spiritual side of one's nature and to achieve a higher order of courtly moral behaviour is Reality; to seek immediate, one-sided and ephemeral pleasure, which forms no part of such an order, is Illusion.

William's attack on Ovid is matched by Marcabru's attacks on the tyranny of carnal *Amors* and of *Fals'Amors*. In the *tenso* with Uc Catola, about whom we know very little, he says: 'Ovid shows here, and the course of events proves it . . . that Love is more attracted to decadent men.' Uc Catola professes the benefits of an Ovidian-type love which pleases the senses: 'When I am weary and sad and my fair love [*bon'amia*] welcomes me with a kiss as I undress, I depart from her feeling healthy and happy and healed.' But Marcabru likens such love to the carnal pleasures of the wine press (VI, 45–56).

Marcabru's opposition to the irrational quality of Ovidian love may also explain his attack on the school of Eble of Ventadorn,[24] whose poems have not survived: 'No more will I commit myself on behalf of the compositions of Lord Eble which [who] uphold[s] foolish meaning against reason' (XXXI, 73–6).

Marcabru is by no means alone in decrying the *mores* of his time. John of Salisbury (*Policraticus*, III, XIII, and VI) attacks the courtly layabouts, and Bernard of Cluny (or Morlaix), Etienne de Fougères and others vituperate against the excesses of all classes of society. But Marcabru's moralising has a specific purpose; he believes that 'whole' love in the sense of *Fin'Amors* will provide happiness for the man who finds it, and stability for a society which is disrupted by amoral licence. He gives to *Fin'Amors* the moral virtue that Cicero saw in the love, or *amicitia*, which cannot exist except among good men (*De Amicitia*, V, 18), which springs from nature rather than from need (VIII, 27), and to which we are most attracted by virtue, 'than which nothing is more lovable' (*Nihil est enim virtute amabilius*) (VIII, 28). The unswerving constancy that we seek in *amicitia*, says Cicero, is maintained by loyalty (*fides*), and a man cannot be loyal whose nature is full of twists and turnings (XVIII, 65). The good man allows no feigning or hypocrisy in *amicitia* (XVIII, 65), which depends also on reverence, its brightest jewel, for it is a fatal mistake to believe that *amicitia* opens wide the door to every passion and sin (XXII, 83–4). Do not, says Cicero, commit your love too quickly or attach it to unworthy men. Those men are worthy of friendship who have within their own souls the reason for their being loved (*Digni autem sunt amicitia, quibus in ipsis inest causa cur diligantur. Rarum genus!* . . ., for most men recognise nothing good in human experience unless it brings some profit (XXI, 79–80)).[25]

The courtly virtues[26] which sustain Marcabru's idea of Fin'Amors[27] distinguish it from and raise it above other forms of profane love. If we put together an imaginary composite portrait of the true lover or *fis amaire* we should see a man who possesses or is endowed with *Jovens*, youthfulness of virtue, generosity of spirit and freedom from petty meanness, and who has *valors* or innate moral worth, in a courtly sense. Such a man needs *conoissensa*, the power of discriminating between the good and the bad, the whole and the fragmented, the true and the false, and he needs the rational quality of *mesura* in order to follow the right path which *conoissensa* shows him, and direct himself to a real life suited to his *natura*, talents and position, instead of a false life based on illusion. He must be inspired by *Jois* which demands a positive search for a happiness which, through its constancy and freedom from deceit, will give him an assurance of security and harmony within himself and in his outward social behaviour. He must reject a sterile and passive attitude to life. He must be able to recognise the virtues required by Fin'Amors, of which the chief is loyalty, and must accept, consciously in his mind, the merits of Fin'Amors, and subject himself willingly to its discipline which rejects 'fragmented' thinking and any desire which has self-gratification as its only purpose. He must recognise the carnal and spiritual sides of his nature and assimilate carnal desire to his vision of Fin'Amors. If he does this, he will improve in courtly virtue and will live *letz, cortes e sapiens*; happy in the feeling of stability, reassurance and freedom from sin and folly which is given by this love; wise through knowing himself and thinking in a 'whole' way, and *cortes* by living according to *cortesia*, which is both the sum total of all the courtly virtues and their manifestation in social behaviour. This courtly moral excellence will earn him *pretz*, which is the esteem or reputation given him by society.

The fuller meaning of some of these virtues, *Jois, Jovens, Conoissensa* among others, becomes clearer with later troubadours, and all these qualities vary in importance and shades of meaning as troubadour poetry and courtly society evolve and change, but the great merit of Marcabru is that he allows us to see that *cortesia* is not merely a social *courtoisie* but a rationalised system of values. *Jois, Jovens*, and other courtly terms had been current at the time of Guilhem IX, and Marcabru with his vision of the golden past laments the absence of these virtues because of which, he says, life is degraded. It is probable that Marcabru, who was learned in the arts of eloquence, deepened the meaning of existing courtly terminology by relating it to the Christian precepts for living a 'whole' life. He was influenced in this by contemporary thinkers such as William of Saint Thierry, who, steeped in the classical, and possibly Hispano-Arabic literature then available, were analysing Love in all its manifestations and effects on the body, mind and spirit of man.

Marcabru's abstract ideal of *Fin'Amors* is more important to him than the physical reality or the idealised vision of the *domna*. If *Lanquan fuelhon li boscatge* (xxviii, MS. C only) is correctly attributed to him, he can turn his hand to the conventional love lyric as well as to the genres of the *pastorela, congé,* Crusading song and burlesque poetry. But it remains the task of other troubadours to put the ideal of *Fin'Amors* into practice. With his moralising outlook, swayed by clerical misogyny, Marcabru sees the *domna* more readily in the image of Eve than of the Virgin Mary. His exalted idealism has as companion a harsh and precise observation of life, and his praise of virtue goes with an ardent attack on *basse-cour* behaviour. In the real life of the court, in what may be his late poems, he finds little *cortesia*, but much courtly pretence:

> De tals sa·n vei enrazigatz,
> Los fols, e·ls savis deceubutz
> Per los acropitz penchenatz
> Que tot jorn demandon salutz,
> E demandon aco per ces;
> C'anc nuills francs hom non dec sofrir
> C'aitals gastaus fumos tengues.   (xxxix, 57–63)

For I see men who are rooted [in wickedness], fools and wise men deceived by the squatters with combed out hair who demand greetings all day and demand them as tribute. Never should any man with a whole mind tolerate the upkeep of such dissipated, smoky-minded people.

Righteous anger turns to resignation in *Pus s'enfulleyson*:

> E s'ieu cug anar castian
> La lor folhia, quier mon dan;
> Pueys s'es pauc prezat si·m n'azir,

Semenan vau mos castiers
De sobre·ls naturals rochiers
Que no vey granar ni florir.   (XLI, 25–30)

And if I think that I can continue to castigate their folly [sinfulness], I am seeking to harm myself. And since people care little if I grow angry, I am constantly sowing my reproofs on what are, by their very nature, rocks from which I see no seed or blossom come forth.

He continues:

I commend myself to God. How can one trust oneself to this inconstant world [lo segle cazen e levan]? (XLI, 37–8)

Marcabru is one of the most original and important of all medieval poets. He can write, as in A la fontana del vergier (I), with pure and direct lyrical feeling, but he also has the spirit of Dante's eagle reaching for the stars. His vision of Fin'Amors and of a way of life controlled by mesura and sustained and expressed by cortesia, influences all later troubadours and through them the development of courtly ideas in Western Europe. Marcabru's ideas are not new, but their expression in such evocative and varied language and rhymes in what is, so far as we know, an early stage in the evolution of cultivated lyric poetry, other than Latin, in Western Europe, is the mark of an outstandingly inventive poetic genius, in whom there can be seen already many of the ideas and qualities of Jean de Meung.

The Generation of 1170

4

Bernart de Ventadorn

ABOUT 1170 AT PUIVERT, when all were *iogan rizen* 'playing and laughing', Peire d'Alvernhe passed in mocking review the troubadours of his day, Peire Rogier, Guiraut de Bornelh, Bernart de Ventadorn, Raimbaut d'Aurenga and others, who may have been present at some formal occasion which has been interpreted, probably wrongly,[1] as a halt on the road to Aragon of the wedding procession of Eleanor, daughter of Henry II, and her retinue.

These poets, with Peire d'Alvernhe, represent a transitional stage in the development of troubadour poetry. Much more than the early troubadours, Guilhem IX, Marcabru and Jaufre, they feel the need to conform in subject-matter and style to an increasingly powerful courtly convention. About 1170 the individual search for *Jois* on an abstract level of imagination or memory, and the individual moral striving to escape from the burden of sensuality, expressed in highly allusive language, is rivalled by a poetry which accepts the courtly canon of Love, and the allusive style is gradually displaced by the easy, direct courtly style of the *trobar leu*. Metaphysical ways of expression and thought are in retreat before the worldly demands of courtly patrons and audiences.

The here-and-now standards of the courtly audience, which impoverished troubadour poetry, also ensured a welcome for it throughout the courts of Europe. The poet who was most appreciated and imitated abroad, especially in Northern France, was Bernart de Ventadorn, archetype of the courtly troubadour. Peire d'Alvernhe says of him:

> E·l tertz, Bernartz de Ventedorn,
> q'es menre de Borneill un dorn;
> en son paire ac bon sirven

per trair'ab arc manal d'alborn,
e sa mair'escaldava·l forn
et amassava l'issermen.[2]   (XII, 19–24)

And the third, Bernart de Ventadorn, who is a hand's breadth less than Borneill. For his father he had a serving man skilled at shooting with the long bow of laburnum, and his mother heated the oven and gathered twigs.

The Provençal *vida*, using this stanza, tells us:

Bernart de Ventadorn came from Limousin [which today is Corrèze and Haute Vienne] from the castle of Ventadorn. He was a man of poor birth, the son of a hired man [*sirven*] who was a stoker and heated the oven to bake the bread in the castle. And he became a handsome and skilled man, and he knew well how to sing and compose, and he grew to be courtly and accomplished . . .

The *vida* tells us also that his lord the viscount of Ventadorn (probably the famous *Ebolus cantator*, friend and poetic rival of Guilhem IX) honoured him for his singing and composing, but sent him away when he discovered his love for the young viscountess; Bernart was welcomed by the young Duchess of Normandy (Eleanor of Aquitaine) and composed many fine songs about her; when Henry II took her to England Bernart stayed with the 'good count Raimon of Toulouse', and when the count died Bernart entered the order of Dalon, a Cistercian abbey near Hautefort where Bertran de Born also retired, and there he died.[3]

We know little about Bernart's life from other and less romantic sources: his poetic career spans Aquitaine, including Limousin and Poitou, and the new rich centre of troubadour poetry at Toulouse; he addressed love songs to Eleanor of Aquitaine and may have been present at the coronation of Henry II and Eleanor in Westminster Abbey in 1154; and he found patronage with Count Raimon V of Toulouse. There is no information about him after 1173, which is the last possible date of composition for Peire d'Alvernhe's poem *Cantarai d'aquestz trobadors*.

Bernart is the first great troubadour who accepts completely the *service d'amour* and addresses his songs of love entirely to a lady of exalted rank. When Marcabru attacks the tyranny and deceits of sensual love, *Amors*, and suggests an alternative, *Fin'Amors*, in which sensual desire is controlled by reason and *mesura*, he is, for a courtly audience, attacking the idea of the *domna* in her physical and sensual being in favour of an abstract and idealised concept of supreme *Fin'Amors*, and this would scarcely have endeared him to Eleanor of Aquitaine. Bernart accepts the tyranny of *Amors*, which he sees as an Ovidian god of love shooting his darts of pleasure and pain, and he accepts suffering as the way to greater happiness in love. His submission to the *domna* is feudal and complete; happiness lies in the reward of a glance, a love token, a kiss, the sight of her naked body. The *domna* is almost synonymous with *Amors*; she holds the power of happiness and sorrow, life and death, she is a deity whose mercy can release him from the prison in which *Amors* has set him. Bernart proclaims his devotion to *Amors* and the *domna* with mind and body, and his entire natural being. He sings of the shades of sorrow, joy, disillusionment and hope, that he feels for the *domna* whom he must desire as aspirant (*fenhedor*), suppliant (*precador*), recognised suitor and trusted associate (*entendedor*), and finally, but rarely, accepted lover (*drut*). The framework of love is fixed by social formalities, but Bernart's lyric genius is anything but social or formal. To situations which demand mannered elegance he reacts with impassioned poetic feeling and the seeming artlessness of direct and largely monosyllabic poetic language. It would be as wrong to see him as a completely 'social' poet, a troubadour and play actor of the courtly establishment, as to think of him as a 'Wordsworth of the twelfth century'. He has both qualities: he must win reputation and patronage by using the ideas and terminology to which his courtly audience is accustomed and he must give release to the ebullient lyric genius within him. *Himmelhoch jauchzend, zum Tode betrübt*, he feels the edge of joy and despair as sharply as any Romantic poet. As a courtly poet, presumably of low birth, he must reveal this power of feeling within the courtly conventions of *Amors*, to which his intense and vigorous poetry lends life and richness. Not to love or feel delight leads, he thinks, to death in life, the condition that Raimbaut d'Aurenga calls 'flabby-hardened', *flacs-endurzitz*; and personal courtly virtue (*valors*) must perish in a society which is thus half dead through lack of feeling. Bernart's courtly submission and intense feeling are both apparent in *Non es meravelha* (**xxxi**):

Non es meravelha s'eu chan
melhs de nul autre chantador,
que plus me tra·l cors vas amor
e melhs sui faihz a so coman.
cor e cors e saber e sen
e fors'e poder i ai mes;
si·m tira vas amor lo fres
que vas autra part no·m aten.

Ben es mortz qui d'amor no sen
al cor cal que dousa sabor;
e que val viure ses valor
mas per enoi far a la gen?
ja Domnedeus no·m azir tan
qu'eu ja pois viva jorn ni mes,
pois que d'enoi serai mespres
ni d'amor non aurai talan.

Per bona fe e ses enjan
am la plus bel'e la melhor.
del cor sospir e dels olhs plor,
car tan l'am eu, per que i ai dan.
eu que·n posc mais, s'Amors me pren,
e las charcers en que m'a mes
no pot claus obrir mas merces,
e de merce no·i trop nien?

Aquest'amors me fer tan gen
al cor d'una dousa sabor:
cen vetz mor lo jorn de dolor
e reviu de joi autras cen.
ben es mos mals de bel semblan,
que mais val mos mals qu'autre bes;
e pois mos mals aitan bos m'es,
bos er lo bes apres l'afan.   (XXXI, 1–32)[4]

It is no wonder if I sing better than any other singer, for my heart draws
me more to love and I am better suited to do its bidding. Heart and body
and knowledge and mind and strength and power have I devoted to it;
the bridle draws me so much to love that I do not look around elsewhere.

That man is dead indeed who does not feel in his heart some sweet
delight of love; and of what use is it to live without worth except to bore
people? May God Almighty never hate me so much that I may ever live
for a day or a month after I am guilty of being a dullard and having no
desire for love.

In good faith and without deceit do I love the fairest and the best. I sigh
from my heart and weep tears from my eyes; because I love her so much
I harm myself. What more can I do, if Love takes me captive and if the
prison in which it has set me can be opened by no key except mercy, and
if in her I find no mercy at all?

This love smites my heart so graciously with a sweet delight: a hundred
times a day do I die of grief and come back to life another hundred times

for joy. My hurt has indeed a fair appearance, since it is worth more than any other happiness. And since my hurt is so pleasing to me, the happiness after the suffering will be good.

Helpless, dependent on the mercy of his *domna*, he makes his feudal submission:

> Bona domna, re no·us deman
> mas que·m prendatz per servidor,
> qu'e·us servirai com bo senhor,
> cossi que del gazardo m'an.
> ve·us m'al vostre comandamen,
> francs cors umils, gais e cortes!
> ors ni leos non etz vos ges,[5]
> que·m aucizatz, s'a vos me ren.   (49–56)

Noble lady, I ask of you nothing but that you should accept me as your servant, for I will serve you as I would a noble lord, whatever reward may come to me. Behold me at your command, you who are noble, kind, joyous and courtly. You are no bear or lion that you should slay me if I surrender to you.

Bernart cannot dissimulate his love; in Ovidian fashion, the sight of his lady causes his eyes, face and complexion to change their appearance, and he trembles like a leaf in the wind. Beset by love, he cannot reason about it:

> non ai de sen per un efan,[6]
> aissi sui d'amor entrepres.   (45–6)

I have not as much sense as a child, so much am I the captive of love.

In *Amors, e que·us es vejaire?* (IV) Bernart plays his courtly role of debating with *Amors*:

> Amors, e que·us es vejaire?
> trobatz mais fol mas can me?
> cuidatz vos qu'eu si' amaire
> e que ja no trob merce?
> que que·m comandetz a faire,
> farai o, c'aissi·s cove;
> mas vos non estai ges be
> que·m fassatz tostems mal traire.   (IV, 1–8)

Love, what do you think? Can you ever find anyone more foolish than me? Do you think I can be a lover and never find mercy? Whatever you command me to do, I will do, for that is right. But it is not at all becoming of you to make me suffer all the time.

He formally declares his love for the most beautiful woman in the world. He would rather suffer hanging than love a lady from whom he can expect no happiness; but against *Amors* there is no defence. Yet *Amors* can reward, and his lady might deign to see and hear him:

> Grans enois es e grans nauza
> tot jorn de merce clamar;
> mas l'amor qu'es en me clauza,
> no posc cobrir ni celar.
> las! mos cors no dorm ni pauza
> ni pot en un loc estar,
> ni eu no posc plus durar,
> si·lh dolors no·m asoauza.   (41–8)

It is a great tribulation and sorrow to ask for mercy every day, but I cannot cover up or hide the love which is enclosed within me. Alas! my heart does not sleep or rest and cannot stay in one place, and I cannot endure any longer, if my grief is not assuaged.

His sighs would have slain him swiftly, more than a year ago, were it not for her kindly look, which redoubled his desires. Bernart turns from courtly to everyday language to reproach his *domna*:

> No·n fatz mas gabar e rire,
> domna, can eu re·us deman;
> e si vos amassetz tan,
> alres vos n'avengr'a dire.   (57–60)

You do nothing but jest and laugh about it, my lady, when I ask anything of you; and if you were as much in love as I, you would be compelled to say more than that.

The *Amors* which commands and tyrannises is synonymous with the social pressure of Bernart's situation at the centre of life at court. To please his patroness, he must see her as the epitome of beauty and grace, and to satisfy her, his audience and himself, and distinguish himself from the lesser rhymesters, he must show the true and intense quality of his feeling. *Amors* provides the structure for his poem, but the pleasure for his audience and his own poetic and social success must come from the total effect of a composition in which words and melody, rhymes, courtly doctrine, personal feeling and musical accompaniment are harmoniously bound up and integrated.

In En cossirer et en esmai (XVII) Bernart's theme is similar but his treatment of it is less stilted:

> En cossirer et en esmai
> sui d'un'amor que·m lass'e·m te,

que tan no vau ni sai ni lai
qu'ilh ades no·m tenh'en so fre,
c'aras m'a dat cor e talen
qu'eu enqueses, si podia,
tal que, si·l reis l'enqueria,
auria faih gran ardimen.

Ai las, chaitius! e que·m farai?
ni cal cosselh penrai de me?
qu'ela no sap lo mal qu'eu trai
ni eu no·lh aus clamar merce.
fol nesci! ben as pauc de sen,
qu'ela nonca t'amaria
per nom que per drudaria,
c'ans no·t laisses levar al ven. (XVII, 1–16)

I am careworn and dismayed by a love which binds and holds me, so that however far I go in any direction, it holds me instantly in its bridle, for now it has given me the purpose and desire to woo, if I am able, a lady whose favour a king would be bold to seek.

Alas, wretched captive! and what shall I do? And what counsel shall I take about myself? For she knows not the hurt I suffer and I dare not ask her for mercy. Ignorant fool! You have little wisdom indeed, for she would never love you either in name or in fact, for she would rather let you be carried off by the wind.

He will not confess his love. To die for love is *cortezia*:

que mout m'es grans cortezia
c'amors per midons m'aucia; (30–1)

for it were a deed of great courtesy if love for my lady slew me.

Reason argues with love in his heart:

What wrong does my lady, if she knows not what befalls me?
God, she should have known that I die for love of her.
How?
From my uncouth behaviour and my churlish tongue's silence. (33–40)

What joy from her glance!

que·l seus bels douz semblans me vai
al cor, que m'adous'e·m reve. (43–4)

for her fair, sweet look goes to my heart and soothes and heals me.

Burning with desire he leaves her, to declare his love in writing.

In *Per melhs cobrir* Bernart rebels with a courtly conceit against *Amors* and the strength of his desire. Song and delight conceal his sorrow although he dies of love (1–6). Love has chosen a *domna* and has forced him to love her; may she turn her eyes to her liege man! The beauty of her lips, eyes, brow, hands, arms and all the rest of her perfection, causes him torment and anguish. Resenting his desire, he remains subject to it, not knowing his destiny:

> A mo talen volh mal, tan la dezire,
> e pretz m'en mais, car eu fui tan auzatz
> qu'en tan aut loc auzei m'amor assire,
> per qu'eu m'en sui conhdes et ensenhatz.
> e can la vei, sui tan fort envezatz:
> vejaire m'es que·l cors al cel me salha.
>
> Dins en mo cor me corrotz e·m azire,
> car eu sec tan las mias volontatz.—
> mas negus om no deu aital re dire,
> c'om no sap ges com s'es aventuratz.
> que farai doncs dels bels semblans privatz?
> falhirai lor? mais volh que·l mons me falha!
>
> (XXXV, 25–36)

I detest my desire, so much do I desire her, and I esteem myself more because I was so bold and set my love in so high a place that I am pleasing and well mannered. And when I see her, I am so happy that my heart seems to leap to the sky.

Within my heart I am enraged and angry with myself for following my desires so much. But no man should say such a thing for one knows not at all the fate that is in store. What shall I do about these fair and friendly looks? Shall I fail to respond to them? I prefer that the world should fail me.

In *Lancan vei per mei la landa* he laments the ignorant desire (*nescis talans*) which impels him to address a lady who snubs him:

> be m'auci mos nescis talans,
> car sec d'amor los bels semblans
> e no ve c'amors lh'atenda. (XXVI, 12–14)

My ignorant desire slays me, for it follows the fair appearances that love makes and does not see what Love may have ready for it.

He longs for the ceremony of the royal *couchée*: may God make her want to welcome him! May she order him to her bedside to remove her shoes, on his knees, humbly, if she deigns to offer him her foot (29–35).

With *Amors* which is ephemeral and scornful (XLV) he can play the courtly game in Ovidian style; deceived, he will deceive (XIX); since love is urgent, let cunning avail both lady and lover:

per Deu, domna, pauc esplecham d'amor!
vai s'en lo tems, e perdem lo melhor!
parlar degram ab cubertz entresens,
e, pus no·ns val arditz, valgues nos gens!   (XXXIX, 45–8)

By Heaven, my lady, we achieve little in love. Time passes and we are losing the best! We should be talking with secret signs, and since boldness avails us not, let cunning be our aid!

Bernart's hope of happiness in love is centred on the physical presence of his *domna*, her look, love token or kiss, or the promise of more. Love is contained here on earth, and the *domna* enjoys the supreme authority which Marcabru gave to his abstract ideal of *Fin'Amors*. For Bernart *Fin'Amors* is no lofty ideal which will show the lover the inadequacy and the foolish burden of his sensual desire; it is a true love that is felt in the heart, and the inspiration of song:

Chantars no pot gaire valer,
si d'ins dal cor no mou lo chans;
ni chans no pot dal cor mover,
si no i es fin'amors coraus.   (XV, 1–4)

Singing can scarcely be of any worth if the song does not proceed from within the heart, and song cannot proceed from the heart if there is in it no true and heartfelt love.

He attacks those who blame *Amors*:

Amor blasmen per no-saber,
fola gens; mas leis no·n es dans,
c'amors no·n pot ges dechazer,
si non es amors comunaus.
aisso non es amors; aitaus
no·n a mas lo nom e·l parven,
que re non ama si no pren!   (15–21)

Foolish people blame Love through ignorance. But this does not harm it, for Love cannot decline unless it is common love. That is not love; love which is such that it loves no one unless it takes [from them] has no more than the name and appearance of love.

Fin'Amors has no concern with the venal love of women –
aquelas c'amon per aver e son merchandadas venaus:

En agradar et en voler
es l'amors de dos fis amans.
nula res no i pot pro tener,
si·lh voluntatz non es egaus.
e cel es be fols naturaus
que de so que vol, la repren
e·lh lauza so que no·lh es gen.   (29–35)

In giving pleasure and in desiring does the love of two faithful lovers consist. Nothing can avail in love if the desire to love is not equal. And that man is indeed a born fool who blames it for what it desires and advises it to do what is displeasing to it.

With this mention of the fols naturaus 'a fool by his very nature' who blames Love for its sensual desires and turns these in a direction which is not pleasing to it, Bernart may be referring to Marcabru's wish to control and refine the carnality of Amors and raise it above the plane of the senses. In this case Peire d'Alvernhe may have Bernart in mind when he attacks those who call Marcabru a fool for not recognising his own nature and realising why he is born (XIII, 40–2).

If this interpretation is correct,[7] Bernart is acting as the spokesman for Amors which springs from the 'natural' desire of the senses. In Lo gens tems de pascor he says: 'Alas! of what use is my life if each day I do not see in bed beneath the window my true and natural joy [mo fi joi natural], her body white as Christmas snow, so that we may measure ourselves against each other?' (XXVIII, 33–40). This conflict between Bernart's courtly view of love and Marcabru's idea of love as part of the natural order of life antedates by a century the contrast between the First and Second Parts of the Roman de la Rose by Guillaume de Lorris and Jean de Meung.

Fin'Amors, for Bernart, is the love of two faithful lovers (XV, 30), and Love, which is unconcerned about a man's strength or weakness, wealth or poverty, abhors the company of pride. Pride decays, and Fin'Amors guides the lover. Fin'Amors is love that is sincerely felt. Love is humility, patience and fidelity, and all men, regardless of birth or position, are equal in its service:

> Mas en amor non a om senhoratge,
> e qui l'i quer, vilanamen domneya,
> que re no vol amors qu'esser no deya;
> paubres e rics fai amdos d'un paratge;
> can l'us amics vol l'autre vil tener,
> pauc pot amors ab ergolh remaner,
> qu'ergolhs dechai e fin'amors capdolha. (XLII, 15–21)

But in love a man has no supremacy, and if he seeks it there, he woos like a churl, for love desires nothing unseemly. It puts poor men and rich on the same footing, and, when one lover wants to decry another, love cannot remain long in the company of pride, for pride decays and true love gives the lead.

Marcabru saw Fin'Amors as a fount of moral and spiritual goodness which lit up the world. Bernart sees love as a source of light for his own heart, offering him 'improvement' in the sense of personal happiness, reassurance and freedom from dismay and confusion. His happiness from Fin'Amors and his lady's promise afflicts his senses and turns the world upside-down:

> Ara no vei luzir solelh,
> tan me son escurzit li rai;
> e ges per aisso no·m esmai,
> c'una clardatz me solelha
> d'amor, qu'ins el cor me raya;
> e, can autra gens s'esmaya,
> eu melhur enans que sordei,
> per que mos chans no sordeya.
>
> Prat me semblon vert e vermelh
> aissi com el doutz tems de mai;
> si·m te fin'amors conhd'e gai:
> neus m'es flors blanch'e vermelha
> et iverns calenda maya,
> que·l genser e la plus gaya
> m'a promes que s'amor m'autrei.
> s'anquer no la·m desautreya?   (VII, 1–16)

Now I cannot see the light of the sun, so much are its rays darkened for me. I am not at all distressed by this for a light as brilliant as the sun shines upon me from the love which casts its rays into my heart; and although other people are confused and dismayed I grow better rather than worse, and so my song does not decline.

The meadows seem to me green and scarlet as in the sweet maytime. So firmly does true love keep me happy and joyful that the snow is white and scarlet blossom to me and the winter is the calends of May, for the most gracious and joyous lady has promised to grant me her love. Will she not go back on her word to me again?

Fin'Amors is the natural prey of the savai, the 'base' men, for whom Jovens and Jois have no meaning:

> c'aras s'ajoston li savai
> e l'us ab l'autre cosselha
> cossi fin'amors dechaya.   (19–21)

for now base men come together and take counsel one with another to see how true love may be impaired.

The quotations already given from Bernart's poetry show him as an exemplary courtly lover, court poet and courtly play-actor; he does feudal homage to his exalted lady, admires her beauty, desires her body, seeks the reward of a glance or kiss, is saddened by the treacherous heart beneath her eyes, by her pride, her mockery and her other lovers, and seeks happiness with a new *domna* who may console him for the traitress who deceived him. These are the topics of courtly love, of so-called *amour courtois*. They are the prescribed courtly responses to each social and emotional situation in love and they dominated the love poetry of the Northern French *trouvères* in the late twelfth and thirteenth centuries and the thinking of many nineteenth-century scholars of troubadour poetry. Bernart did not invent this code of mannered responses which is found in the many closed and refined societies in which Love imposed a system of social behaviour. The system which Bernart accepts and uses depended on the social and emotional supremacy in Love of the *domna* and was probably developed, under the influence of Ovid, Cicero and possibly Hispano-Arabic love poetry, at the court of Poitou in the eleventh century. The niceties of etiquette in Love were certainly debated at this court, for Guilhem IX uses and burlesques the form of the love debate. Andreas Capellanus,[8] for all his benevolent irony, has also given us a vivid impression of Eleanor's court, for which Bernart composed, as it debated the finer rules and problems of love casuistry and the proper social and emotional procedure in Love. This 'courtly' love is concerned primarily with the psychology and social responses to a love that is based on sensual desire: the lady or her innate sense (*carestia*) of herself as *domna* preserves distance between herself and the suitor, who improves in patience, humility and the other courtly qualities which are needed to please and impress and win some reward as token of her favour. This pattern of behaviour is concerned with love felt and desired on the plane of the senses. The higher aspiration to spiritual forms of love based on reason, *mesura*, ideas of moral excellence and abhorrence of *cupiditas*, were probably developed separately from this code of social and sensual love, but came into conflict with it and influenced it through Marcabru and Jaufre Rudel from about 1140 to 1170. The aspiration to a higher, spiritual form of love is found in Hispano-Arabic literature, but, as we have seen with Marcabru, it enters troubadour poetry probably through the scholastic philosophers of the early twelfth century. The analogies

between profane spiritual love and Christian love, between
adoration of the domna and of the Virgin Mary are apparent in
the allusive poetry of Marcabru and Jaufre Rudel, but they are
present in Bernart de Ventadorn only in the profane form of
his adoration of his lady, in a feudal supplication which may
just possibly have religious overtones.

Bernart is the first troubadour who uses these courtly
commonplaces of Love extensively, and he gives them life
with his imagery, and powers of self-dramatisation and
feeling. He does not, like Peire d'Alvernhe or Marcabru, in
parody, send a bird messenger to his lady. He identifies himself with the bird:

> Ai Deus! car no sui ironda,
> que voles per l'aire
> e vengues de noih prionda
> lai dins so repaire?
> bona domna jauzionda,
> mor se·l vostr'amaire!
> paor ai que·l cors me fonda,
> s'aissi·m dura gaire.
> domna, per vostr'amor
> jonh las mas et ador!
> gens cors ab frescha color,
> gran mal me faitz traire!   (XLIV, 49–60)

Ah God! why am I not a swallow so that I might fly through the air and
come out of the deep night there into her room? Noble and joyous lady,
your lover is dying! I fear that my heart may melt within me if this lasts
only a little longer for me. Lady, for love of you I join my hands in adoration! You, who are gracious and of fair complexion, make me suffer great
hurt.

His art is dramatic; he is the actor on the courtly scene and
his lady the foil and the reason for his lyrical play-acting: he is
the swallow flying out of the deep night like a bird-lover in
Celtic romance; he dies; his heart melts; he kneels in adoration. He follows his lady like a leaf in the wind (III, 32–3); he
hurls himself at the bait like a fish (XII, 8); he lives in pain like
a man dying in the flames (III, 63–4); he will wear down his
lady's hard and untamed heart like the drop of water falling
and hollowing the hard stone (XVI, 38–40) – and he acknowledges the Ovidian source of this image.[9]

Jois is central to his character and his poetic creation. It is
an inner force which seeks enjoyment in life, powerful and
self-perpetuating but needing an object on which to crystal-

lise. More than any other troubadour except Bertran de Born, Bernart can exteriorise his feelings dramatically through natural objects; the lark, the nightingale or the *domna*. He seeks some natural object through which he can express *Jois*, which is both the desire and the experience of joy, and *ira*, its attendant sorrow.

Bernart takes nature's summer mood as the model of behaviour for the courtly man. Nature gives herself to *joi* and any man who is not interested in *joi* and *amor* leads a mean, base life:

> La dousa votz ai auzida
> del rosinholet sauvatge,
> et es m'ins el cor salhida
> si que tot lo cosirer
> e·ls mals traihz qu'amors me dona,
> m'adousa e m'asazona;
> et auria·m be mester
> l'autrui jois al meu damnatge.
>
> Ben es totz om d'avol vida
> c'ab joi non a son estatge
> e qui vas amor no guida
> so cor e so dezirer;
> car tot can es s'abandona
> vas joi e refrim'e sona:
> prat e deves e verger,
> landas e pla e boschatge.   (XXIII, 1–16)

I have heard the sweet voice of the nightingale in the woods and it has pierced to the depths of my heart so that it sweetens and soothes for me all the care and the sufferings that love gives me. And hurt as I am, I truly have need of the joy of others.

Every man who does not dwell in a state of joy and does not direct his heart and his desire towards love, leads a base life, for all that exists abandons itself to joy, and sounds and resounds: meadows, gardens and orchards, *landes*, plains and bosks.

In his anger against Love which has scorned and rejected him, the joy of the nightingale makes him die of desire:

> Ai las! com mor de talan!
> qu'eu no dorm mati ni ser,
> que la noih, can vau jazer,
> lo rossinhols chant'e cria,
> et eu, que chantar solia,
> mor d'enoi e de pezansa,
> can au joi ni alegransa.   (XLV, 8–14)

Alas! how I die of desire! I cannot sleep morning or evening for at night when I go to lie down the nightingale sings and calls, and I, who was wont to sing, die of sorrow and grief when I hear joy and delight.

Or the nightingale can waken him, overwhelmed by feelings of joy, and disturbed by thoughts of love:

> Pel doutz chan que·l rossinhols fai,
> la noih can me sui adormitz,
> revelh de joi totz esbäitz,
> d'amor pensius e cossirans;
> c'aisso es mos melhers mesters,
> que tostems ai joi volunters,
> et ab joi comensa mos chans. (XXXIII, 1–7)

For the sweet song that the nightingale sings, at night when I am asleep, I awake quite out of my mind with joy, though I think and reflect about love; for my greatest virtue is that I always welcome joy and my song begins from joy.

Bernart's feelings respond to the moods of Nature which had led Marcabru to moral thoughts about man. He identifies himself with the woods and the oaks which come into leaf, and with the blossom:

> autresi·m chant e m'esbaudei
> . . . e reverdei
> e folh segon ma natura.[10] (XXIV, 6–8)

in just the same way do I sing and rejoice. . . and renew my foliage in accordance with my nature.

With the new leaves, the blossom and the nightingale and thoughts of his lady, he is oppressed by exuberant joy, which turns into instant despair:

> Can l'erba fresch'e·lh folha par
> e la flors boton'el verjan,
> e·l rossinhols autet e clar
> leva sa votz e mou so chan,
> joi ai de lui, e joi ai de la flor
> e joi de me e de midons major;
> daus totas partz sui de joi claus e sens,
> mas sel es jois que totz autres jois vens.
>
> Ai las! com mor de cossirar!
> que manhtas vetz en cossir tan:
> lairo m'en poirian portar,
> que re no sabria que·s fan.
> per Deu, Amors! be·m trobas vensedor:
> ab paucs d'amics e ses autre senhor.
> car una vetz tan midons no destrens
> abans qu'eu fos del dezirer estens? (XXXIX, 1–16)

When the fresh grass and the leaf appear and the blossom buds on the bough, and the nightingale high and clear raises its voice and begins its song, I have joy for it and joy for the blossom and joy for myself and greater joy for my lady, on all sides I am enclosed and circled by joy, but this is joy that conquers all other joys.

Alas! how my thoughts slay me! for many times I am so deep in thought that thieves could carry me away and I should know nothing of what they do. Love, in the name of God, you find me vulnerable, with few friends and with no other lord. Why just once do you not put constraint on my lady, before I am killed by desire?

Joy robs him of his senses when his lady looks at him:

> C'ab sol lo bel semblan que·m fai
> can pot ni aizes lo·lh cossen,
> ai tan de joi que sol no·m sen,
> c'aissi·m torn e·m volv'e·m vire.   (XXVII, 28–31)

For merely from the kindly look she gives me, when she is able to and opportunity allows, I have so much joy that I do not feel I am a person, so much do I turn and twist and spiral.

It is not entirely a courtly conceit that leads Bernart to describe his desire (*talans*) as *nescis* and himself as being *fol* and *nesci*. *Nescis* 'ignorant, not knowing' is the quality of naivety which obeys natural instinct without reflection or recourse to *sen* 'wisdom and common sense'. The man who is *nescis* obeys the instinctive desire for *Jois* on the plane of the senses and does not rationalise it in accordance with a higher spiritual ideal of love. He may be chided for this *foudatz* by a reflective poet such as Marcabru, and Guilhem IX, it may be remembered, burlesques the distinction between *sen* and *foudatz* by riding *foudatz* to the extremes of bawdiness.

When Peire, who is probably Peire d'Alvernhe, upbraids Bernart in *Amics Bernartz de Ventadorn* for renouncing Love and song for love of a false woman, his words are not entirely satirical: 'Bernart de Ventadorn, my friend, how can you forbear to sing when you hear the young nightingale rejoicing night and day in this way. Hear the joy it displays! All night it sings beneath the blossom, it is more intent on love than you' (II, 1–7). Bernart is wayward and humorous: 'I like sleep and rest more than listening to the nightingale', but Peire, the reflective poet, blames Bernart for his lack of control, and his *foudatz*:

> Bernartz, foudatz vos amena,
> car aissi vos partetz d'amor,
> per cui a om pretz e valor.   (II, 43–5)

Bernart, foolishness misleads you since you depart in this way from love through which a man has reputation and worth.

For Bernart joy excludes wisdom and reflection:

> c'anc pois qu'eu l'agui veguda,
> non agui sen ni mezura.   (VIII, 23–4)

for ever since I saw her I have had neither wisdom, nor a sense of proportion.

Marcabru and Jaufre Rudel regretted the *fols fais* of their moral errors in love: Bernart says that the man in love must err, but he is guiltless because good sense is not to be found in love:

> E s'eu en amar mespren,
> tort a qui colpa m'en fai,
> car, qui en amor quer sen,
> cel non a sen ni mezura.   (XVI, 29–32)

And if I err when I love, the man who blames me for this is wrong, for the man who looks for good sense in love has neither good sense nor a sense of what is fitting.

For Bernart *mesura* lies in accepting that the fool must act foolishly, as Marcabru said, and must gather the branch that will beat and strike him (XLII, 29–31). Bernart cannot turn away from his folly, for love takes from him all awareness of what he does, and he rejects reflection which turns his joy to pain:

> Amors, aissi·m faitz trassalhir:
> del joi qu'eu ai, no vei ni au
> ni no sai que·m dic ni que·m fau.
> cen vetz trobi, can m'o cossir,
> qu'eu degr'aver sen e mezura
> (si m'ai adoncs; mas pauc me dura),
> c'al reduire·m torna·l jois en error.
> pero be sai c'uzatges es d'amor
> c'om c'ama be, non a gaire de sen.   (XIII, 19–27)

Love, you make me tremble so violently that because of the joy I have I do not see or hear or know what I am saying or what I am doing. A hundred times do I discover, when I think about this, that I ought to have good sense and a sense of proportion (and I do have this, but it lasts but a little time for me), for, when I contemplate it, my joy turns to pain. But I know well that it is the custom in love that the man who loves well has scarcely any good sense.

The heart that is overcome by joy is thrown out of joint with nature:

Tant ai mo cor ple de joya,
  tot me desnatura.
flor blancha, vermelh'e groya
  me par la frejura,
c'ab lo ven et ab la ploya
  me creis l'aventura,
per que mos pretz mont'e poya
  e mos chans melhura.
tan ai al cor d'amor,
de joi e de doussor,
per que·l gels me sembla flor
  e la neus verdura.   (XLIV, 1–12)

I have my heart so filled with joy that it throws me out of joint with nature. The cold appears to me as blossom, white, scarlet and yellow, for my happiness increases with the wind and the rain, so that my reputation climbs and rises and my song improves. I have in my heart so much joy and sweetness from love that the ice appears to me as blossom and the snow as greenery.

Bernart dramatises and acts out his *foudatz* with good humour and light irony: 'I can go about without clothes, naked in my shift, for true love protects me from the cold wind [11–16], but the man is a fool who acts immoderately and behaves unbecomingly [17–18]; I have taken heed of my behaviour since I have wooed my present *domna*. And good sense will help me to tell lies about the source of the joy which inspires, opens and completes my song' [1, 1–32].

Earlier troubadours, such as Guilhem IX and Jaufre Rudel, consciously sought a greater joy in the forgetfulness of their identity in dream or meditation. For Bernart it is the over-powering effect of *Amors* and *Jois* that robs him of his senses and his awareness of his being. To convey this self-forgetful-ness he identifies his feelings with those of the lark:

Can vei la lauzeta mover
de joi sas alas contral rai,
que s'oblid'e·s laissa chazer
per la doussor c'al cor li vai,
ai! tan grans enveya m'en ve
de cui qu'eu veya jauzion,
meravilhas ai, car desse
lo cor de dezirer no·m fon.

Ai, las! tan cuidava saber
d'amor, e tan petit en sai!
car eu d'amar no·m posc tener
celeis don ja pro non aurai.

tout m'a mo cor, e tout m'a me,
e se mezeis e tot lo mon;
e can se·m tolc, no·m laisset re
mas dezirer e cor volon.

Anc non agui de me poder
ni no fui meus de l'or'en sai
que·m laisset en sos olhs vezer
en un miralh que mout me plai.
miralhs, pus me mirei en te,
m'an mort li sospir de preon,
c'aissi·m perdei com perdet se
lo bels Narcisus en la fon.   (XLIII, 1–24)

When I see the young lark moving its wings for joy in the ray of the sun
so that it forgets itself and lets itself fall for the sweetness that goes to its
heart, alas! such great envy comes to me of anyone whom I may see
rejoicing, I wonder that forthwith my heart does not melt with desire.

Alas! so much did I think that I knew about love, and so little do I
know, for I cannot abstain from loving her from whom I shall never have
reward. She has stolen my heart from me and has stolen myself from me
and herself and the whole world. And when she stole herself from me she
left me nothing except desire and a heart filled with longing.

Never did I have control over myself, nor was I my own master from
that moment when she let me look into her eyes, into a mirror that pleases
me greatly. Mirror, since I beheld myself in you, my deep sighs have
slain me, for so did I lose myself as fair Narcissus lost himself in the
fountain.

The lark forgets itself for joy and lets itself fall; just so does
the poet, when he sees himself in the eyes of his *domna*, lose
control of his senses, and feel himself removed from himself
and the world around him. When his lady removed herself
from him, he was left with nothing but pain and desire. Since
no other *domna* will help him with his lady, he will attack
them all (25–32), and since his lady has slain him, he will
reply to her through death:

mort m'a, e per mort li respon,
e vau m'en, pus ilh no·m rete,
chaitius, en issilh, no sai on.   (XLIII, 54–6)

she has slain me and through death I reply to her, and go away, since she
does not keep me in her service, a wretched captive, into exile, I know
not where.

The sense of the numinous is absent from Bernart's poetry.
Unlike Jaufre Rudel he is not escaping from the sorrow of
everyday to seek a greater joy in the imagination and the
spirit. Bernart's *Jois* is here in this world, visible, tangible, to

be known through his senses and expressed through the living image. If he is cut off from the joy of this world, the joy of the court, he dies as a poet who must express through the world around him his violent poetic feelings and desire for joy. His idea of happiness is bounded by the court, by Amors and the domna, and, unlike Jaufre Rudel, he cannot escape to the contemplation of love on a higher plane. Deprived of joy of the senses, he escapes into 'death' since he no longer exists within himself as a person who can feel anything but sorrow. In Non es meravelha he sees that man as dead who cannot feel some sweet delight of love in his heart, and he calls on God never to hate him so much that He will allow him to live for a day or a month if he is guilty of having no joy or desire for Love (XXXI, 9–16).

In courtly terms Bernart is acting out the folly of the lover when Amors first strikes him at the sight of the beloved and all his controls disappear so that he loses himself like fair Narcissus. The courtly canon demanded that the rational qualities of sen and mesura should rescue the lover from the disorder of his senses. When the lover in the First Part of the Roman de la Rose looks at the pool and falls in love with the reflection of the rose in the two pebbles, Amors demands that he should accept the rules of love before he approaches the rose. Bernart refuses to use sen and mesura. His escape from the 'dire confusion' of love, which for him is not a moral disturbance but an emotional turmoil and despair, is an escape into 'death'.

Death in the sense of exile from Jois, song, the domna and the life of the court is obviously a courtly conceit, which is used by Chrétien when Lancelot is imprisoned in the tower. It is a poetic device which was overworked by many later amants martyrs in the North of France from Gace Brulé to Charles d'Orléans. But if we accept that Bernart is alive with intense and colourful feelings, it is apparent that his role as court poet and entertainer, soupirant to an exalted and unrewarding domna such as Eleanor of Aquitaine, wife of two kings, must have led him to an impasse, in which desire for the feeling of Jois was constricted so much by the courtly pressure of rational control, sen, mesura and carefully ordered behaviour, that the only escape for him as an individual and a poet lay in withdrawal. Bernart is not a contemplative and balanced observer of court life; he lives the life of the court but cannot disguise his chagrin or numb his feelings with courtly pretence. He compares his case to that of Tristan who suffered many griefs for Yseut the fair (XLIV, 45–8), and this is partly true, since Tristan is driven by the *foudatz* of the love potion to uncontrollable passion for Yseut. Tristan's attempt to control his sorrow by *sen* and *mesura* through marriage to Yseut of the White Hands drove him to an impasse from which he escaped into the dream world of *per cuda* love for the statue of Yseut the Fair.

This pattern of excessive joy that brings forgetfulness of all except the *domna*, of unrequited love, of joy turned to unbearable pain and the wish for renunciation and 'death', occurs elsewhere in Bernart. In *Can lo boschatges*, joy for the spring brings restless unease, but his heart's root is bound tight by his lady:

> d'un gran joi me creis tals oblitz
> que ves re mais no·m posc virar.
> noih e jorn me fai sospirar,
> si·m lassa del cor la razitz.
>
> Per midons m'esjau no-jauzitz,
> don m'es l'afans greus a portar,
> qu'e·m perdrai per leis gazanhar,
> et er li crims mout deschauzitz.
> las! que farai? com sui träitz,
> si s'amor no·m vol autreyar!
> qu'eu no posc viure ses amar,
> que d'amor sui engenöitz.   (XL, 5–16)

from a great feeling of joy such oblivion grows within me that I cannot turn myself to anything else. Night and day she makes me sigh and binds up the root of my heart.

Because of my lady I rejoice, having had no enjoyment, and the pain of this is hard to bear, for in order to win her I shall lose myself and this will be an uncouth crime on her part. Alas! what shall I do? How I am betrayed if she will not grant me her love, for I cannot live without loving, for I was sired by love.

Bernart's despair moves to a climax:

> Domna, s'eu fos de vos auzitz
> si charamen com volh mostrar,
> al prim de nostr'enamorar
> feiram chambis dels esperitz!
> azautz sens m'i fora cobitz,
> c'adonc saubr'eu lo vostr'afar
> e vos lo meu, tot par a par,
> e foram de dos cors unitz!

Ai! can brus sui, mal escharnitz!
qu'eu no posc la pena durar,
de tal dolor me fai pasmar,
car tan s'amistat m'esconditz!
ab bel semblan sui eu träitz.
que·m val? res no·m pot chastiar!
mortz venh'a sel qui·m vol blasmar
qu'eu no l'am mortz e sebelitz!

Car forsatz m'en part e marritz,
leu m'auci, mas greu fui noiritz,
tal ira·m sen al cor trenchar,
car me mor e volh trespassar,
mas ses leis no serai gueritz!   (57–77)

My lady, if I were to be heard by you with the same tenderness that I wish
to show you, we would make an exchange of our souls at the beginning
of our love! Pleasing good sense would have been granted to me at that
moment so that I should then have known about your feelings and you
about mine, sharing completely, and we should have been united in our
two hearts.

Alas! how dark I feel, scorned and ill used! I cannot endure the pain
which makes me faint with such grief because she denies me her love so
completely! I am betrayed by the fair illusion of kindness that she showed
me. What can I do? No one can teach me! May death come to the man
who blames me for not loving her when I am dead and buried.

Since I depart from her sad and constrained, she kills me easily although
I was nurtured [by love] with difficulty. I feel such sorrow cutting my
heart, for I am dying and wish to pass away since without her I shall never
be healed.

Bernart's lament for his 'betrayal' by his lady and his desire
for death may be a courtly commonplace, but the tragic
quality of the poetry, emphasised by the rich vowel sounds,
recalls Tristan dying on the cliff when he hears from Yseut of
the White Hands that the sail of the ship is black. In his desire
for shared happiness of the heart in equal love, and his acceptance and desire for physical death and burial when he realises
that such happiness is not possible, Bernart greatly extends
and intensifies the conventional courtly situation.

The only remedy for the death-wish is patience and endu-
rance. In Bel m'es can eu vei la brolha, he desires and sighs for his
lady, but his mood switches abruptly from the superficial and
conventional:

e car ela no sospira,
sai qu'en lei ma mortz se mira,
can sa gran beutat remir.

Ma mort remir, que jauzir
no·n posc ni no·n sui jauzire;
mas eu sui tan bos sofrire
c'atendre cuit per sofrir. (IX, 38–44)

And because she does not sigh, I know that my death is mirrored in her when I behold her great beauty.

I behold my death since I cannot find joy with her and am not joyful because of her. But my patience is so long that I hope to succeed by enduring.

In *Amors enquera·us preyara* Bernart again illuminates a conventional courtly situation with the intense expression of his distress:[11]

Soven plor tan que la chara
n'ai destrech'e vergonhoza,
e·l vis s'en dezacolora,
car vos, don jauzir me degra,
pert, que de me no·us sove.
e no·m don Deus de vos be,
s'eu sai ses vos co·m chaptenha,
c'aitan doloirozamen
viu com cel que mor en flama;
e si tot no·m fatz parven,
nulhs om menhs de joi no sen. (III, 56–66)

Often do I weep so much that my face is distraught and covered in shame, and my face is drained of colour because I am losing you, in whom I should rejoice, so that you do not think of me. And may God give me no happiness from you if I know how I may lead my life without you, for I live in pain as much as the man who dies in the flame, and although I do not let this appear, no man feels less joy than I do.

Bernart, like Arnaut Daniel, describes his suffering not only on the courtly plane, but with personal feeling, so that death through love can be *cortesia* (XVII, 30–1), or it can be the feeling of sorrow cutting into the heart because one is dying and wishes to die (XL, 75–6).

In *Lo tems vai e ven e vire* Bernart reconciles his 'personal' and 'social' reactions to his courtly dilemma. His personal response is pique at his lady's carefree neglect of a sorrow which makes him renounce song. The opening lines are remarkable for their monosyllabic words and thin, sad, alliterative sounds giving the insistent beat of passing time, like Walther von der Vogelweide's *Owê war sint verswunden alliu miniu jâr?*:

Lo tems vai e ven e vire
per jorns, per mes e per ans,
et eu, las! no·n sai que dire,
c'ades es us mos talans.
ades es us e no·s muda,
c'una·n volh e·n ai volguda,
don anc non aic jauzimen.   (XXX, 1–7)

The time goes and comes and turns through days, through months and through years, and I, alas! know nothing to say about it, for my desire is always one. It is always one desire and does not change, for with it I desire and I have desired one woman from whom I never had enjoyment.

Bernart is resigned:

Ja mais no serai chantaire
ni de l'escola n'Eblo,
que mos chantars no val gaire
ni mas voutas ni mei so;
ni res qu'eu fassa ni dia,
no conosc que pros me sia,
ni no·i vei melhuramen.   (22–8)

Never more will I be a singer, nor belong to the school of lord Eble, for my singing is of little help, and my warbling and my tunes; nor do I know of anything that I may do or say that will bring me advantage, and I see no chance of improvement in these matters.

Marcabru attacked Eble's poetic art for its folly, and when Bernart says that he will no longer sing or follow this school of poetry, he is probably renouncing what Guiraut de Bornelh calls *bella foudatz*, the desire to feel joy and to express immediate feeling without rational control, and to accept the suffering that this brings:

Bernart continues:

Si tot fatz de joi parvensa,
mout ai dins lo cor irat.
qui vid anc mais penedensa
faire denan lo pechat?   (29–32)

Although I pretend to be joyful I have within me a heart full of sorrow. Who has ever seen penitence being done before the sin?

Bernart's personal self protests, but his courtly self triumphs. He accepts his lot. He will never leave his lady; the empty ear of corn sways to and fro when the grain has gone:

Ja no·m partrai a ma vida,
tan com sia sals ni sas,
que pois l'arma n'es issida,
balaya lonc tems lo gras.   (43–6)

As long as I live I will never depart from her, as long as I am healthy and well, for after the grain has gone from it the ear of corn sways for a long time to and fro.

The song is bound up, ending as it began with his one desire for his lady alone. May God who created her physical perfection grant him her love!

Bernart's originality and greatness lie in his lyric power and ability to express with immediacy his feelings of joy, sorrow, rebellion, acceptance and humility. His images are sparse, living, evocative, and the most memorable part of his creation. They are above all dramatic, and Bernart feels as the lark feels when it hovers and falls, as the victim in the flames, the leaf following the wind, the swaying empty ear of corn. As court entertainer and troubadour he accepts the formal social cadre represented by the *domna* and the rules of *Amors*, but his lyric genius uses and passes beyond this framework. The source of his poetry is the *Jois* within him and the desire to give expression to this unformed inner elation, and *Amors* and the *domna* are primarily no more than means to this end. It is himself that he sees when he looks into his lady's eyes, in hope and love (XLIII, 19–20) or in despair (IX, 39–40).

Bernart has humour and common sense, but he is not a reflective poet. He is not interested, on the poetic level, in any clash between the demands of love of God and Christian morality and profane love of the *domna* and courtly values. His poetry is not *entiers*: he accepts the courtly plane and all its values. Life, love, nature, his lady, have meaning for him as they affect his senses. He lives and composes on this plane and writes appropriately in the *leu* style, not hinting, as earlier troubadours had done, at wider levels of meaning with allusive words or constructions. When, in his imagination, he projects himself into a dramatised situation, image and feelings are sharply observed through his senses. Because of his natural instinct and gifts, and probably in response to the tastes of his courtly, worldly audience, he is a poet of *foudatz*, and *foudatz* for his generation of poets appears to mean a willingness to be carried along by desire, feeling and love of *Jois*, like the leaf following the wind, without rational controls beyond the immediate demands of formalised courtly society. He can pretend to simulate joy when he is in despair, but even this superficial control is paper thin. His 'naive' quality and his apparently ingenuous ways of thought and desire (*nescis talans*) must have provided a pleasing and refreshing contrast with the intricate courtly etiquette of his day, but *foudatz* without *sen* is not the mark of the complete courtly lover and poet, as Chrétien de Troyes hints in his *D'Amors qui m'a tolu a moi* in reply to Bernart's *Can vei la lauzeta mover* (see p. 150). Bernart delights in the *vergier d'amour*, looks into the pool of Narcissus, is wounded by Love's darts, kisses the rose-bud and is rebuffed by *Dangier*, but he must remain in recreant or patient mood outside the tower in which *Bel Accueil* is imprisoned. *Raison* cannot help him to win the courtly prize, nor can his vision of a love which is inspired by mutual desire and is equally shared in mind and body. He is incapable of the sustained pretence of courtly, Ovidian artifice in love. He does not praise *jovens*; he is the spirit of *jovens*.

5

Raimbaut d'Aurenga

RAIMBAUT, COUNT OF ORANGE (c. 1146–73) was brought up under the guardianship of the great lords, Bertran des Baux and Guilhem de Montpellier. Although he was the nominal lord of Orange, Omelas, Courthézon and many other castles, he was impoverished by his inheritance of debts, his duty to bestow largesse, and the inflationary economic crisis caused by the growing wealth of the towns. He borrowed money on whatever possessions were not already mortgaged and held restricted court, probably at Courthézon,[1] where he was the friend and patron of Guiraut de Bornelh, Peire Rogier, and possibly Bernart de Ventadorn.

Peire d'Alvernhe, who gave pride of place in his *Cantarai d'aqestz trobadors* to poets of clerical status and low birth, leaves Raimbaut to the ninth position:

> E·l novens es en Raembautz,
> qe·s fai de son trobar trop bautz;
> mas eu lo torni en nien,
> q'el non es alegres ni chautz.   (XII, 55–8)

And the ninth is lord Raimbaut who grows too happy about his poetry: but I care nothing for it [him] since it [he] is neither gay nor warm.

Peire is jesting with the key-words *bautz* and *chautz* from Raimbaut's songs,[2] but he may have in mind the thoughtful disposition which another troubadour, Peire Rogier, advised the youthful Raimbaut to enliven:

> No·us fassatz de sen trop temer,
> per qu'om digua: 'trop es senatz',
> qu'en tal luec vos valra foudatz
> on sens no·us poyria valer;
> tant quant aurez pel saur e bai
> e·l cors aissi fresquet e gai,
> grans sens no·us er honors ni pros.
>   (ed. C. Appel, VIII, 29–35)

Do not inspire too much fear by your wisdom so that people say: 'he is too wise', for on some occasions folly will help you and wisdom can be of no avail. As long as your hair is gold and brown and your body is fresh and joyous, great wisdom will bring you no honour or advantage.

Peire Rogier's words may have inspired Raimbaut to try the courtly whirl that deadens thought:

> Aissi ai bastit en gaug
> Mon cor nou e fresc,
> C'ades sort e saill e tresc
> Si q'apenas veig ni aug. (XXI, 15–18)

I have so raised up my new and fresh heart to enjoyment that I continuously jump and leap and dance with the result that I can scarcely see or hear.

Raimbaut was a lesser ruler than Guilhem IX, but as a poet he shares many of his qualities. He has the same independence of spirit and the same self-doubt and quest for happiness, the same mistrust of Amors as a social system and the half-formed desire to come to terms with it. He laughs at convention, prefers the brilliant and the unexpected to the banal and finds excitement in fine beginnings (bels comens). He knows that death is close, that tot es niens, and he has the ironical bawdiness that conceals melancholy. But Raimbaut is enriched by what he has inherited from Guilhem IX, Marcabru and Jaufre Rudel, and at a time when troubadour ideas on love, happiness and poetic style were uncertain, he expresses in depth, in youthful, outspoken and tempestuous tones what was tentative, hinted at and embryonic in Guilhem IX.

Raimbaut does not look for happiness in an escape from the reality of his everyday existence. He does not wish to lose his identity in flight to a dream world, to the consolation of memory, or to self-oblivion in nature or in death, in the manner of either Guilhem IX, Rudel or Ventadorn. He does not, like Marcabru, find an outlet for dissatisfaction in abstract moralising. His central aim as a poet is to retain his personal identity and to clarify it by understanding and describing the external reality of nature, the vices of society that oppress him and his struggle for personal happiness against the forces of doubt and sorrow.

Raimbaut lives intensely and rationally within the compass of his earthly existence. To the question: why do I love? he replies:

Qar? No sai qant m'ai a viure,
Per qe mon cors al cor liure;
E sapcha·n guidar dretz fil
Mos volers, e non s'ature
Mas en valen seinhoril;
Qu'om no·s iau de son cortil.　　　　　(IV, 7–12)

Why? Because I do not know how long I have to live, and so I surrender
myself to my heart. May my desire know how to guide me with a straight
thread and come to a halt only in the realm of worth, for joy is not to be
found in one's own backyard.

Raimbaut is intoxicated by the sound and meanings of
separate words, which he weaves together in new and sudden
combinations, and he abhors pretence and artificiality. The
qualities of *Jois* and *Jovens* alone can remove the film and rust
with which deceit and slander coat his life:

Cars, bruns e tenhz motz entrebesc!
Pensius – pensanz enquier e serc
Com si liman pogues roire
L'estraing röill ni·l fer tiure,
Don mon escur cor esclaire.
Tot can Jois genseis esclaira
Malvestatz röill'e tiura
E enclau Joven e serga
Per qu'ira e jois entrebesca.[3]　　　　　(I, 19–27)

Precious, dark and tinted words do I interweave! Deep in thought and
thinking actively I enquire and seek for a means of filing and wearing
away the alien rust and the evil film, so that I may give light to my sombre
heart. *Malvestatz* rusts and puts its film over all that *Jois* best lights up,
and it shuts in *Joven* and seeks a way of mixing up sorrow and joys.

Jois for Raimbaut is not the static ideal of an elusive happiness. It is the joy felt by the heart that is *jovens* in the active
pursuit of its own particular moment of happiness. *Jois* is the
innate force that inspires the search for happiness and the
pleasure in the search, as well as the happiness that is sought
and found. Such a positive seeking for *Jois* is the only bearable
way of life for Raimbaut, and the only escape from the film
and rust of flaccid, unformulated desires (*flacs volers*) and the
insensitive apathy of the people who are *flacs endurzitz*, flaccid
within their hardened shell. To be like these people is anathema. When joy has fled, he turns to the lady who has
betrayed him:

Volretz que torn flacs – endurzitz
O que demer?　　　　　(VIII, 35–6)

Will you want me to become flaccid – hardened, or commit some unworthy act?

The knowledge that happiness can never be complete brings self-doubt and weariness to the pursuit of Jois, and in *Car vei qe clars* this is symbolised by the lassitude induced by paralysing heat:

> E·l sols blancs, clars,
>   Veg qe raia
> Cautz, greus, secs, durs et ardenz,
> Qe·m frain totz mos bons talens.
> Mas una voluntatz gaia
> D'un franc joi, qe·m mou Dezirs,
> No vol c'ap flacs volers viva.
>
> Ges no m'es clars
>   Ni m'esquiva
> Est jois, don faz lez sospirs,
> Ni sai s'anc mi valc mos dirs
> Ni mi noc; e tem qe·m viva
> Enaisi trop lonjamens
> L'amors qe·il tenc meja gaia.
>
> Mos cors es clars
>   E s'esmaia!
> Aici vauc mestz grams-iauzens,
> Plens e voigz de bel comens;
> Qe l'una meitatz es gaia
> E l'autra m'adorm Cossirs
> Ab voluntat mort'e viva.
>
> C'us volers clars
>   Qe·m caliva
> M'espeing enant en Faillirs!
> Mostra Temers que jauzirs
> Val mais al home qe viva
> Qe cortz gaugz; per q'espaventz
> S'altempr'ab voluntat gaia.   (IX, 8–35)

And I see the sun, white, bright, shining, hot, harsh, dry, hard and burning, so that it shatters all my good intentions. But a gay longing for a noble joy which Desire awakes in me, does not wish me to live with flabby longings.

This joy, for which I sigh, happy, is neither bright nor evasive towards me, and I do not know whether I was ever helped or harmed by speaking of it; and I fear that the half-joyful love that I bear her may live too long like this within me.

My heart is bright and is afraid! So I go around half grieving-rejoicing, full and empty of fine beginnings; for the one half is joyous and the other is lulled for me by sombre reflection with a longing that is dead and live.

For a bright desire that burns me impels me forward to acts of transgression! Fear shows that a state of joy is worth more than brief pleasure to the man who wishes to remain 'alive', so that terror is tempered by a longing that is joyous.

Raimbaut's sharp, harsh, monosyllabic description of the sun which deadens thought, and his skilful rhyme scheme constructed on the refrain words *clars, gaia* and *viva*, conceal the fact that, in meaning if not in expression, this is an archetypal courtly poem of *Fin'Amors*. In the four stanzas which have been quoted, *voluntatz gaia* opens and closes, and 'binds up' the discussion of the poet's predicament. Faced by the choice between *voluntatz gaia, franc joi, dezirs* and, on the other hand, *flacs volers*, his response is simple: joy is all. He will devote himself to the joy that comes from one particular desire rather than the mindless and unformulated sensual desiring of *flacs volers*. But the courtly dilemma remains. Bright, sensual desiring urges him to 'transgress' and expose himself to the nothingness of happiness that is soon lost. *Temers*, or the hesitation caused by fear of this, restrains him; he will remain in a state of gay and courtly longing (*voluntatz gaia*) and the lasting enjoyment (*jauzirs*) which this brings, for one cannot love with *Fin'Amors* (*finamenz*, 48) without a great and joyful fear. The lover, accepting the need for *Temers*, must remain *gramsiauzens* 'sorrowing-rejoicing' and *Jois* must remain in *Dezir*, the specific desire that is not fulfilled. *Temers* represents a state of feeling and is inspired by *Cossirs*, the power of thought and reflection which dulls *volers clars* and keeps *dezir* alive. In this way the lover's longing dies because *Cossirs* rejects *volers*, and it lives (l. 28) because *Cossirs* shows the way to *jauzirs* through desire unfulfilled. The lover's mind must control his general sensual desire (*volers*), however sharply it burns him. Raimbaut, like Jaufre Rudel and Marcabru, chooses *Fin'Amors* as the way to lasting happiness, but he does not suffer the moral pangs that afflicted these earlier poets. His delicate analysis of his psychological state in the allegorical picture of *Dezirs, Volers, Voluntatz, Jois, Temers* and *Cossirs*, as they react lightly against one another, is, in simple form, the whole art of the psychological allegory of love which Guillaume de Lorris unfolded later in his *Roman de la Rose*, and *Temers* in Raimbaut restrains the lover as *Jalousie* restrains the lady in Guillaume de Lorris. Raimbaut's *Car vei qe clars* is remarkable for the skill with which a conventional theme is enfolded in unconventional vocabulary, and subtle personal feelings and desires are made to assert themselves in the face of nature's blinding force.

Raimbaut sees in Fin'*Amors* the love that allows a man to live *letz, cortes e sapiens*, but Fin'*Amors* is the way to personal happiness in everyday life and not, as with Marcabru, an abstract, moral and quasi-religious ideal. In *Ara non siscla* Raimbaut feels joy in his mind and not his senses; no nightingale or oriole sings, and no flower appears in the forest.

> C'a pauc lo cors no·m n'avanta.
> Q'esquirols non es, ni cabrols,
> Tan lieus com eu sui, q'el test
> M'es la joia q'eu cercava. (XIV, 15–18)

My body almost escapes me; no squirrel or goat is as lively as I, because the joy I sought is in my mind.

His joy is real and live, and, unlike his former dream joy, it increases while he is awake; it rejuvenates, reassures and protects him from anguish and suffering:

> Car a midonz atalanta
> Qe·m loing dols! E serai ben fols
> S'eu totz temps ab leis non rest,
> Pos frain ma dolor plus brava;
> Si qe fais ni afans
> No·m pot esser dans,
> Ni maltraigz no·m dol paucs ni grans. (8–14)

For my lady desires that grief should depart from me. I shall indeed be a fool if I do not remain with her for ever, since she tames my wildest pain, so that neither the burden, nor the sorrow can harm me, or suffering or grief whether great or small.

May God who reserved this lady for him never grant him anything more. Raimbaut addresses his *domna* as he might have addressed the Virgin Mary, and he implies a comparison between his own period of suffering (39) and the forty days that Christ suffered in the wilderness (29):

> C'ap ton cor q'el mieu se planta,
> Sai qe·m tols – car donar no·m vols –
> Domna, que Jois pais e vest,
> Tot l'enjan q'a me portava.
> Gen lo·m trais. Sain Johans!
> Ar m'en creis talans
> Don cairai el sol ablasmans. (36–42)

For with your heart which enters into mine and stays there, I know, Lady whom Joy nurtures and clothes, that you rid me of all the deceit that I endured on my own – and that you have no wish to inflict it on me. Graciously you took this away from me. By Saint John,[4] my desire to be with you now grows so much that I shall fall swooning to the ground.

God reappears in *Ben sai c'a sels seria fer* (XXII), when Raimbaut joyfully remembers a sweet evening of kisses:

> Quan la candela·m fetz vezer
> Vos baizan rizen, a! cal ser! (XXII, 65–6)

When the candle allowed me to see you, as we kissed and laughed, ah! what an evening!

But happiness is short: 'What shall I say if Love declines when kisses are gone? Alas! May God who has given me a joyous evening, never allow me to see this' (44–8).

Raimbaut's reference to God here is more than a commonplace. God and *Amors* are juxtaposed. *Amors* is powerful and unfathomable and grants moments of delight as well as deceit and harm. God is generous in His desire for the lover's happiness: 'God shows great restraint in not raising her, kissing, up to Him. But He does not wish to take her from me or do her any wrong' (XXII, 25–7). *Amors* is associated with the 'rust' as well as the delights of life, God with the brightness of unalloyed and lasting joy. God stands in the background as the giver and protector of this refining and purifying love, which is *Fin'Amors* (XXII, 33).

This love which brings self-improvement and is supported by God as the superior counterpart of *Amors* recurs in *Dona, si m'auzes rancurar*. Raimbaut has been refused any favour other than a kiss and accepts the courtly compromise sadly but rationally:

> Bela doussa dona (si·us par
> Qu'ieu no vailla tant enquera
> Que·m dejatz ab vos colgar)
> Neis del be que fag m'avetz
> No fo anc re si temetz
> C'aiatz faillit; qu'ieu faillira
> E tanh meils que·ill mortz m'en me
> Que ja vos faillatz per me. (XXVI, 33–40)

Fair, sweet lady, if it seems to you that I am not yet worthy to lie with you, there was never anything in the kindness that you have shown me that might lead you to fear that you have sinned; for I should sin, and it would be better for death to take me away, rather than that you should ever sin on my account.

He offers his lady a declaration of Fin'*Amors*:

> Per que·us deu ben esser plus car,
> Mas mos cors ves vos s'esmera
> Si que res no i pot camjar. (49–51)

I should indeed be the more dear to you, the more my heart is purified in my relation to you, so that nothing can change within it.

Would that God might impose this ideal of pure love on all men!

> Dona, Dieu saubr'ieu ensenhar
> So don totz molt meillurera
> Que tolgues c'om en amar
> No pogues far tortz ni vetz
> . . . . .
> Que no i fail qui fortz sospira
> Ni trop au ni sent ni ve,
> Ni conois ni sap ni cre. (57–60, 62–4)

My lady, I could tell God how every man might be greatly improved if He were to take away from man the power to commit wrong and sinful acts in love...for a man commits no sin when he sighs deeply, or hears or feels or sees too much, or has too much discernment, knowledge or trust.

Raimbaut also describes the conflict between tyrannical and deceitful *Amors* and the lover's personal desire for lasting happiness. In *En aital rimeta prima* (II) he sees two ways of life, the one grating, scolding, blaming, and the other constant, believing in *Jois*, rejuvenation and a life that is free of rust and film. *Amors* shuts love within his heart where it burns fiercely and painfully; *Jois* lies in the hope that his aloof and cowardly lady will release this love from its furtive concealment and allow it to be free and open. In *Apres mon vers* (IV) Raimbaut temporises with *Amors*. It is only one way to *Jois*, but it is the best, and although it makes him *trist-alegre* and steals *Jois* from him, he will obey its commands. He submits to his lady, and may God, the ultimate source of help, aid him to find *Jois* with her.

Raimbaut composed many songs in which he is the submissive lover (III, V, VI, VII, VIII, XII, XXII, XXIX, XXX, XXXIII). In *Ara·m so* (XXIX) he aspires, with a *dezir* that is free of sensuality, towards a distant love: God granted him this lady, and his disciplined love makes him discreet and careful of her reputation. He enlarges on this idea in *A mon vers* (XXX): without

Dezir, Amors is not *Amors* but merely carnal satisfaction. It is God who rules the heavens and gave dominion on earth to his lady.

But Raimbaut's lucidity of mind and feeling for his personal destiny hold him back from the role of exemplary courtly lover. 'Grieving-rejoicing, loving unloved and living on thin air' (VI, 29–31), he knows that *Amors* cannot give him personal happiness: 'Why does desire not die, since I must die? May God quickly cast out desire' (XXXIII, 25–32).

Raimbaut, like Guilhem IX, has an acute sense of self-irony, and the jesting *joglar* stands beside the doubting poet:

> E soy fols cantayre cortes
> Tan c'om m'en apela ioglar.　　(XXIV, 33–4)

And I am such a foolish courtly singer that they call me *joglar*.[5]

Guiraut de Bornelh in his *planh* on Raimbaut's death praises the folly that concealed his wisdom:

> A! bels amics essenhatz,
> 　nescis als fatz
> e duitz e savis als membratz!
> 　　(Appel, *Chres*, p. 122)

Ah! fair and learned friend, ignorant in the eyes of fools and educated and wise to men of judgment.

and in the same poem:

> Ar es morta bella foudatz,
> 　e iocx de datz
> e dons e domneys oblidatz;
> per vos si pert pretz e dechai.　　(41–4)

Now is fair folly dead, and games of dice and gifts and wooing forgotten, fine reputation is ruined and in decay.

In *Ben s'eschai* Raimbaut claims the cloth crown of the *joglars*, and treats unconventionally the courtly *topos* of the *domna* as a source of poetic inspiration:

> Per midonz ai cor estout
> 　Et humil e baut;
> Car s'a lieis non fos d'azaut
> Ieu m'estera en luoc d'un vout:
> Que d'als non pensera mout
> Mas manjera e tengra·m chaut
> Et agra nom Raembaut.　　(XXI, 29–35)

145

Because of my lady my heart is bold, humble and joyous, for if I were not pleasing to her, I should stand around like the statue of a saint, thinking of nothing but how I should eat and keep myself warm, and answer to the name of Raimbaut.

With a light heart he asserts his supremacy as a lover:

> Don d'amar dic:
> Qu'am si ses tric
> Lieys qu'amar deg,
> Que·l miels adreg
> (S'eron sert cum l'am finamens)
> M'irion sai
> Preguar hueymai
> Que·ls essenhes cum aprendens
> De ben amar;
> E neus preguar
> M'en venrion dompnas cinc cens.   (XVII, 34–44)

And so I speak of loving, for my love for her whom I ought to love is so free of deception that men who are most skilled in love – if they were aware of how perfectly I love her – would come here to entreat me now to instruct them like apprentices in the art of true loving; and even five hundred ladies would come to entreat me for this.

Raimbaut, like Guilhem IX, mocks himself with mingled *sen* and *foudatz*, and his abrupt, malicious humour must have gained much in performance. In *Pos trobars plans* his distant lady causes him turmoil which he describes in literary parody of Guilhem IX and Jaufre Rudel:

> Sains Julians!
> Con vauc torban!
> Soi serrazis o crestians?
> Qals es ma leis?
> Non sai . . .   (XVI, 41–5)

By Saint Julian! How I go around in turmoil! Am I Saracen or Christian? What is my religion? I know not . . .

A brief plea to God to intercede, and then the flat aside to his lady, and his audience:

> Pauc soi certans!
> (Ves qe·us reblan,
> Domna.) De vos so molt londans!   (49–51)

I am so uncertain. (See how I woo you, my lady.) I am very far from you.

In *Lonc temps* (XXVIII) Raimbaut claims that he is impotent, and parodying *amor de lonh* pushes the theme of Joy in Desire to the limit of farce: 'I hasten to tell my secret...and to relieve husbands who cast me black looks of trouble and sorrow and care...so that every man is a proven fool who is bothered if I woo his wife — why remove me from her? — since no harm comes to him if my unhappy sighs are re-doubled...if I never have the power to add to happiness in bed, I now grow fat merely from desiring and seeing, since I seek nothing else. I should like the countess at Monrosier to hear of my perfect joy.'[6]

In *Assatz sai d'amor* Raimbaut is caustic about the deceits of conventional courtly society, the ladies who favour glib and treacherous suitors, and the *auctores* who profess the art of courtly love. Raimbaut turns courtly service upside-down in his parody of arts of love that depend on social etiquette:

> Si voletz dompnas guazanhar,
> Quan querretz que·us fassan honors,
> Si·us fan avol respos avar
> Vos las prenetz a menassar;
> E si vos fan respos peiors
> Datz lor del ponh per mieg sas nars;
> E si son bravas siatz braus!
> Ab gran mal n'auretz gran repaus.   (xx, 17–24)

If you want to win ladies and if, when you want them to do you honour, they make you a base, mean reply, begin to threaten them. And if they make you worse replies, give them some fist in the middle of their nose. And if they are uncouth, be uncouth! Through doing great evil you will have great repose.

Raimbaut, himself, will treat all ladies as if they were his sisters, and remain:

> Humils e simples e leyaus,
> Dous, amoros, fis e coraus.   (39–40)

Kind and honest and loyal, gentle, loving, true and sincere.

but his presumptive pupils must abstain from such behaviour which is madness, and leads to grief, pain and tears. He jests with a secure mind for he 'loves' nobody and does not know what 'love' is. His secret in love is his ring Lady, *Anels*, who keeps him radiantly happy. Raimbaut is rejecting conventional social *Amors* and its unheeding preference for suitors who lack true quality but obey its rules; his security of mind lies in a secret personal love for a *domna* he can trust. Conventional courtly behaviour, mechanical and unfeeling, is part of the deceit and *Malvestatz* that casts rust and film over life.

Raimbaut makes this clear in *Als durs, crus, cozens lauzengiers* (XXXVII) in which he brackets men who are *cortes ufaniers* with the gossips and scandalmongers (*lauzengiers*). Both types of men are enemies of *Jois*. The man who is *ufaniers* is ostentatious, vain and insincere, and the man who is *cortes ufaniers* is skilled in the Ovidian tactics of courtly etiquette, but he lacks true feelings.[7] Raimon de Miraval, a self-styled authority on courtly love in the next generation of troubadours, had the insight to see that he was exposing himself to the charge of being *cortes ufaniers*. Such people who esteem rules and conventions more than *Jois* and nobility of spirit are anathema to Raimbaut, because they do not feel. They are the parasites of the rapidly evolving courtly society of the South, and many troubadours, like Raimbaut, attack the success with which their mechanical social wooing is rewarded. Raimbaut turns from *Amors* which is based on social convention to *Fin'Amors* which is less socially exposed, more personal, secret and loyal. In his plea for sincere feeling in love, Raimbaut is close to Peire Rogier, and antedates Guilhem de Montanhagol.

Raimbaut understands clearly the conflict between the social pressure of courtly convention and the desire for personal happiness that perplexed the troubadours of his generation. As a nobleman with his own small court, he is in a stronger position than Bernart de Ventadorn, and he rejects social *Amors* and the increasing power of courtly dogma in favour of individual *Jois* and the ideals of Guilhem IX and Jaufre Rudel:

> D'autres n'i a que van estiers,
> Que·s fa quecx cortes ufaniers;
> Que per outracujar mot fat
> O cuj'aver mielhs guazanhat
> Cel qu'a plus la lengua lata
> En dir de partir l'amistat
> De cels en cui Jois s'afata.   (XXXVII, 29–35)

Others there are who behave in a different way, for each one sets up as a courtly expert so that with foolish presumption a man imagines he is superior to all if he has the widest tongue for saying things which break up the love of those in whom Joy is budding.

Such men are charlatans:

Tal cug'esser cortes entiers
Qu'es vilans dels quatre ladriers,
Et a·l cor dins mal ensenhat;
Plus que feutres sembla sendat
Ni cuers de bou escarlata
Non sabon mais que n'an trobat –
E quecx quo·s pot calafata.   (43–9)

Such a man thinks himself perfect in courtly ways and is a churl on all
four sides, and his feelings within him are badly bred. No more than felt
is like taffeta or ox-hide like fine scarlet, are they aware of anything but
what they have invented about this subject, and each one of them caulks
and fills in as best he may.

May God curse them and do an act of *caritas* thereby (50–4)!
Cortesia for Raimbaut is not skill in courtly etiquette, but the
quality of feeling which shows in every action of the man who
is *cortes*.

Raimbaut's rejection of the conventional spring opening
for his song *Non chant* is not just a device to startle his audience.
He is cocking a snook at the conventional declaration of love
which such openings introduce and at the courtly poets, such
as Chrétien de Troyes, who rejected the uncontrollable passion of Tristan for Yseut, which fascinated courtly audiences,
in favour of a love which was disciplined by the mind and
beneficial to the individual and society. Raimbaut wishes to
love, like Tristan, outside society and out of harmony with
nature:

Non chant per auzel ni per flor
Ni per neu ni per gelada,
Ni neis per freich ni per calor
Ni per reverdir de prada;
Ni per nuill autr'esbaudimen
Non chan ni non fui chantaire,
Mas per midonz en cui m'enten,
Car es del mon la bellaire.   (XXVII, 1–8)

I do not sing for bird or blossom or snow or frost, or even for cold or
heat or for the meadow that grows green again; nor for any other cause
of joy do I sing, nor have I sung, but for my lady to whom I aspire because
she is the fairest in the world.

He has drunk the potion of Tristan's love:

De midonz fatz dompn'e seignor
Cals que sia·il destinada.
Car ieu begui de la amor
Ja·us dei amar a celada.

Tristan, qan la·il det Yseus gen
E bela, no·n saup als faire;
Et ieu am per aital coven
Midonz, don no·m posc estraire.   (25–32)

I make of my lady my feudal lady and lord, whatever may be my fate.
Since I have drunk that love, I must love with secrecy. Tristan, when the
fair and gracious Yseut gave him this love, could not do otherwise. And
in such a way as this do I love my lady from whom I cannot part.

Chrétien de Troyes, in his song *D'Amors qui m'a tolu a moi*,
which is a riposte to Bernart de Ventadorn's *Can vei la lauzeta
mover*,[8] also takes up this challenge of Tristan-type love:

Onques del bevraje ne bui
don Tristans fu anpoisonez,
mes plus me fet amer que lui
fins cuers e bone volantez.
            (Bartsch, *Chres* [10th edn], XXXII, 28–31)

Never have I drunk the potion with which Tristan was poisoned but[9] a
true heart and whole desire make me love more than he did.

Chrétien is advocating *Fin'Amors* against *amour-passion*, and
Raimbaut, when he affects the role of a Tristan-type lover, is
insisting with humorous force that love must be felt in the
heart of the individual lover for the individual *domna*. Such
love exists, as Tristan's had done, outside the conventions of
courtly society, and the intrigues of the *lauzengiers*, the *cortes
ufaniers* and the *domnas* themselves.

Amors has become for Raimbaut the allegory of the powerful tyranny exercised on him in order to make him conform
to the conventional courtly frustrations and deceits imposed
by the *domna* in love affairs which are openly discussed in
courtly society and have *pretz* or social reputation as their aim
rather than *Jois*. Raimbaut is looking for an individual and
secret way to happiness, outside courtly society, with a *domna*
who will be loyal and trustworthy. It is in this sense of a
secret love which is withdrawn from and hostile to society
that his love is like that of Tristan for Yseut.

Raimbaut prefers to use the active phrase *amar finamens*
rather than the abstract *Fin'Amors*. He dislikes the thought that
love and poetry may be *comunaus*, or shared by all. He desires a
secret and personal relationship with his *domna*, in a delicate
balance in which he will find comfort and reassurance, desire
will be controlled and neither assuaged nor tormenting, and

his lady will be loyal and protective and offer permanence to
their love. He wishes to love with Tristan's intensity of feeling,
but without his bravery against his enemies.

As a poet Raimbaut desires the continuous excitement of
technical change and innovation, and as a lover he rejects the
convention of courtly social love because it is not only ordinary and *comunaus* but 'unreal' and ephemeral. He looks for
lasting happiness with a *domna* of like mind who is not ruled
by *Amors*, the figurehead of sensual and social love. The search
for personal *Jois* inspires both his poetry and his love.

With Raimbaut the conflict between *Fin'Amors* and *Amors* is
no longer a moral conflict between a disciplined, aspiring and
ultimately beneficial love and a sensual, tyrannical love that
is harmful to the individual and society. Raimbaut moves
away from the idea of a love that brings benefits to society.
He sees the conflict from his own independent point of view.
He chooses personal happiness and rejects submission to
courtly conventions, but when he denies the tyranny of
Amors as a code of social behaviour, Raimbaut is going against
the trend of courtly tastes which within a generation dictate
an abrupt change in troubadour ideas on love.

Raimbaut also resists courtly fashion in his defence of the
trobar clus, in the famous *tenso Ara·m platz* with Guiraut de
Bornelh:

> Ara·m platz, Giraut de Borneill,
> Que sapcha per c'anatz blasman
> Trobar clus, ni per cal semblan.
> Aiso·m digaz,
> Si tan prezatz
> So que es a toz comunal;
> Car adonc tut seran egual.   (XXXI, 1–7)

Now it pleases me, Guiraut de Bornelh, to know why and for what reason
you keep blaming the obscure style. Tell me whether you esteem so much
that which is common to all, for then all men will be the same.

Raimbaut's scorn for the foolish and ignorant people who
cannot discern what is most precious in poetry is close to that
of Martial in his Epigrams (II, LXXXVI):

> turpe est difficiles habere nugas
> et stultus labor est ineptiarum.
> scribat carmina circulis Palaemon:
> me raris iuvat auribus placere.

'Tis degrading to undertake difficult trifles; and foolish is the labour spent on puerilities. Let Palaemon write poems for the general throng; my delight is to please listeners few and choice.[10]

This *tenso Ara·m platz* was composed when the *clus* style was going out of favour. The *clus* style had two main features. The first and rarer quality was the interweaving within a poem of more than one level of meaning, and the gradual revealing, to the percipient listener, of the hidden meaning or meanings. As the poem developed, the beginning and end of the 'hidden' meaning, which with Marcabru was usually a moral truth, were bound up (*lassatz*) with key words. The second feature of this style was the use of words coloured with meanings which often had Christian or Biblical connotations. Courtly audiences preferred the clear or *leu* style, and Guiraut de Bornelh, who in this *tenso* defends the clear style, was himself reluctantly forced by public demand to give up the *clus* style.[11] The *trobar clus* varied in its aims from one generation of poets to the next, and at the time of this *tenso* it was probably applied by poets such as Peire d'Alvernhe to a debased form of poetry which was artificially obscure and void of meaning, or to poetry in which individual words, rather than the whole poem, were rich with dark and delicate nuances of personal meaning. This appears to be the case with the only extant poem of Raimbaut, *Cars, douz e fenhz*, which could be termed *clus*. This type of *clus* poetry is what Raimbaut is defending against Guiraut de Bornelh, and with its emphasis on rich and rare words and combinations of words, and exotic rhyme-words at the expense of concealed and sustained moral truths, it foreshadows the so-called *trobar ric* of Arnaut Daniel.

Raimbaut's sense of irony and hatred of the banal impel him to the *bella foudatz* which shocks through its use of the unexpected. His *gap*, *Escotatz mas no say que s'es*, is composed in stanzas of six lines with a final throwaway line of prose in mocking or bawdy style in the manner of Guilhem IX.

Escotatz, mas no say que s'es,
Senhor, so que vuelh comensar.
Vers, estribot, ni sirventes
Non es, ni nom no·l sai trobar;
Ni ges no say co·l mi fezes
S'aytal no·l podi'acabar,

Que ia hom mays non vis fag aytal ad home ni a femna en est segle ni en l'autre qu'es passatz. (XXIV, 1–7)

Listen, my lords, but I know not what this is that I want to begin. It is not a *vers, estribot* or *sirventes*, nor can I invent a name for it. Nor do I know at all how I should set about composing it if I could not finish it in such a way...for never did anyone see such a thing composed by man or woman in this century or the last one.

Raimbaut, using the *no say que s'es* technique of the schools that Guilhem IX had parodied, is mocking the nicely formulated genres of the literary pundits, and at the same time the vapourings of precious poets covering their inadequacy with new names for old genres.[12]

He amplifies his burlesque of current genres and styles:

> Que ben a passatz quatre mes,
> (Oc! e mays de mil ans so·m par)
> Que m'a autrejat e promes
> Que·m dara so que m'es pus car.
> Dona! Pus mon cor tenetz pres
> Adossatz me ab dous l'amar.
Dieus, aiuda! *In nomine patris et filii et spiritus sancti!* Aiso que sera, domna?
>
> (22–8)

For a good four months have passed (yes! and it seems to me more than a thousand years) since she granted me the assurance and promised me that she would give me what is most dear to me. My lady, since you hold my heart captive, sweeten the bitterness for me with sweetness. God help me! In the name of the father, the son and the Holy Ghost! What will this turn out to be, my lady?

The first two solemn lines are a parody of the *planh*. Thus Gaucelm Faidit on the death of Richard Cœur de Lion:

> Mortz es lo reis, e son passat mil an,
> c'anc tant pros hom non fo, ni no·l vi res.
>
> (ed. J. Mouzat, L, 10–11)

The king is dead and a thousand years have gone since a man of such worth existed or was seen by anyone.

Raimbaut moves swiftly from the mock-heroic to a parody of precious courtly style. In the line *Adossatz me ab dous l'amar*, *l'amar* is a commonplace pun on three levels, 'bitterness', 'loving' and 'the sea', used by Bernart de Ventadorn and worked to death, possibly with humorous intention, by Chrétien de Troyes in *Cligés* (ed. Micha, 538–57). Raimbaut flies into mock despair at his flat pun: 'God help me!...' he seeks absolution: *in nomine patris*...and binds up his song with its beginning: 'what is this song going to be?'

In the next stanza Raimbaut goes from words of *amor de lonh* in the style of Jaufre Rudel, through commonplace praise of his lady, to bawdy rejection of her and the concept of distant love:

> Qu'ieu soy per vos gays, d'ira ples;
> Iratz-jauzens me faytz trobar;
> E so m'en partitz de tals tres
> Qu'el mon non a, mas vos, lur par;
> E soy fols cantayre cortes
> Tan c'om m'en apela ioglar.

Dona, far ne podetz a vostra guiza, co fes n'Ayma de l'espatla que la estujet lay on li plac.[13]   (29–35)

For because of you I am gay and full of sorrow; you make me compose, sad and rejoicing as I am, and for the sake of you I have left three women of such quality that except for you they have no equal in the world. And I am such a foolish courtly singer that they call me *joglar*. My lady, you can do as you like, as lady Ayma did with the shoulder blade when she stuck it there where it pleased her.

The wisdom behind Raimbaut's folly and his extra-ordinary versatility in rhyme and versification come together in his most remarkable and, possibly, his last poem,[14] *Ar resplan la flors enversa* (XXXIX). The intricate rhyme scheme that he develops is not unlike the one that Arnaut Daniel adopted for his *sestina*. Raimbaut takes eight rhyme-words and repeats them in alternate stanzas in two different grammatical forms. The words are: *enversa / enverse*; *tertres / tertre*; *conglapis / conglapi*; *trenca / trenque*; *siscles / siscle*; *giscles / giscle*; *joys / joy* and *croys / croy*. Stanzas I and II are linked by a play on words, which is a form of internal rhyme, in lines 3. *flors / flor*; 4. *cotz / cautz*; 6. *fuelhs / fulhat* and 8. *vey / vey*. Stanzas II and IV both have *plan* in line 2, and stanzas I and V have *rancx* in line 2.

> I Ar resplan la flors enversa
> Pels trencans rancx e pels tertres,
> Cals flors? Neus, gels e conglapis
> Que cotz e destrenh e trenca;
> Don vey morz quils, critz, brays, siscles
> En fuelhs, en rams e en giscles.
> Mas mi ten vert e jauzen Joys
> Er quan vey secx los dolens croys.
>
> II Quar enaissi m'o enverse
> Que bel plan mi semblon tertre,
> E tenc per flor lo conglapi,
> E·l cautz m'es vis que·l freit trenque,

E·l tro mi son chant e siscle,
E paro·m fulhat li giscle.
Aissi·m suy ferm lassatz en joy
Que re non vey que·m sia croy –

III Mas una gen fad'enversa
(Cum s'eron noirit en tertres)
Que·m fan pro pieigz que conglapis;
Q'us quecx ab sa lengua trenca
E·n parla bas et ab siscles;
E no y val bastos ni giscles
Ni menassas; – ans lur es joys
Quan fan so don hom los clam croys.

IV Qu'ar en baizan no·us enverse
No m'o tolon pla ni tertre,
Dona, ni gel ni conglapi,
Mas non-poder trop en trenque.¹⁵
Dona, per cuy chant e siscle,
Vostre belh huelh mi son giscle
Que·m castion si·l cor ab joy
Qu'ieu no·us aus aver talan croy.

V Anat ai cum cauz'enversa
Sercan rancx e vals e tertres,
Marritz cum selh que conglapis
Cocha e mazelh'e trenca:
Que no·m conquis chans ni siscles
Plus que folhs clercx conquer giscles.
Mas ar – Dieu lau – m'alberga Joys
Malgrat dels fals lauzengiers croys.

VI Mos vers an – qu'aissi l'enverse,
Que no·l tenhon bosc ni tertre –
Lai on hom non sen conglapi,
Ni a freitz poder que y trenque.
A midons lo chant e·l siscle,
Clar, qu'el cor l'en intro·l giscle,
Selh que sap gen chantar ab joy
Que no tanh a chantador croy.

Now the upside-down blossom shines through the sharp ridges and the hills – which? Snow, ice and frost which burns and torments and cuts, so that I see that the sharp cries, calls, songs and warblings are dead in the leaves, in the branches and twigs. But Joy keeps me green and rejoicing now when I see that the wretched and churlish men are withered.

For I turn things upside down for myself so that the hills seem fair plains to me and I consider the frost as blossom, and it seems to me that the warmth cuts the cold and the thunderclaps are songs and whistlings to me, and the twigs appear to me covered in foliage. I am so firmly bound up in Joy that I can see nothing that seems base to me.

Except for a stupid race of people, upside down as if they had been reared in the hills, who do me more hurt than frost. Each one of these cuts with his tongue and speaks low and with whistlings. And neither stick nor twig helps in this, nor threats; – on the contrary, their joy comes from doing things which make people call them churls.

Neither plains nor hills, my lady, nor ice nor frost prevent me from laying you back and kissing you, but powerlessness keeps me from it. My lady, for whom I sing and whistle, your fair eyes are the rods which so chastise my heart with Joy that I dare not have a churlish desire towards you.

I have gone about like an upside-down person, searching rocks and valleys and hills, saddened like one whom the frost impels onwards and kills and splits; for neither song nor high warbling has won me over any more than the rod wins over the false clergy. But now – I praise God – Joy takes me into her dwelling in spite of the false and churlish slanderers.

Let my poem go – for so do I turn it upside down that neither woods nor hills may hold it – there where a man feels no frost, and cold has no power to destroy. Let it be sung and warbled to my lady, clearly so that its shoots may enter her heart, by a man who can sing graciously and joyously, for it befits no churlish singer.

Raimbaut is using the commonplace of the world upside down as framework for a song which in technique and meaning is a culmination of all his other poems, a serious review of the absurdity of life and his faith in the victory of *Jois* over *Malvestatz*, of light and warmth over what is dark, cold and base. As Love had put nature out of joint for Bernart de Ventadorn, so Joy now puts together the bare winter scene, the *quils*, *critz*, *brays* and *siscles* of thin birdsong and the high-pitched, twittering slanderers.

Raimbaut is lucid and assured as he turns the winter scene upside down. The *Jois* in his mind discards the harsh winter image of nature and the baseness that coats life with rust. He is so firmly bound up in joy in *Ar resplan* that nothing can seem amiss; the thunderclaps are birdsong and the warm cuts the cold. He sees good in everything – except the stupid upside-down people who cut with their tongues.

In stanza IV no external harshness of nature, ice or frost can restrain him from laying his lady back with his kisses. But *non-poder* keeps him from it, not impotence, but the lover's loss of mastery over his natural self and his loss of identity once he looks into his lady's eyes. With Bernart de Ventadorn the imagery was passive, the lover seeing himself in his lady's eyes, as in a pleasing mirror (XLIII, 17–20), but Raimbaut dramatises the conflict within him so that his lady's eyes chastise, blame and correct his heart with such joy that he dares not feel base desire towards her.

Raimbaut is submitting to a love that is Fin'Amors and is rejoicing in the hope of living *letz, cortes e sapiens*. He sings of his search for this happiness in life. He has wandered among crags, valleys and hills, sad and tortured by frost, refusing to be lured from his path by song, but now, and he praises God for this, Joy at last gives him shelter and happiness and he sends his *vers* to the lady in whose presence cold has no power to hurt.

Ar resplan is a triumphant song. Raimbaut feels that he has found personal *Jois* and has won the battle against the things in life that are base, harsh, mean, cold and cutting. In this sense it is the victorious counterpart to the more abstract *Cars, douz e fenhz* in which Joy and Reputation wilt before the evil people, and rust and film corrupt. *Ar resplan*, like Arnaut Daniel's *sestina, Lo ferm voler*, is no mere technical *tour de force*. The discipline of the style sets off the rigour with which Raimbaut matches the winter cruelties of nature and the harshness of life offered to the person who seeks happiness by traversing the wilderness. *Anat ai cum cauz'enversa* ('I have gone about like an upside-down person') is no formalised poetic trick; it means what it says. Raimbaut, the entertainer and *joglar*, caustic, learned and full of *bella foudatz*, has a real sense of the vanity of life. Bred to the courtly system, he views it in a wide and distant perspective. He holds fast to the ideals of *Jovens* and *Jois* and the search for the ultimate happiness that earlier troubadours called *lo mielhs*. All that is contrary to *Jovens* fills him with sadness and doubt, so that in his sharp-minded self-knowledge he is full and empty of fine beginnings, *grams-iauzens, trist-alegre*, and with intense and uncertain desire, a *voluntat meja gaia*, is seeking personal happiness. He refuses to move from his own path for the delights of nature, song, society or *Amors*. He finds harmony and reassurance through his rational approach to life and love, his *sabers*, as Peire d'Alvernhe would say. He feels sharply the counter-balancing forces in life, loyalty and deceit, true feeling and the harsh shell of the *flacs-endurzitz*, the warmth that cuts the cold, the aspiration of controlled desire and the tyranny of undisciplined longings, and he finds joy through rejecting the uncertainties of *Amors* and of the courtly world for his idea of Fin'Amors, the special, secret and personal love for a loyal domna.

Raimbaut was not mentioned by Dante as a troubadour who might serve as a model for writers in the vernacular tongue. The reasons for this are not unclear. Dante is looking for an auctor, an authority on Love and a master in the art of composing poetry in the vernacular, and he finds him in Arnaut Daniel. Raimbaut is a precursor, a brilliant non-conformist experimenter, who, owing much to Marcabru in nature imagery and the use of startling compound words and allegory, has within him a bold youthful inventiveness and intoxication with the sound, meaning and power of individual words. Add to this his quest for happiness of the mind, his gaiety and melancholy, and he becomes for us one of the most sympathetic poets of the Middle Ages.

Guiraut de Bornelh, on Raimbaut's early death, praised his wisdom, merriment and bella foudatz:

> Dels vostres trobars esmeratz,
>   de las bontatz,
> del pretz, del sen, de las rictatz
> en degran esdevenir iai
> sel cui pieitz vai.
> (Appel, Chres, LXXXIII, 49–53, pp. 122–3)

When they think of the poems that you refined and made perfect, of your acts of kindness, your fame, wisdom, and splendid works, those people who are suffering most will be compelled to be joyful.

6

Peire d'Alvernhe

IN *Cantarai d'aqestz trobadors* Peire d'Alvernhe in jocund mood reviews the foibles of the poets of his day and in the last stanza he, or another poet, sings:

> Peire d'Alvernge a tal votz
> que canta de sus e de sotz,
> e lauza·s mout a tota gen;
> pero maïstres es de totz,
> ab c'un pauc esclarzis sos motz,
> c'a penas nuils hom los enten.[1]   (XII, 79–84)

Peire d'Alvernhe has such a voice that he sings high and low and praises himself greatly in the presence of everyone. Yet he is the master of all, provided that he makes his words a little clearer, for scarcely anyone can understand them.

The Provençal biographer says that Peire came from the diocese of Clermont, was wise and well educated and the son of a burgher, handsome and pleasing in his person.

He composed and sang well and was the first good troubadour who existed beyond the mountains [i.e. of Provence], and he composed the best melodies for *vers* that had ever been invented...He was considered the best troubadour in the world before Guiraut de Bornelh came. He praised himself greatly in his songs and blamed other troubadours...He led his life for a long time in this world, in noble society, and then he repented [var. MS. R, 'became a monk'] and died.[2]

Peire composed between 1150 and 1180. He attended the court of Raimon V of Toulouse where he must have known Bernart de Ventadorn. In 1158, in the spring and summer, he was at the court of Castille, which he had already visited during the reign of Alfonso VII. In the summer of 1159 he was at Barcelona, and he knew the court of Ermengarda of Narbonne. He may also have spent some time in Northern France.[3]

Like other troubadours, Peire Rogier, Peire Cardenal, Aimeric de Belenoi, Gui d'Uisel, Uc Brunet and Gausbert de Poicibot, Peire d'Alvernhe was a cleric before he turned to poetry, and Bernart Marti in his attack on Peire's boast that his poetry is *entiers*, 'whole' or 'perfect', accuses him of apostasy:

> E quan canorgues si mes
> Pey d'Alvernh' en canongia,
> A Dieu per que·s prometia
> Entiers que pueys si fraysses?[4]
> Quar si feys fols joglares,
> Per que l'entier pretz cambia.
>
> (ed. E. Hoepffner, v, 31–6)

And when Peire d'Alvernhe entered a canonry as a canon, why did he promise himself entirely to God and then break his word? For he changed into a foolish minstrel and impairs this perfect reputation.

The conflict between the secular and religious life determines Peire's attitude to his poetry. He is no brave, impulsive warrior in love, such as Bernart de Ventadorn, but a troubadour of *saber* and *sen*. He disciplines feeling and desire according to the orders of *mesura*, the rational control of the senses which Marcabru commended to the follower of *Fin'Amors* who wished to live *letz, cortes e sapiens*. Unlike most troubadours of the twelfth century who keep love of God and love of the *domna* on separate planes which meet only when the exalted *Fin'Amors* felt for the *domna* is expressed in terms which can be associated with love of God and the Virgin, Peire refuses to accept the co-existence of the courtly and the Christian ways of life. He recognises the conflict between present delight in the Joy of the Court and the desire for eternal salvation, and in face of the reality of death and fear of damnation he renounces courtly *Jois* in favour of love of God. Bernart de Ventadorn, Bertran de Born and Folquet de Marseille, who finally embraced the religious life, must have felt this conflict, but Peire alone among twelfth-century troubadours expresses it clearly, and thereby justifies his claim that his poetry is 'whole' and 'integrated' (*entiers*).

So far as love of the *domna* is concerned, Peire is more poet than lover. He feels none of Bernart's extreme joy and sorrow in love. Peire submits to *Amors* in the hope that he will find an assured contentment and will feel *segurs* within the frame-

work of courtly society and within himself. *Jois* for him is not
the quest for individual ecstasy or the hope of ultimate
happiness (*mielhs*) in this world. Peire is a meditative and contemplative poet of subtle and gentle lyricism, and *Jois* controlled by *mesura* offers him social and moral balance and the
hope of a quiet mind.

Peire's ideas about love and happiness, which are in the
direct tradition of Marcabru and Jaufre Rudel, may be seen
more clearly if we look first at those poems which are concerned primarily with *Amors*, then at those which deal with
Fin'Amors and *amor de lonh*, and finally at his poems about the
choice between the love and joy of this world and Christian
love of God.

Peire's *Ab fina ioia comenssa* begins like Bernart's *Ab joi mou lo
vers e·l comens*, but in place of Bernart's robust cries of joy and
delight at his lady's fair and laughing lips, Peire, in pale imitation of Jaufre Rudel, cherishes the memory of love, gratefully
and patiently:

> D'amor ai la sovinenssa
> e·ls bels digz: ren plus no·m dona;
> mas per bona atendenssa
> esper c'alcus iois m'en veigna;
> ·l segles vol c'om si capteigna
> segon que pot sempres faire
> q'en breu temps plus asazona
> q'a pro d'aisso don ac fam. (III, 9–16)

From love I have the memory and the fair words: it gives me nothing
more. But if I wait patiently and with good disposition I hope that some
happiness may come to me from it. The world wishes a man to behave in
the way that is natural to him and, if he does this, joy will soon ripen for
him and he will possess an abundance of what he hungered for.

He deserves no more than a kindly look and words of welcome from his lady:

> ni·s taing que tant aut mi ceigna
> ni tant rics iois m'endeveigna
> on coven us emperaire:
> pro fai car sol gen mi sona,
> ni car sofre q'ieu la am. (20–4)

nor is it fitting that I should gird myself in such an exalted way or that
such splendid joy should befall me as that which an emperor considers
his due. She helps me merely by addressing her gracious words to me and
by allowing me to love her.

Although Peire does not preach the virtue of *mesura*, as Marcabru had done, he puts it into practice: patience and hope are all that is due to him and happiness lies in recognising and accepting this. He repents without having sinned and asks for a forgiveness which his lady refuses. He rejects despair, and calls on God for a help which goes beyond the help he ostensibly needs with his *domna*:

> que perdutz es desperaire;
> per c'ai esperanssa bona:
> pel nostre Don mi reclam. (38–40)

for the man who despairs is lost [damned], and so I keep my fair hopes and call upon our Lord.

Although Peire is affecting the *amant martyr*, the afflictions of Love are less important than concern for his own poetic excellence:

> Ab fina ioia comenssa
> lo vers qui bels motz assona
> e de re no·i a faillensa;
> mas no m'es bon qe l'apreigna
> tals cui mos chans non coveigna,
> q'ieu non vuoill avols chantaire,
> cel que tot chan desfaissona,
> mon doutz sonet torn'en bram. (1–8)

This song which brings fair words into harmony and is without flaw of any kind is inspired by perfect joy. But I am not pleased that anyone to whom my song is not suited, should learn it, for I do not want a churlish singer who sets every song out of joint to turn my sweet melody into harsh howling.

Peire's concern with the art of *trobar* is again evident in *Chantarai pus vey* in which he chooses the path of patient, faithful and 'purifying' service to his lady. The flight of his lark is no symbol of ecstasy and self-oblivion but a muted, contrived image of the rise and fall of birdsong, and his words are chosen for the harmony of their matching vowel sounds and consonants rather than poetic feeling:

> Belh m'es quan l'alauza se fer
> en l'ayr, per on dissen lo rays,
> e monta, tro li·s bel que·s bays
> sobre·l fuelh que branda·l biza,
> e·l dous temps – qu'anc bona nasques! –
> entruebre·ls becx dels auzelhos,
> don retin lur chans sus e ios. (IV, 8–14)

I am happy when the lark hurls itself into the air, there where the ray of the sun descends, and climbs up until it is pleased to lower itself on to the leaf which is shaken by the wind; and the gentle season – fairer than any that was ever born! – begins to open the beaks of the young birds so that the notes of their song rise and fall.

Peire's other song of submission to *Amors*, *La fuelhs e·l flors*, has far more life. In the season of abundance, the birdsong and the dew that lights the bough bring joy and delight and desire for wisdom:

> qu'entendemens
> mi ven e voluntatz
> d'esser sabens
> de mais en mielhs assatz.   (v, 7–10)

so that the aspiration and desire comes to me to be wise, more and increasingly much more so.

However wise and skilful the poet may be, his gifts cannot be prized unless they are inspired by the lasting, dynamic joy that is denied to the man without wisdom and peace of mind.

> Quar ses gaug grans sabers ni purs
>   ni gienhs ginhos
> non er aut elegutz;
> per que ie·m cre en cent augurs
>   iauzens ioyos
> e iauzens mantengutz
>   contra tals gens
> cuy falh sciens'e patz.   (11–18)

For, if joy is absent, great and pure wisdom and subtle artistry will never be chosen as excellent; so that I believe by a hundred signs that I am rejoicing and in a state of joy, and sustained in a state of rejoicing in contrast to those people in whom knowledge and peace of mind are absent.

Peire's joy is complete:

> Qu'ab lo plus gent ioy vau segurs   (21)

for it comes from the assurance that the wise, unchanging intelligence and beauty of his lady will shield him from the harsh words of angry men and foul-mouthed slanderers: the *domna,*

> don sapiens
> suy e mai melhuratz
> d'autres sinc cens
> d'amor enamoratz.   (57–60)

because of whom I am wise and more greatly improved than any other five hundred men who have fallen in love with love.

She gives him poetic supremacy:

> Que cum l'aurs resplan e l'azurs
> contra·l fer ros
> desobre los escutz
> mi det do, tro lai ont es Surs,
> qu'ieu sobriers fos
> als grans et als menutz
> dels esciens
> de trobar ses fenhs fatz,
> don sui grazens
> ad aquilh don m'es datz.   (61–70)

For just as gold and azure shine in the rusty iron of shields, so has she given me the gift which, from here to Tyre, makes me supreme over the poets, great and small, who know how to compose without foolish imaginings. And I am grateful to her through whom this has been given to me.

'Improved' by fin'amistatz and sheltered by his lady from the strife of fals'amistatz, supreme in the poetic art which is concerned with 'real' themes and not with foudatz, nien and cuda, Peire chooses to live letz, cortes e sapiens. This poem of reasoned self-praise masquerading as courtly praise of the lady who has granted him his gifts, may have provoked Bernart Marti's attack on Peire in D'entier vers far ieu non pes.

Peire's sabers buds and new Jois blossoms and bears fruit at the onset of winter:

> Deiosta·ls breus iorns e·ls loncs sers,
> qan la blanc'aura brunezis,
> vuoill que branc e bruoill mos sabers
> d'un nou ioi qe·m fruich'e·m floris;
> car del doutz fuoill vei clarzir los garrics,
> per qe·s retrai[5] entre·ls enois e·ls freis
> lo rossignols e·l tortz e·l gais e·l pics.   (VII, 1–7)

At the approach of the short days and the long evenings when the white air grows dark, I want my knowledge to branch and bud with a new joy which bears fruit and blossoms for me; for I see the woods lightened through loss of their gentle leaves, so that, in the midst of these vexed and cold times, the nightingale, the thrush, the jay and the pie withdraw.

Peire, like Marcabru and Jaufre, is opposing a pure 'distant' winter love to a 'close' sensual summer love. He finds pleasure in thoughts of his lady:

Contr'aisso m'agrada·l parers
d'amor loindan'e devezis
car pauc val levars ni iazers
a lui ses lieis cui es aclis;
c'amors vol gaug e guerpis los enics,
e qui s'esgau a l'ora q'es destreis,
be·m par q'a dreit li vol esser amics.   (8–14)

At this season the appearance of distant love pleases me and I will explain
this, for getting up and going to bed have small value for the man who is
without the lady to whom he is devoted. For Love desires enjoyment and
deserts the mournful, and it seems to me that Love is right in wishing to
befriend the man who rejoices at that moment when he is oppressed.

Seeing and believing and knowing that Love, with its deceits
and pleasures, tears and laughter, makes a man, whether he
likes it or not, fat or lean, rich or poor, Peire prefers what he
has (15–20), which in this case is the thought of his lady and
his hidden, distant love. In her presence he is uncourtly and
timid:

Ges ieu non sai los capteners
mas soffre, c'una m'a conquis
don reviu iois e nais valers,
tals que denan li·m trassaillis;
car no m'enqier de dir, me·n ven destrics,
tan tem qe·l mieils lais e prenda·l sordeis;
on plus n'ai cor, mi pens: car non te·n gics?[6]   (22–8)

I do not know the right ways to behave, but I suffer because I have been
conquered by a lady through whom such joy comes back to life and such
worth is born that I tremble in her presence. Harm comes to me because
I do not woo with words, so much do I fear that I may abandon what is the
best and accept the worst. When I most aspire to her, I think: 'Why do
you not give this up?'

The thought of her is pure joy:

So es gaugz e iois e plazers
que a moutas gens abellis
e sos pretz mont'a grans poders
e sos iois sobreseignoris,
q'enseignamens e beutatz l'es abrics:
dompneis d'amor, q'en lieis s'espan e creis,
plens de dousor, vertz e blancs, cum es nics;
per q'ieu mi pens: ia non te·n desrazics,
quan mi conquis en loc on ilh me seis
plus que se·m des Franssa lo reis Loics.   (43–52)

This is delight and joy and pleasure that she is pleasing to many people,
and that her fame rises mightily and the joy she gives is supreme, because

courtly knowledge and beauty are her shield and the service of love, which in her expands and grows, full of sweetness, green and white as snow.

So that I think: 'Never uproot yourself from her, since on that occasion when she crowned me she overcame me more completely than if king Louis had given me France.

The *dompneis d'amor* that is green and white as snow binds up the initial image of new joy fruiting in the short days and long evenings of winter when the white air grows dark. Peire is rationalising his position as troubadour to a famous and successful courtly *domna*. He is choosing distant love, not, like Guilhem IX, as a temporary mental escape from the banality and convention of *Amors*, or, like Jaufre Rudel, as a refuge from the moral burden of close, sensual love, but as a way of saving himself from the frustrations and *foudatz* of *Amors* that afflicted Bernart de Ventadorn. This is what Peire means by his *sabers*. *Jois* for him is not ecstatic awareness of the inexpressible, but measurable delight in creating happiness and security for himself in the courtly situation. He rejoices in his lady's social reputation, in her courtly accomplishment, and the supreme *joie de la cour* that she bestows, and he rejoices in his status as her troubadour, in his poetic prowess and in his *sabers*, the rational power that he applies to his life and which appears to have the importance for Peire that *mesura* had for Marcabru. Peire uses *mesura* on only one occasion (I, 117) and with the meaning of measurement, and *Fin'Amors*, which was both Marcabru's shield against amoral, promiscuous love and the way to happiness through the rationalisation of carnal desire, has now become for Peire d'Alvernhe the only choice for the troubadour who seeks to please his lady and his audience, and keep for himself the serenity, wisdom and happiness that will guarantee poetic and courtly success. This serenity is disturbed by 'close' love, but is restored by thoughts of the lady's courtly excellence and her assurance of protection (VII, 28 and 50).

Peire reverses the theme of *amor de lonh* in *Rossinhol, el seu repaire*. He bridges the distance from his lady with his Ovidian messenger, the nightingale, who gives warning that whiteness, like the blossom on the branch, will soon lose its first freshness (I, 55–7).

Peire turns the courtly poem of distant love upside-down. He makes the lady declare her love and her vision of happi-

ness, her wish to feel *Jois* and to be *segura*, to find peace in converse with her lover and self-forgetfulness in her dream. The
lady who feels *amor de lonh* for her suitor may be a literary
device to startle and amuse a courtly audience, or Peire may
be using, perhaps unconsciously, the pre-courtly tradition of
the lady sorrowing at the departure of her knight which we
find in Marcabru's *A la fontana del vergier* and Der von Kürenc-
berc's *Ich zôch mir einen valken*:

> Fort mi pot esser salvatge
> quar s'es lonhatz mos amis,
> c'anc ioi de negun linhatge
> no vi que tan m'abelis;
> > trop viatz
> > fo·l comiatz,
> mas, s'ieu fos segura,
> > mais bontatz
> > n'agr'asatz:
> per qu'ieu n'ai rancura.
>
> Que tan l'am de bon coratge,
> c'ades, s'eu entredormis,
> ab lui ai en guidonatge
> ioc e ioi e gaug e ris;
> > e·l solatz
> > c'ai em patz
> no sap creatura,
> > tan quan iatz
> > e mos bratz
> tro que·s trasfigura. (1, 71–90)

It is harsh that my lover has gone, for never have I seen a joyous person of
any lineage who was so pleasing to me. The leave-taking was too swift,
but if I had felt secure, he would have received many more kindnesses
from me, and for this reason I grieve.

For I love him so dearly that, as soon as I am half asleep, I have, with
him as my guide, disport and joy and delight and laughter, and no creature
knows of this converse that I have in peace as long as he lies in my arms
until he is transfigured.

She continues:

> non vueill autr'aver conquis;
> mos cuidatz
> es bos fatz. (94–6)

I do not wish to have conquered any other man: my imaginings are a
fine reality.

In two further songs Peire rejects the disturbance of mind

and feeling caused by 'close' love. *Al dessebrar del païs* (II)
describes Peire's delight and sorrow at the moment of leaving
his love (*m'alegr'e m'irays*). Jaufre had thought that he would
feel *iratz e gauzens* at the imaginary parting from his lady; he
would be sad at losing her *solatz* and physical presence, yet
would rejoice at the prospect of remembering this love. Peire
is sad at being betrayed and dismissed from the sweet, pleasing, and perhaps allegorical land, where joy is wooed most
intensely and reputation is most loved. He knows that he
could lie about this love to which he was so close (*vezis*), but
he rejoices that he is embittered towards love, for now he is
equipped for any new undertaking:

> D'esser hueymais m'esbaudis
> pus amars m'enamarzis;
> qu'ara·m sent de totz assays
> vertz e blancs e brus e bays,
> e m'albir
> e dic vos d'amor nems conia
> que paors es de perir
> lai on li es ops que lonia. (II, 33–40)

Now I rejoice in existing since false loving makes me bitter; for now I feel
green and white and dark and bay coloured, and I believe and I tell you
about love that is too pleasing, that a man fears that he will perish at the
moment when he must depart from it.

He rejects his lady: let her go with her false laughter where
she pleases; she will never see him again. He must leave this
pleasant land of courtly joy, and were it not that he desires to
vex her, he would have retired to a canonry – and made her
victory complete (41–8). He concludes:

> Senher n'Estrieu, qui s'aconia
> de trop human ioy iauzir,
> mal fai[7] qui non lo calonia. (49–51)

My lord Estrieus, if a man finds pleasure in enjoying too much human
happiness, anyone who does not blame him acts wrongly.

Peire's rhymes (-*is*, -*ays*, -*onia*), his use of the phrases and
words *m'alegr'e m'irays* (4), *camis* (17), *Sarrazis* (18), *vezis* (25)
and the device of a refrain word (*conia*), make it clear that he
had Jaufre Rudel in mind when he composed *Al dessebrar del
païs*. But he twists and develops Jaufre's theme. Jaufre in *Belhs
m'es* rejected the confusion and burden of sensual or 'close'
love and turned to *Fin'Amors*, and in *Lanquan li jorn* he sought

joy in separation from 'close' love and the illumination of the
mind through the memory of distant love. Peire finds joy in
freedom from dominant 'close' love, but he also sees danger
in too great a delight in human love, and the line *que paors es
de perir* (39) implies that earthly love which is too pleasing
may lose a man his hope of salvation. Peire demands distance
in love in order to preserve his mental, social and spiritual
self.

Peire knows that false love which belongs to the churls and
cowardly layabouts will betray him too. He opens *En estiu*
with a sensual summer scene in the style of Marcabru:

> En estiu, qan crida·l iais
> e reviu per miei los plais
> jovens ab la flor que nais,
> adoncs es razos c'om lais
> fals'amor enganairitz
> als volpillos acropitz:
>
> Li sordeior e·il savais
> n'an lo mieills e·l meins del fais:
> pauc so prezon, qui·s n'irais.
> Amarai, mas non puosc mais,
> que de tal amor sui guitz
> don sai que serai trahitz.   (IX, 1–12)

In summer when the jay cries out and Youth is reborn with the blossom
that buds among the meadows, it is right that false, deceitful love should
be left to the cowardly squatters.

These unvirtuous and despicable men have the best and the least of the
burden: they care little for the anger of others. I will love since I cannot do
otherwise, for I am led by a love which I know will betray me.

In Marcabru's *Pax in Nomine Domini* the cowards and *crup-en-
cami* hog their hearths and refuse the *lavador* and the tests that
God sets for the bold and the gentle, and Peire may have
intentionally introduced a similar nuance of Christian meaning, for his next stanzas are enigmatic:

> Pres ai estat en caslar,
> ab so que no·i aus estar,
> e pero non puosc mudar
> de mos enemics no·l gar;
> ja non serai assaillitz,
> q'en auta roch'es bastitz.
>
> Si·l portiers me vol iurar
> c'autre non i lais intrar,
> segur poirai gerreiar;

mas al sagramen passar
tem que serai escarnitz,
que mil vetz i sui faillitz.   (13–24)

I have been held prisoner in a castle although I do not dare to stay in it,
and yet I cannot help defending it against my enemies; I shall never be
attacked, for it is built on a high rock.

If the gatekeeper will swear to me that he will not allow anyone to
enter it, I shall be able to wage war with assurance, but should he break
his oath, I fear I shall be scorned, for I have failed in this matter a thousand
times.

These stanzas, which use the feudal language of a chatelain
who sets out for war and entrusts his castle and his lady to the
loyalty of his gate-keeper, are composed in the style of the
riddle-poem or *devinalh* and can be interpreted in different
ways. The image of the castle and the tower in Jaufre's *Pro ai
del chan* has been seen as religious symbolism,[8] and Peire's
castle built on a high rock may possibly have a Christian
meaning as D. Scheludko suggested[9] when he understood
these lines as a contrast between *Amor dei* and *Amor mundi*. A.
Jeanroy saw the castle as the *domna*.[10] These interpretations
were rejected by A. del Monte who took the castle as the illusion of love which imprisons the poet against his wish; from
the *auta rocha* (18), the lonely place to which he has raised
himself, the poet defends this illusion of love against reality,
whilst fearing that passion, as it has done before, may prevent
him from returning from reality to illusion.[11]

Peire is not, however, concerned to any great degree with
the theme of illusion and reality. He listens to his mind, and
recognises and rationalises the good and the bad he sees
around him. If he flees, it is from the fear that the pleasures of
earthly love may overpower him. This may suggest another
meaning for this passage. The castle is *Amors* or close love in
which he does not want to stay although he will defend it,
and at the same time the castle, as Jeanroy suggested, is the
domna who is the symbol of this love, and is so exalted that
having raised himself to her level he will be protected from
attack. The gate-keeper is the poet's rational control, the
sabers which prevents sensual desire from entering and dominating this love. If *sabers* is disloyal, he will fail as he has done
a thousand times before. The enemies of the poet (16) are his
sensual desires and the slanderers who are poised to attack
him with accusations of *Fals'Amors*.

Such an explanation of the castle and the gate-keeper as psychological allegory in the style of Guillaume de Lorris has the merit that it fits the context of the poem. The two stanzas in question amplify the meaning of the lines immediately before them in which Peire admits that he is destined to love and be guided by a love which will betray him. They also introduce the following stanzas in which he prays that he may find the consolation which comes from loving with a peaceful mind:

> A Dompnidieu qier solatz
> per q'ieu si'enamoratz,
> q'en aital hora fui natz
> c'anc non puoc amar en patz. (IX, 3 1–4)

From Almighty God I seek the solace of falling in love, for I was born under such a star that I can never love with peace of mind.

He prays that Love may deceive him, and so cure him:

> Amor mi lais Dieus trobar
> on ia no·m posc afiar,
> e qant ieu la tenrai car,
> ill pens de mi enganar;
> c'adoncs mi tenc per garitz,
> qan mi ment tot cant mi ditz. (37–42)

May God let me find a love in which I can never place my trust, and when I hold this love dear may she be thinking about deceiving me; for I shall consider myself cured at the moment when everything that she says to me is a lie.

'The man who imagines that he can find a different sort of love', he continues, 'has much riding to do, for as far as the sky encloses the sea, women can scarcely be found who are not fickle to their lovers and husbands. A man who is guided by such love must always sorrow' (43–50).

In another enigmatic poem, L'airs clars, which he calls a song that is not obscure (vers non-clus) composed to a new tune (sos novelhs) so that everyone may sing it, Peire advises the cultivation of happiness as the right path to a moral life:

> Qu'ira ni grans cossiriers
> non obra boneza,
> qu'ans es dans e destorbiers:
> non obra proeza;
> que, cum totz mals encombriers
> mou de cobezeza,
> atressi sortz totz faitz niers
> d'embronquar, qui·l veza.

Doncx qui de gaug a dezirier,
ben tengua a dreyt so semdier
e l'ir'e l'avol parven lays
als malvatz ni als sers savays.   (VI, 13–24)

For sorrow and mournful thoughts do not produce goodness; rather do
they create harm and disturbance, and nothing that has a noble value. For
just as every evil obstacle is caused by cupidity, so does every dark deed
proceed from a morose condition, if one makes a habit of it. Then let that
man who desires to be joyful hold firmly to his right path and leave
sorrow and a wretched countenance to the wicked and the despicable serfs.

A man must not only reject sorrow for joy, but must choose
between two joys:

Mas dels dos ioys es ops sens
e reconoyssensa,
e l'us es abaissamens
e l'autre creyssensa.
E s'oms es lo mon seguens
vir se on mais l'agensa,
qu'ayselh sos faitz es grazens
qu'es ses repentensa;
qu'aital es de gaug ufanier
— qui·lh sec e defug l'autr'entier –,
cum del can cuy cazec del cays
la carns, quan l'ombr'e l'aigua·l trays.

Perque qui del ioy munda
s'apropch'e s'aferma
si: 'era·l terras', non l'a,
que, quan creys mais, merma;
quar, s'amors fon bona ia,
qui no·m pliu ni·m ferma,
que no m'o menta dema,
don l'amars s'azerma
fors cum volva a descordier?
ieu no sai; *mas* e sent e quier
l'amor on non a ren biays,
on ma bon'esperansa·m pays.   (25–48)

But with these two joys there is need for intelligence and discernment;
the one is degradation and the other is increase. And if a man is a follower
of the ways of the world, let him turn his attention to that joy which
brings him most happiness,[12] for his deed is pleasing if it is done without
need for repentance; for that man makes a show of his enjoyment when
he pursues it and flees the other perfect joy, like the dog whose meat fell
from its mouth when the shadow in the water betrayed him.

Therefore if a man approaches worldly joy and reassures himself with
the words: 'Now you shall possess it', he has it not, for when it increases
most, it decreases. For, if love was once kind, if no one can pledge me or

assure me that it will not lie in what it says to me tomorrow, then to what end does loving lead except to change into discord? I do not know, but I feel and seek that love in which there is nothing awry, a love in which my fair hopes may nourish me.

What is the joy that is degradation, is ephemeral and decreases when it grows, and proceeds from a love that is lying, inconstant and disturbing? And what is the perfect joy which comes from the love in which nothing is amiss and which Peire apprehends and seeks but does not know? An obvious answer is that one joy belongs to this world and the other to the next. But although Peire may be hinting at the Augustinian division of love into *amor mundi* and *amor dei*, he explicitly states that his song is *non-clus* and therefore not concerned with hidden levels of spiritual meaning. This is a worldly song, in clear language, such as knights sing (8–12), and the two joys of which Peire speaks are almost certainly worldly: the transitory happiness of sensual *Amors* and the perfect, secure happiness that comes from *Fin'Amors*, a happiness which brings joy to the man who gives himself to it without pretence, harsh countenance or fickle desire (49–52), and which has such worth that all fine reputation does homage to it. The symbol of this supreme happiness is the rose:

> que, cum resplan roz'en rozier
> gensetz d'autra flor de vergier,
> sobra sobre totz ioys sos iays
> del maior gaug qu'anc nasc ni nays.　　　(57–60)

for, as the rose on the rose tree shines forth more graciously than any other flower in the orchard, so does the joy from this greatest delight that ever existed or exists, excel all other joys.

Peire's poem *L'airs clars* is part of the continuing conflict between *Amors* and *Fin'Amors* which was postulated by Marcabru and developed in a personal, lyrical way by Jaufre Rudel. Peire judges logically: the well-being of society depends on good and excellent deeds which are inspired by *Jois*; if a man is to engage in the affairs of the world he must seek the greatest *Jois*, which rewards the sincerity and constancy that it demands. Peire, like Guilhem de Montanhagol in the next century, is pleading rationally for the courtly discipline of *cortesia* against undisciplined and illusory pleasure. *Jois* for Bernart de Ventadorn means the happiness which brings self-forgetfulness and attendant sorrow, but for Peire it has become the secure contentedness of the individual within himself and within society.

Peire accepts the rules and limitations of courtly values in order to achieve a serene mind that is free from the turmoil of *Amors*, and in *Be m'es plazen* he develops this courtly quietist theme:

> ab motz alqus
> serratz e clus .... (VIII, 4–5)

with words that are locked and shut.

We know from Guiraut de Bornelh and Raimbaut d'Aurenga, who were Peire's contemporaries, thât the *trobar clus* was under attack in their day. The *clus* style was essentially concerned with hinting at the extra meanings suggested by 'coloured' words and the gradual unfolding of levels of meaning which were usually associated with moral problems and especially the conflict between the flesh and the spirit and illusion and reality. It is probable that the courtly and 'this-worldly' direction which was given to troubadour poetry by Eleanor of Aquitaine and was exemplified in the songs of Bernart de Ventadorn, led to a revulsion from the allusive and often moralising poetry of the *clus* style. A courtly audience, as we see from Guiraut de Bornelh and Raimbaut d'Aurenga, would appreciate more readily a song composed in the clear or *leu* style, and this development in courtly taste may have been strengthened by the emergence of a false *clus* style, such as we can detect in Bernart Marti, which was concerned with intentionally obscure virtuosity with words rather than the gradual revealing of a higher moral meaning. Courtly taste increasingly demands the *canso* which is composed on the one level of love for the *domna* and rejects the *vers clus* with its several planes of meaning. From about 1170 the *clus* style begins to go out of fashion. A newer generation of more conventionally courtly troubadours is less preoccupied with their individual search for happiness; moral doubts about sensual love are stilled by submission to the rules of *Amors* such as they are prescribed by Andreas Capellanus, and poetic composition becomes the plain task of singing orthodox courtly songs for an earth-bound audience. Such is the art of the great courtly troubadours like Gaucelm Faidit, Raimon de Miraval and Peire Vidal, and of scores of lesser courtly poets who write in the decades remaining before the onset of the Albigensian Crusade. Peire d'Alvernhe is most decidedly not of their number, and this is why he uses without shame words that are *serratz e clus* in a poem *Be m'es plazen* (VIII) which is directly in the tradition of Marcabru, Jaufre Rudel, and even of Guilhem IX.

I   Be m'es plazen
     e cossezen
    que om s'ayzina de chantar   3
     ab motz alqus
     serratz e clus
    qu'om no·ls tem ja de vergonhar.   6

II   D'aut chai em bas
     qui per compas[13]
    no sap lo segle demenar;   9
     e ben hi falh
     qui tan trassalh
    que non hi puesc'a temps tornar.   12

III   Ben es auras
     totz crestias
    que ia nems si vol encombrar,   15
     ni sobre·l cays
     leva tal fays
    que corren no·l puesca portar.   18

IV   Qu'ieu sai e sen
     mon escien,
    e vuelh vos en tot castiar,   21
     per trop captens
     val hom mot mens
    e ten hom plus vil son afar.   24

V   Mais am un ort
     serrat e fort
    qu'hom ren no m'en puesca emblar   27
     que cent parras
     sus en puegz plas:
    qu'autre las tenh'ez ieu las guar.   30

VI   Que·l reprochiers
     es vertadiers
    que dels antics auzi comtar: 33
     lo ric al ric,
     e l'om mendic. . . :
    quecx d'eis semblan troba son par.   36

VII   De tot can suelh
     amar, me tuelh
    e so qu'ei amat desampar,   39
     qu'ieu non am re
     ni autre me
    e cug me totz d'amor lonhar.   42

VIII   Qu'arreire temps
        ai amat nemps
        e vuelh m'en atrazach layssar;   45
        non aura grat
        qui m'a amat
        ni en cor m'avia d'amar.   48

IX   Qu'ieu ai un cor
        et un demor
        et un talan et un pessar   51
        et un amic
        vas cui m'abric
        et a cuy me vuelh autreyar.   54

X   Si mal m'en pren
        per eys mon sen,
        cug a ma vida follejar;   57
        apres ma mort
        no·m fass'om tort
        d'aquo qu'ieu ai ad oblidar.   60

XI   Daus manhtas pars
        me for'afars
        en prendre o en gazanhar;   63
        fers e parvenz
        es mos talenz
        vas m'amiga qu'eu tenc plus car.   66

XII   . . .
        amors de lonh,   70
        tan gran besonh
        qu'ai de tener e de balhar.

I find it pleasing and fitting that a man should try to sing with words that are locked and shut, and not fear to use them out of a sense of shame.

That man falls from high to low estate who with a pair of compasses cannot deal with life in this world; and he is greatly mistaken if he leaps forward so far that he cannot get back in good time.

Any Christian man is a fool who wishes at any time to burden himself too greatly, and to raise higher than the level of his mouth a load so heavy that he cannot carry it at a run.

For I know and feel, for sure, and wish to correct you absolutely about this, that by undertaking too much a man is worth much less, and his way of life is held more cheaply by others.

I prefer a garden, strong and closed in so that nothing can be stolen from me, to a hundred open gardens, high on smooth hill tops, which someone else may own and I look at.

For the proverb is true that I have heard related from the Ancients: the rich with the rich and the mendicant man. . . . : each one finds a partner in his own likeness.

I am taking myself away from all that I was wont to love and I abandon all that I have loved, for I do not love anyone and no person loves me, and I am minded to remove myself entirely from love.

For in the time that is past I have loved too much and I wish to cease from this forthwith; whoever has loved me or whoever desired to love me will receive no thanks.

For I have one heart and one dwelling and one desire and one belief and one friend towards whom I go for shelter and to whom I wish to grant myself.

If ill befalls me through this intention of mine, I think I shall be acting like a fool during my life; after my death let no man blame me for that which I have to forget.

On all sides my life would be taking and gaining; fierce and visible is my desire for my beloved whom I hold most dear.

. . . love from afar, so great a need do I have to possess and to give.

This poem has been interpreted as a *congé* before departure to the monastic life, as a *de contemptu mundi*, and as a poem in which Peire seeks spiritual peace within the courtly ethic without any sure feeling that this ethic is the right one. A. del Monte[14] sees its theme, in the context of Peire's other works, as the abandonment of empirical loves and as dedication to solitude of the spirit and to love for the sake of love, as pure nostalgia, and the cult of the interior being as a norm of life. But in the wider context of earlier troubadour poetry we can see that this poem is an amalgam of expressions from Marcabru, Guilhem IX and Jaufre Rudel.[15]

Behind Peire's use of 'coloured' words and *clus* style the central theme of *Be m'es plazen* is revealed as Marcabru's ideal of *mesura*, the rational ordering of one's personal life and the avoidance of the immoderate impulse, the task that is too demanding and the burden that is too heavy to carry with ease. As Jaufre in *Belhs m'es l'estius* rejoiced at being *descargatz de fol fais*, so Peire desires to avoid the foolish burden of the many loves inspired by *Amors*. The *ort serrat e fort* which he prefers to the hundred open gardens in the possession of other men, hints at love for the Virgin Mary, but is intended to be the single love, the *amigua* to whom he will now give and devote himself. As Jaufre, in order to return to a sense of his own *valor*, said:

> E non iray jamai alhor
> Ni non querrai autrui conquistz,   (IV, 10–11)

so Peire decides to remove himself from *Amors* (42) and from the taking and gaining that is part of the worldly burden and of *Amors*. He turns away from his earlier loves to the one friend in whom is all his belief and desire (49–54). He equates his fierce longing to abandon the taking and gaining involved in the 'many directions of love' (*manhtas pars*) with his desire to 'own and to give' (71–2) which can be realised in 'distant' love for the *amigua* whom he holds most dear. We cannot tell whether this *amigua* (66) or the *amic vas cui m'abric* (52–3) or the *ort serrat e fort* (25–6) is a real love or a creation of his imagination or the Virgin Mary. And this difficulty in finding a clearcut interpretation is not surprising since Peire has constructed this poem on the three planes of love, physical, imaginary and spiritual, which can be discerned in the songs of the early troubadours. He rejects ephemeral casual loves in return for solace of the heart and mind that comes from yielding himself so completely to a single love that he may find forgetfulness of the tribulations of everyday life. Behind this single undiversified love which is Fin'*Amors* there are overtones of Christian love of God and of the Virgin Mary which are conveyed, as in Jaufre Rudel, by coloured words such as *crestias*, *ort serrat* and *abric*. Behind Peire's joy in his distant, detached love there hovers the hope of Christian happiness. Peire thinks more widely than Jaufre. Peire justifies his rejection of a world that is too demanding, and his longing for security of mind and spirit, within the general human need to encompass and see this earthly life in the round and so avoid the interminable getting and spending of men who are too busied with the things of this life to think about its meaning. Peire takes his concept of distant love from Jaufre Rudel but his urge to give moral warning, to *castiar*, comes from Marcabru, and he acknowledges this indebtedness in his early poem *Bel m'es quan la roza floris* (XIII), which was composed between 1157 and 1158:[16]

> Sel que·l ioi del setgle delis
> vei que son pretz dezenansa;
> fils es d'avol criatura,
> que fai avol demonstransa:
> e per tan non baisa·l col!
> Quar gitatz es a noncura,
> estai mais entre·ls savais.
>
> Per mi non dic, tan m'abelis,
> quan vei molt gran alegransa.
> Amors vol c'a longias dura,
> e non pot aver fizansa,[17]
> si·l carnal amar non vol;

quar vei que cors non a cura
mas de senhor que engrais.

Chantador, lo vers vos fenis:
aprendetz la comensansa.
Marcabrus per gran dreitura
trobet d'altretal semblansa,
e tengon lo tug per fol,
qui no conois sa natura[18]
e no·ill membre per que·s nais. (22–42)

I see that the man who destroys the joy of the world is impeding his own reputation; he is the son of a churlish creature and gives churlish proof of this: and yet he does not lower his neck! Because he is given over to indifference he remains for ever among the despicable.

I do not say this about myself, so much pleasure do I find in seeing great delight. That man desires love that lasts a long time, and yet he can have no confidence unless he desires carnal loving, for I see that the body cares only for the lord who grows fat.

Singers, I finish this song for you; learn the beginning [of all this]. Marcabru through his great sense of what was right composed in this very fashion, and they all think of him as a fool who does not understand his own nature or realise why he is born.

These lines, as has been suggested above (p. 120), may be seen as the riposte to an attack on Marcabru by Bernart de Ventadorn in his *Chantars no pot gaire valer* (xv, 29–35). Bernart called that man a *fols naturaus*, 'a fool by his very nature', who blames Love for its sensual desire and turns desire in a direction which is displeasing to Love.

As Marcabru had distinguished between different types of love according to the different ways of thinking which they inspired, Peire judges them according to the happiness they produce. The *ioi del setgle* (22) is the joy which in *Be m'es plazen* is to be found if one removes oneself from sensual love (viii, 42) and too great a preoccupation with worldly striving (viii, 22–4). The man who, in *Bel m'es quan la roza*, destroys this happiness of the mind which rejoices in the world, demonstrates unashamedly his base extraction – and this may be a personal gibe against Bernart – and his lack of interest in a higher happiness of the mind (22–8). Peire is implicitly accusing such a man of what Marcabru called *frait cuidar* 'fragmented thinking'.

In the context of this argument the line: *amors vol c'a longia dura* (31) takes on its proper meaning as the direct riposte to Bernart's declaration (xv, 29–35) that the essence of love lies in giving pleasure and in sensual desire and that anyone who blames it for this is a born fool. Once more the controversy between *Amors* 'sensual, close and transitory love' and *Fin'Amors* 'disciplined, distant and lasting love' is apparent. Peire, who, as we have seen, is intent on finding great and lasting happiness, advocates a love that is *Fin'Amors* and he rejoices when he sees great happiness and delight (29–30). But this happiness, which belongs to the mind, is destroyed by the man who has no sense of reassurance unless he loves carnally. Such a man, Peire adds ironically, is attempting an impossible compromise when he desires that sensual love shall be long lasting. Peire's bitter intention is apparent in his use of the word *amar* which for Marcabru was synonymous with lowly and even venal love. 'Carnal love' (33) here is not St Bernard's idea of the proper love of the physical self that is demanded by *necessitas*, but the love of the carnal senses which, according to William of St Thierry, must be controlled by reason in order that sense, mind and spirit may love in an integrated way. This is what Marcabru meant by *entiers cuidars* or integrated thinking, and this is the way in which Peire d'Alvernhe is composing, as he imitates Marcabru and praises him for his *rectitudo* (*per gran dreitura*) and the awareness of what Gerard Manley Hopkins would call his 'selfhood', and the reason for his having been born. Peire's high ideal of the 'joy of this world' depends on this approach to life and love which is a complete synthesis of the sensual, the mental and the spiritual. In extreme form, this is also the joy which St Francis of Assisi, an admirer of troubadour poetry, felt for the world as created by God. This is what Peire, like Marcabru, understands by *natura*, and in this he is directly opposed to Bernart's idea of *natura* as natural desire on the single plane of the senses.[19]

In the important song *Gent es* (x) Peire praises the wisdom, intelligence and self-knowledge which are the only guides to happiness:

> Gent es, mentr'om n'a lezer,
> s'enans de son mielhs a faire,
> que, quan s'aizina·l cuidaire,
> tal hor'es larcs de voler,
> e qui enans es avertitz
> que l'aguaitz li sia yssitz,
> non es ges del tot muzaire.

Contr'aso deu aparer
en cuy sens es alberguaire,
que sciensa no pretz guaire
s'als ops non la vey valer;
doncs ar er de mi sentitz
lo sabers don suy tequitz,
s'er fis o mesclatz de vaire.

Qu'el segl'ai fag mon plazer
tan qu'en suy de trop peccaire,
et ar agrada·m n'estraire,
pus Dieus pro·m n'a dat lezer;
qu'esser pot hom descauzitz
e non es ops n'an delitz
per oltracujat vejaire;

Pueys Dieus so·m laissa vezer
en que puesc esser miraire
de mo mielhs e·l sordeis raire.
Hon om plus a de saber,
hon maier sens l'es quesitz,
et aquelh par plus falhitz
qu'a sos ops n'es enguanaire.

Mas s'ieu en saubes lo ver
be sai, for'ancar compaire
de ioven et enquistaire.
Sil ric, cuy degra chazer
en grat, fan vis esbauditz,
mas si·l fals segl'es mestitz
que·il fait son pauc contra·l braire.

E mentr'usquecs pot querer
luy qu'es vers Dieus e salvaire
mout es endreg si bauzaire,
pus o met en nonchaler;
que mager gratz n'es cobitz
qui fer s'escolp que feritz,
d'aitan suy ben esperaire.

So fera plus a temer,
per que suy meravilhaire
qu'hom non es Dieu reguardaire,
tro qu'es tan prosmatz al ser
que·l iornals l'es escurzitz;
e s'adoncx no·l ven complitz
non cug que pueys se n'esclaire.

Amors, be·m degra doler,
si negus autr'enginhaire
mas lo dreituriers iutiaire
de vos me pogues mover;

que per vos er'enriquitz,
essaussatz et enantitz
e pel senhor de Belcaire.

Mas so non pot remaner,
cortez'amors de bon aire,
don mi lais esser amaire,
tan m'agrada a tener
lai on vol sanhs esperitz;
e pueys el mezeys m'es guitz,
no·us pes s'ab vos non repaire.

Qu'ieu sai, tan rics governaire
no·m denhes en guit aver
— Peire d'Alvernhe so ditz —
no de·us for'enquer partitz
ni per autr'amor camiaire.

While a man has the opportunity, it is good that he should strive to achieve his greatest happiness, for when the man who is given to illusory thoughts takes his ease, he is, at that moment, generous with sensual desire; and the man who is aware that the ambush is coming towards him, is not at all an idle gawper.

In this situation, it must become apparent in whom wisdom dwells, for I do not esteem knowledge if I do not see it proving its worth when it is needed; so that I shall now realise whether the reasoning power by which I am impelled, is pure or adulterated.

For in this world, I have had so much pleasure for myself that I am a great sinner, and now I am pleased to withdraw from it, since God has given me the opportunity to do so; for a man can be base and need not be destroyed because of his unreasoned opinions,

since God allows me to see where I can behold my utmost happiness and shear away the worst. The more knowledge a man has, the more is intelligence demanded of him, and that man appears to have failed and sinned the most who deceives himself about his own needs.

But if I could know true happiness here in this world, I would continue to be the consort and wooer of Youth. These noblemen, to whom I ought to be pleasing, have joyful faces, but this false world is so wicked that deeds count for little against the braying.

And every man who is still able to seek Him who is true God and saviour, is a great deceiver towards himself, if he is unmindful of this; for great appreciation rather than injury is granted to the man who accuses himself harshly, and from this I have great hopes.

What is most to be feared, and for this reason I am filled with wonder, is that a man pays no heed to God until he has come so close to the evening that the daylight has grown dark for him; and if the daylight does not then come to him in its completeness, I do not believe that he will find enlightenment afterwards.

Love, I ought indeed to grieve, if, apart from the just Judge, any intriguer could separate me from you; for by you I was enriched, exalted and advanced, and by the lord of Beaucaire.

But this cannot last, courteous and gentle love, with whom I cease to be a lover, so much does it please me to aspire there where the Holy Spirit wishes; and since it is my personal guide, may you not be grieved if I do not dwell with you.

For I know that if such a powerful leader had not deigned to act as my guide – Peire d'Alvernhe is saying this – I would not yet have been separated from you, nor would I have been fickle because of any other love.

Peire resolves in courtly song the conflict between profane and divine love, their attendant ways of life and the happiness they provide. Marcabru has compromised over this question with his idealised vision of a *Fin'Amors* which co-exists on a separate plane of the mind and spirit with the Christian love of God which it resembles in its virtues, restraints and promise of personal improvement and happiness. Jaufre Rudel in *Quan lo rossinhols* (1) turned his back on the delights of *Amors* to seek his greater happiness by following God to Bethlehem. For Peire *Amors* is joy, delight and courtesy, but, like the later poet of *Flamenca*,[20] he sees its limitations and the need for *saber* and *sen* which can warn a man of the approaching evening and lead him to the hope of salvation. Every man has the personal duty not to drift like the *cuidaire* and *muzaire*, but to use rational judgment to choose lasting happiness, to obey the guidance of the Holy Spirit and escape the darkness and fear of damnation.

Peire's rational approach to his problems and doubts makes him the most outspoken of those troubadours, like Jaufre Rudel, Marcabru and Arnaut Daniel, who may be called metaphysical and whose aspiration to a higher level of joy than that of love of the courtly *domna* is conveyed almost invariably in an allusive, *clus* style of poetry. This genuine 'dark' style was also intended to bring out meanings which give a rounded and whole view of earthly joy and eternal joy.

In *Sobre·l vieill trobar* Peire uses this style in place of the clear, expository style of *Gent es* and again treats the theme of the two joys:

> Sobre·l vieill trobar e·l novel
> vueill mostrar mon sen als sabens,
> qu'entendon be aquels c'a venir so
> c'anc tro per me no fo faitz vers entiers;
> e qui non cre qu'ieu sia verdadiers
> auja dese con estau a razo.   (XI, 1–6)

On the subject of the old and new styles of composing I wish to demonstrate my view to people who are wise and rational, so that those who are to come may understand well that integrated poetry was not composed before me, and if anyone does not believe that I am telling the truth, let him hear forthwith how this can be justified by reason.

Peire's claim *anc tro per me no fo faitz vers entiers* was taken up by the author of his *vida* who calls him *lo meillor trobador del mon, tro que venc Guirautz de Borneill*[21] and, perhaps by way of the *vida*, by Dante for whom he was one of the *antiquiores doctores* (*De Vulgari Eloquentia*, I, X, 3). *Vers entiers* is poetry which is perfect and integrated in theme as well as technique. For Rabanus Maurus (*De clericorum institutione*, PL, cvii, col. 385) *integritas lectionis* meant the ability to understand all the meanings of figurative speech, and for Peire d'Alvernhe allusive and apparently obscure and dark poetry must be composed in such a way that it leads to an awareness of truth. For Peire this truth is wider than the knightly morality or the spiritual integrity of the individual; it is the realisation which comes to those who are mentally alive (*saben*) about the ephemeral and the eternal in matters of love and happiness.

This is what Peire means when he twists the phrase 'the bread and the knife' which Guilhem IX had applied to sensual love:

> Qu'ieu tenh l'us e·l pan e·l coutel
> de que·m platz apanar las gens;
> que d'est mestier an levat en pairo,
> ses acordier que no·s rompa·l semdiers,
> qu'ieu dic que nier si mostr'[22] els faitz non niers,
> qu'a fol parlier ten hom lui e·l sermo. (7–12)

For I possess the experience and the bread and the knife with which I am pleased to nourish people; for in this profession they have raised up as a model, without agreeing that the path he treads may not be a broken one, a man of whom I say that he shows himself dark in actions which are not dark and who is held to be a foolish prattler of foolish words.

Peire is contrasting the reality (*e·l pan e·l coutel*) of his own experience which also brings nourishment to others, with the pretence to deep experience of the poet whose words are belied by what he does, and who, a mere foolish prattler, has been raised up in reputation despite his lack of moral and spiritual rectitude and poetic inspiration.

The duty of the poet is to please consistently and to avoid contorted sounds and phrases which muddle (13–18). His

own poetic excellence proceeds from the *complitz* quality of
what he says:

> pos qu'es mos trobars tan valens
> . . .
> q'ieu soi raitz e dic qu'ieu soi premiers
> de digz complitz. . .   (20–3)

since my composing has such worth that I am the root source, and I say
that I am the first to use complete expressions. . .

What does Peire mean by *complitz*? He uses the word on two
other occasions:

> Lauzatz si'Emanuel,
> lo reys de terr'e de cel,
> qu'es trinus et unitatz,
> e filhs e sanctz esperitz
> e quasqus payre complitz,
> si q'us noms es et us guitz
> et dieus et homs apellatz.   (XIX, 1–7)

Praised be Emmanuel, the king of earth and heaven, who is the trinity
and the unity, and son and Holy Spirit, and each one a complete father,
so that he is one name and one guide called both God and man.

Complitz also occurs in *Gent es* when Peire speaks with wonder
of the man who ignores God until he has come so close to the
evening that the daylight has grown dark for him:

> e s'adoncx no·l ven complitz
> non cug que pueys se n'esclaire.   (x, 48–9)

and if [the daylight] does not then come to him in its completeness, I do
not believe that he will find enlightenment afterwards.

In both these cases *complitz* refers to a completeness which embraces the earthly and the divine. If we return to *Sobre·l vieill
trobar e·l novel* (XI), we can see that Peire may have such a meaning in mind when he says that he is the root, and the first poet
to speak with 'complete' words. This 'completeness', which
includes the levels of earthly and divine meaning, would be
the mark of the troubadour who, as he says, first composed
integrated poetry (*vers entiers*), and it may help us to understand the meaning of *novel trobar* and *vieill trobar*. Peire is the
prophet of *novel trobar*, and *novel* is a coloured word which can
refer to the New Testament and its teachings. Peire's opponents, who compose in the 'old' style, toil away at dark and
allusive words, but are a flock of sheep (25) because they are
held by the conventional earthly planes of thought, aspiration

and happiness. Peire's art of composing is 'new', his poetry is 'integrated' and his words are 'complete' because his present earthly joy and courtly virtue become part of his hope in a higher ultimate happiness in God (*del mieils qu'es e que fo*, 27). In this idea of exalted courtly joy and virtue as co-existent with and a part of love of God, Peire is the disciple of Marcabru and the obvious precursor of both Arnaut Daniel and especially Guilhem de Montanhagol. The man who meditates joyfully and aspires to a joy that is greater than earthly or courtly happiness will gather his spiritual harvest when the time is ripe (29–30). Once Peire is sure of this ultimate happiness, he encourages and furthers the supreme courtly virtue of generosity of spirit (*Jovens*) and shows Christian generosity by giving his friendship to evil men as well as the good. He speaks of lesser poets:

> Donx com qu'ill sion d'un tropel
> menton tot gent er per las dens,
> qu'ie·m sen sertas del mieils qu'es e que fo,
> enseguras de mon chant e sobriers
> ves los bauzas, e sai que dic, qu'estiers
> no vengra·l gras don a trop en sazo.
>
> Quar er m'abelis e m'es bel
> qu'el mieu ioi s'enant la Iovens;
> e s'ieu ren aic que lur an enviro,[23]
> aisi me·n gic, c'uns gaugz mi creis dobliers
> d'un dous espic qu'es ioios consiriers,
> don m'an amic hueimais li mal e·ill bo.   (25–36)

Therefore however much they may herd together, they are now quite simply lying in their teeth, for I have within myself a sense of reassurance about the greatest happiness that is and that was, I feel sure about my song and superior to the deceivers, and I know what I am saying, for in no other way will the harvest of corn come, of which there is an abundance at the right season.

For now I am delighted and pleased that Youth [generosity of spirit] should find advancement there, in my joy, and if I accepted anything which may be current among them [the herd of lesser poets], so do I renounce this, for a joyfulness increases doubly for me from a sweet ear of corn which is joyous meditation, and because of this, evil and good men now have me as their friend.

Peire sums up in the *tornada*:

> D'aisi·m sent ric per bona sospeiso
> qu'en ioi m'afic e m'estau volentiers,
> et ab ioi pic e gaug mos deziriers
> et ab ioi pic e gaug vueill: Dieus lo·m do.   (37–40)

I feel so rich on account of my good hope that I willingly attach myself to joy and remain in it, and with joy I chisel and gauge my desires and with joy I wish hurt and enjoyment: may God grant this to me.

The enigmatic last line can also mean: 'and with joy I wish for chisel and gauge: may God grant this to me'. In his state of assured Jois, Peire will control and shape his desires, and will welcome physical hurt and spiritual enjoyment as the gifts of God.

We have four religious songs by Peire d'Alvernhe. Two of them, Dieus, vera vida (XVIII) and Lauzatz si' Emanuel (XIX), are hymns of praise to God for his miracles and mercy. In the other two, Cui bon vers (XVI) and De Dieu non puesc (XVII), Peire is haunted by the fear of death and damnation, and hopes and prays for the salvation of his soul. But these two religious songs cannot be considered in a genre separate from his courtly poetry, for in them Peire again faces the problem of the choice between different ways of living and different kinds of love.

Cui bon vers (XVI) is an exercise on the theme of Memento mori: the joys of this world are ephemeral pretence and illusion, and the flesh perishes vilely. Let no man have arrogant, stupid thoughts about the happiness we should enjoy here on earth:

> qu'en pauc d'ora es hom conquis;
> e can ven als deriers sanglotz,
> no li val honcles ni cozis,
> ni metges ab son issarop. (32–5)

for in a short while a man is conquered: and when he comes to the last sobs, no uncle or cousin helps him, or doctor with his syrup.

He uses Marcabru's theme of the cleansing place: 'no count, king, duke or marquess can escape Death, and if they do not first cleanse themselves, before Death closes their face, they will, if they so wish it, delay too long' (46–9)...'I could preach [legir] to you for the whole day, but let us pray to Him who is the beginning and the end that He may keep us from the abyss of Hell and place us there in His Paradise where He set Isaac and Jacob' (50–4).

Peire's claim to be a preacher or instructor may explain why he is called maistres de totz in Cantarai d'aquestz trobadors (see p. 159). He assumes this note explicitly in De Dieu non puesc (XVII): to praise God would be unseemly,

mas pus ylh m'abriv'en valor
ab belh sen si cum *a* parier
ben tanh dir a dreg per s'amor
so qu'al sieu poble a mestier.   (5–8)

but since He impels me forward to increase my worth, with fair wisdom
as He would an equal companion, it is good, right and fitting to say for
love of Him those things which are needed by His people.

'Wherefore I say that a man must consider what he is [*quals es*]
and what he must become, and if a man were to begin to
reflect on this, he would not esteem himself at all' (9–12):

mas l'uelh belh tenon tenebror
e l'esguart gloton desirier,
e·l cors cossenten la folhor
guida l'arm'a mal destorbier.   (13–16)

but darknesses take hold of a beautiful eye and vile desires take hold of a
look, and the body, condoning folly, guides the soul to evil confusion.

And thou must die:

De que·m puesc pro meravillar
cum per se non pren hom albir;
que, quan qu'el tric,[24] l'er a murir
e pel pas ansessor passar;
et en tan estranha flairor
revertis qui·s pus bobansier
qu'als auzens hi a gran feror,
mas huey oblidon aquo d'ier.   (17–24)

I wonder greatly that a man can take no thought for himself, for however
much he delays, he will have to die and pass along the path of his ances-
tors; and the man who lives most splendidly turns back into a smell so
strange that those who are in its presence feel great fear, but they forget
what happened yesterday.

If a man does not cover himself against the Archer, he will
feel the force of the blow (30–1), but it is hard to correct a
man who loves to choose his own hurt (33–4). The man who
wishes to aspire to good as much as to work against evil will
never lose the higher kingdom for the sake of the joy of this
lying world:

quan la carn caitiv'a sabor
l'esperitz pren gran encombrier.   (39–40)

when the wretched flesh is pleasing, the spirit suffers great distress.

The man who shines with wordly wealth and cannot be reconciled with God, is in yet worse plight (41–4); our wisdom, intelligence and senses are God given and their fruits are His (49–56). In resonant tones Peire foresees the Last Judgment:

> Per qu'er escur so qu'ar es clar
> lay on Dieus mostrara·l martir
> qu'elh sostenc per nos a guarir;
> on nos sera totz a tremblar
> lo iorn del iutjamen maior,
> on non aura ren d'ufanier;
> qu'ab gran ioi et ab non pauc plor
> eissens desebran duy semdier. (57–64)

For that will be dark which is now clear when God shows us the martyrdom he suffered for our salvation, when we all have to tremble on the day of the greater judgment when there will be no ostentation or deceit; for with great joy and not a little weeping two paths will diverge for those who are leaving.

Let none be misled by the joy of this world:

> A! co·s pot pauc quascus fiar
> en quan say laissa al transir,
> si·lh eys no so sap devezir
> tan gen que·s puesca profichar;
> e tan breu vid'an li pluzor,
> vilan e clerc e cavalier,
> e tan tost torn'en amargor
> lo ioys d'aquest segle leugier. (81–8)

Ah! how can any man put trust in what he leaves behind in this world when he cannot explain so graciously what profit he may find in it; and most men, churls and clerics and knights, have so short a life and so soon does the joy of this frivolous world turn to bitterness.

In this brilliant and eloquent song, composed at least a generation before Hélinand's *Vers de la Mort*, Peire resolves the conflict between the two joys. Fin'Amors in the qualities of spirit and mind that it demands (*jovens* and *sabers*) may not be incompatible with love of God and may prepare a man's mind for the hope of absolute happiness, but Fin'Amors belongs to this world, and at the Day of Judgment all the joys of this world count for nothing. The man who has lived on co-existent planes of profane and religious love must come to his senses. In the *danse macabre* of a world in which the smell of death itself is transient, he must learn to choose before reaching the moment of darkness.

In his *De Vulgari Eloquentia* (I, X, 3) Dante speaks of the superiority of the Provençal language as the 'more finished and sweeter' medium of vernacular poetry, and names Peire d'Alvernhe and other early learned poets: 'Pro se vero argumentatur alia [lingua], scilicet oc, quod vulgares eloquentes in ea primitus poetati sunt, tamquam in perfectiori dulciorique loquela, ut puta Petrus de Alvernia et alii antiquiores doctores.' Peire is a master of the art of *eloquentia*, as Dante says, but his poetry is also remarkable for the rational force which states explicitly what earlier poets, such as Marcabru and Jaufre Rudel, had implied. Marcabru defined the contrast between carnal love and Fin'Amors but left unclear the dividing line between his ideal of profane Fin'Amors and Christian love of God. He allowed for the easy transference of imagination and poetic feeling from the profane to the religious plane and the attendant use of Christian imagery for exalted profane love that is one of the most appealing qualities of the allusive poetry of the early troubadours. Peire d'Alvernhe marks a further stage in the development of ideas on love in troubadour poetry, when he places sensual love (*Amors*) and Fin'Amors and love of God in perspective, and values them according to the joy that they provide. He assures the victory of Fin'Amors, which is love controlled by the mind and spirit, over the sensual love that seeks self-gratification, but when he comes finally to distinguish between Fin'Amors and Christian love, he builds a wall of *saber* and *sen* between the supreme love of God and all other earthly loves. Fin'Amors for Peire may be compatible with or even assimilated into love of God, and it can evoke exalted feelings and display virtues which are comparable to those of Christian love. But the ultimate happiness of eternal salvation outshines all other joys that are granted by profane love. Peire's rational ordering and redefinition of Marcabru's ideas probably accorded well with the developing taste of the more philosophically minded poets of his day, who, like Chrétien de Troyes in the North of France, were becoming increasingly aware of the spiritual limitations of the courtly code. Peire d'Alvernhe points ahead to the lucidity and supreme eloquence of Arnaut Daniel, whom he influenced greatly, and beyond Arnaut he shows the way to the post-Albigensian troubadours Guilhem de Montanhagol and Guiraut Riquier. Peire's rational thinking marks the close of the early troubadour poetry which sought an elusive, personal and profane ideal of happiness on the planes of the senses, the imagination and the spirit. Jaufre Rudel's moral battle is won and forgotten; the conflict between sensual *Amors* and disciplined *Fin'Amors* is concluded; promiscuous desire (*volers*) is rejected and controlled by reason (*sabers*), and *desirs* is expressed in love for one individual lady who provides *Jois* not as in Jaufre Rudel as a beautiful, illuminating memory, but as a tower and castle built upon a rock, a source of peace and shelter from the vexations of the world. Peire d'Alvernhe is a sign of the way in which *Fin'Amors*, deprived of the courtly society which had nurtured it, will finally be rejected in the late thirteenth century in favour of love of God and the Virgin Mary.

The Generation of 1200

7

Arnaut Daniel

ARNAUT DANIEL was a nobleman of the castle of Riberac in Perigord. Destined by his family to be a *clericus*, he turned poet and became a minstrel,[1] and Raimon de Durfort jests at his lack of clothes and money:

> Pus etz malastrucx sobriers
> non es Arnautz l'escoliers,
> cui coffondon dat e tauliers
> e vay coma penedensiers
> paupres de draps e de deniers.[2]

You are a more unfortunate wretch than Arnaut the scholar who is ruined by dice and the backgammon board, and goes about like a penitent, poor in clothes and *deniers*.

Arnaut may have suffered neglect from the courtly society of his day which preferred the plainer style of the *trobar leu*. The ebullient Monk of Montaudon in his *Pos Peire*, about 1195, covertly derides the audiences who fail to understand Arnaut's 'few foolish words':

> Ab Arnaut Daniel son set
> Q'a sa vida be no chantet,
> Mas us fols motz c'om non enten:
> Pois la lebre ab lo bou chasset
> E contra suberna nadet,
> No val sos chans un aguillen.   (ed. Klein, I, 43–8)

With Arnaut Daniel there are seven, and he never sang well in his whole life with the exception of a few foolish words which are not understood: since the hare hunted with the ox and he swam against the current, his song is not worth as much as a wild rose.

Benvenuto da Imola (1336–90)[3] says that Arnaut, old and poor, sent a fine song to the kings of France and England, and to other lords, and for this was richly rewarded, became a monk and led a blameless life.

Little is known about Arnaut's life. He may have been a friend of Bertran de Born (c. 1140–1202) and one of his poems, *Doutz brais*, has been dated between 1180 and 1187. He was in France in 1180 for the coronation of Philip Augustus and he attended the court of Richard of England,[4] probably at Poitiers between 1189 and 1191 or 1194 and 1199. Benvenuto da Imola says that he lived at the time of Raimon Berenger, count of Provence, who was probably one of the three sons of Raimon Berenger IV (1168–81), and he describes Arnaut as 'vir quidam curialis, prudens et sagax, qui invenit multa et pulcra dicta vulgaria'.[5] As Arnaut is mentioned by the Monk of Montaudon about 1195 but is not in Peire d'Alvernhe's review of the poets of 1170, he may have been born between 1150 and 1160.

Arnaut's fame among poets spread rapidly. Peire Raimon de Toloza (355, 4) and Guiraut de Calanson (243, 9, and 234, 13)[6] imitate him shortly after 1200. Later in the thirteenth century the poet of *Flamenca*, describing his archetypal courtly lover Guillem de Nevers, takes Arnaut as the exemplar of poetic quality:

> Neis Daniel que saup ganren
> No·s pogr'ab lui penre per ren.
> > (ed. Lavaud and Nelli, 1709–10)

Even Daniel who knew a great deal could not compare at all with him.

Arnaut's most famous admirer was Dante. In his *Purgatorio* (XXVI, 115–23) Dante meets Guido Guinicelli whom he calls 'my father and the father of others who are my betters who ever used sweet and elegant rhymes of love', but Guido points to another spirit, who he says was a better craftsman in the mother tongue (*miglior fabbro del parlar materno*). He continues:

> Versi d'amore e prose di romanzi[7]
> soperchiò tutti, e lascia dir gli stolti
> che quel di Lemosì credon ch'avanzi.
>
> A voce più ch'al ver drizzan li volti,
> e così ferman sua opinione
> prima ch'arte o ragion per lor s'ascolti.

In love songs and in romances in the form of proses he surpassed everyone; and let the fools talk who believe that he of Limousin excels.
They turn their faces to the public voice rather than to the truth, and thus they close up their mind, before art or reason can be heard by them.

Dante approaches Arnaut and makes him answer in Provençal:

> Tan m'abelis vostre cortes deman,
> qu'ieu no-m puesc, ni-m vueil a vos cobrire.
>
> Ieu sui Arnaut, que plor e vau cantan;
> consiros vei la passada folor,
> e vei jausen lo jorn, qu'esper, denan.
>
> Ara vos prec, per aquella valor
> que vos guida al som de l'escalina,
> sovegna vos a temps de ma dolor.   (XXVI, 140–7)

Your courteous request pleases me so much that I cannot and do not wish
to hide myself from you.

I am Arnaut who weep and keep singing. With sad reflections I see the
folly that is past and rejoicing I see before me the daylight that I hope
for.

Now I entreat you, by that virtue that guides you to the top of the
stairway, to be mindful in good time of my grief.

'The man of Limousin' whom Arnaut excels is probably
Guiraut de Bornelh whom his *vida* describes as 'meiller tro-
baire que negus d'aquels qu'eron estat denan ni foron apres
lui; per que fo apellatz maestre dels trobadors'.[8] Dante had
certainly praised Guiraut earlier (*DVE* II, 10, 2) as the model
poet of moral uprightness (*rectitudo*), but he chose Arnaut as
the exemplar of the poets who have sung of love. He also
praised Arnaut, with Guiraut de Bornelh and Folquet de
Marseille, as a master of *constructio suprema*, cited Arnaut's *Sols
sui* and admitted his debt to Arnaut for his own sestina *Al poco
giorno*.

In his *Trionfi* Petrarch, who has many lines that are close to
Arnaut's, sees a group of poets of strange appearance and
tongues:[9]

> fra tutti il primo Arnaldo Daniello,
> gran maestro d'Amor, ch'a la sua terra
> ancor fa onor col suo dir strano e bello...

Arnaut is the supreme poet of the *breu chansson de razon loigna*
(XVI, 4) 'the short song with a far theme', and Dante and
Petrarch admire him as their guide in the new art of composing in the vulgar tongue, the supreme craftsman who is
also an *auctor*. In brief words pared to the limit Arnaut reveals a
view of love which appears to be remarkably harmonious. He
is aware of the conflicts and griefs of earlier troubadours who

delighted in antithesis and contrast and who set *Amors*
(*Fals'Amors*) against *Fin'Amors*, *voler* against *desir*, *sen* against
foudatz, *Jois* against *mesura*, the happiness from profane love
against the joy hoped for from God, and the individual desire
to declare one's love against the social need to keep silent.
Arnaut boldly rejects these doubts in favour of absolute submission to *Amors* as the primary source of personal happiness
and poetic inspiration.

Love gives him his theme, as it assails him and puts the
words in harmony with the music (VIII, 9). It has graciously
taught him the arts of its school (XVI, 5). This submission of
himself and his poetry to love is more than a commonplace.
Arnaut accepts the rules of love and is humble before its wayward arrogance:

> Pel bruoill aug lo chan e·l refrim
> e per q'om no m'en fassa crim
>   obre e lim
>   motz de valor
>   ab art d'Amor
> don non ai cor qe·m tuoilla;
>   ans si be·m faill
>   la sec a traill
> on plus vas mi s'orguoilla. (II, 10–18)

Through the woods I hear the song and notes of the birds, and so that I
may not be reproached, I forge and file words of value with the art that is
given by Love from whom I have no wish to depart. On the contrary,
even when he fails me, I follow his trail, the more arrogant he grows
towards me.

He can compose *motz de valor* since Love inspires him with trust
in his own *valor*:

> qu' Amors mi cuebr'e·m cela
>   e·m fai tenir
> ma valor e·m capdela. (III, 14–16)

for Love covers and shelters me, makes me hold to my virtue and guides
me.

Valors here is the awareness of a personal moral integrity
which also has a sense of the need for stability in courtly
society; Jaufre Rudel in similar fashion had praised *Fin'Amors*
for restoring to him his moral sense of self-esteem (IV, 8–11).

But Arnaut sees *Amors* as a power of reassurance, a fortress
against the deceits of the world:

Ar sai ieu c'Amors m'a condug
el sieu plus seguran castel
don non dei renda ni trahug,
ans m'en ha fait don e capdel;
non ai poder ni cor que·m vir'aillors
qu'ensenhamens e fizeutatz plevida
jai per estar, c'a bon pretz s'i atorna.   (v, 8–14)

Now I know that Love has led me to its castle of greatest reassurance, for which I owe neither rent nor tribute; on the contrary it has granted it to me in gift and sovereignty. I have no power, nor any intention to turn away elsewhere, for courtly knowledge and pledged loyalty abide and stay here and turn into fine reputation.

Arnaut has made a true and loyal refuge of Love, from which he has never sought escape; he pleads with Love to spare him its bitter sorrows since he has chosen the best lady in the world and shuns the deceits that might threaten his allegorical castle of stability (15–22):

D'enguan mi tueill e d'enueg fug
per l'amor ab que m'atropel...   (v, 22–3)

I remove myself from deceit and flee from vexation for the sake of Love whose ranks I join.

He will ignore the slanderers. He desires and is desired by his lady, and he will remain loyal (22–8):

et ieu soi cel que·ls sieus digz non trastorna.

And I am a man who does not go back on his words.

Arnaut delights in this love for a particular lady, within the refuge of Love and free from the cares and deceits of the world:

Si l'auzes dir, ben saubron tug
que Jois mi monta·l cor el cel,
quar deport mi creis e desdug
la bela que d'amor apel;
mon bon esper mi dotbla sa valors
quar qui mais val mais dopta far faillida
et ill non es de re trista ni morna.   (29–35)

If I dared say it, everyone would know well that Joy lifts my heart to the heavens, for the fair one whom I entreat in love increases my pleasure and delight. Her worth redoubles my good hopes, for a person of the highest worth fears most to fail in a promise, and she is in no way wicked or moody.

Against falsehood and hypocrisy in Love:

D'aquest'amor son lunh forsdug
dompneiador fenhen, fradel,
pero si·s n'an maint pretz destrug
tal que·s fan cueinte et isnel;
et ieu que soi dels leials amadors
estau jauzens, c'Amors e Jois me guida
lo cor en joi, que aillors no·s trastorna.   (36–42)

From this love hypocritical and infamous suitors are banished far away;
yet, passing themselves off as amiable and lively, they have destroyed
many a reputation; and I, who am one of the loyal lovers, remain rejoicing, for Love and Joy guide my constant heart to joy [to my lady who is
joy].

This poem *Lanquan vei fueill* is the credo of the loyal lover
who is codifying the practical lessons to be learnt from Marcabru's ideal of *Fin'Amors*. Arnaut gives clearer shape to several
themes from Raimbaut d'Aurenga: Love is the fortress and
defence against the sorrows of life; reassurance and lasting
happiness are granted by the *domna* who is incapable of unworthy deeds; *Jois* cleans the rust and film from life and com-
bats deceit and slander; the poet and lover must nurture
valors, or inherent courtly virtue, within himself, and cherish
it in his lady, and must live according to *Jois*, the generously
minded way of life that seeks happiness as a positive good and
leads to *pretz*, which is fine reputation and the social qualities
that go with it.

Only the loyal man may gather the fruits from the tree of
Love:

Amors es de pretz la claus
e de proes'us estancs
don naisson tuich li bon fruich,
s'es qui leialmen los cuoilla;
q'un non delis gel ni niula
mentre qe·s noiris el bon tronc;
mas si·l romp trefans ni culvertz
peris tro leials lo sagre.   (XI, 9–16)

Love is the key to merit and esteem and a shoot of excellent qualities from
which grow all the fruits of goodness, if there is anyone to gather them
loyally, for neither frost nor mist can destroy one of them so long as it is
nourished on the good trunk. But if the treacherous or deceitful man
breaks it, it dies until the loyal man anoints it with balm.

Arnaut's *Amors* is the *Fin'Amors* of earlier troubadours, but
he has not submitted to it without a battle:

Faillirs esmendatz es laus;
et eu senti·m[10] n'ams los flancs
que mais n'ai d'amor ses cuich
que tals q'en parl'e·is n'orguoilla;
que pieitz mi fa·l cor de friula.
Mentr'ella·m fetz semblan embronc,
mais volgr'ieu trair pen'els desertz
on anc non ac d'auzels agre. (17–24)

A sin corrected is a matter for praise, and I have felt within me in both my flanks that I have more love, and I am not imagining this, than the man who speaks and boasts of it with pride; so that it pains me more in my heart than a sharp needle. So long as she gave me a downcast look, I would have wished to be a penitent in the desert where no bird ever nested.

The lover must accept all that Love tells him:

Qui Amor sec, per tal·s liure:
cogul tenga per colomba;
s'ill o ditz ni ver li sembla,
fassa·il plan del Puoi de Doma;
qan d'el plus prop es tant s'apil;
si co·l proverbis s'acoigna,
si·l trai l'uoill, sel puois lo·il oigna;
sofr'e sega ab cor humil. (IV, 33–40)

Let the man who follows Love surrender himself in such a way that he takes a cuckoo for a dove. If Love says this and it seems true to him, let him make a plain of the Puy-de-Dôme. When Love is nearest to him, let him abase himself accordingly; as the proverb tells: Let the man whose eye has been pulled out, bathe the eye of the man who has done this; let him suffer and obey with a humble heart.

For Raimbaut d'Aurenga the upside-down world of the man in turmoil through Love was a place of struggle and of cold, cutting torment relieved finally by warmth. For Arnaut the faithful lover must love absolutely, yielding power over himself and accepting as truth the upside-down world of phantasy to which he is led. The lover must force his mind to painful obedience and humility in order to find Joy. In terms of the *Roman de la Rose* of Guillaume de Lorris, *Raison* must not only be rejected as a counsellor against Love but must be used to bend the mind to accept Love.

Love is aroused through the mind which must accept it:

D'amor mi pren penssan lo fuocs
e·l desiriers doutz e coraus. (XIII, 8–9)

Love's flame, and sweet and heartfelt desire capture me when I reflect.

By teaching him the arts of its school Love has helped Arnaut to mental harmony (XVI, 5–7). It gives him its orders (XVI, 8–28): be faithful and persevere; refuse all other invitations; be like the evergreens, laurel and broom, rather than the violet; like a pilgrim traverse for love the marshes of Beaucaire, and cross the Ebro; eschew error, disloyalty and mockery; honour and celebrate your lady next to God (XVI, 21). This last injunction may be Arnaut's self-reproach for his boast that his love for his lady was more loyal than any man's love of God:

> Non sai un tan si'e Dieu frems,
> ermita ni monge ni clerc,
> cum ieu sui e leis de cui can. (XIV, 25–7)

I know no one, hermit, monk or clerk, who is so constant in love of God as I am constant in love of her of whom I sing.

As the mind sees and controls its reactions to Love and will not rebel against its authority (VII, 1–11) or calculate its service (II, 47), so does it cast a cool eye on Jois, which for Arnaut is a largely mental concept. Jois is no longer exaltation of feeling or aspiration to an unknown happiness, but awareness of a state of reassurance through Love and shelter from the sorrows of the world. The many-hued spring, scarlet, blue, green, white, yellow, puts him in mind to colour his song with a flower such that its fruit will be love, its seed will be joy and its perfume a great freedom from sorrow (XIII, 5–7). Life is good if Joy sustains it (III, 17–18) but Joy is no longer, as with Raimbaut d'Aurenga, the pure exaltation of the spirit shining through the rust and film of life. It is a measurable commodity that is acquired by choosing a domna wisely and showing unswerving loyalty to her and Amors. Perfect joy is rare and joy is swiftly lost if a lover chooses hastily or goes astray. Jois is always exposed to the predatory swoop of Fals'Amors and of the domnas who have no self-esteem:

> Ben greu trob'om ioi desliure,
> c'a tantas partz volv e tomba
> fals'Amors, que no s'asembla
> lai on leiautatz asoma;
> q'ieu non trob ies doas en mil
> ses falsa paraulla loigna,
> e puois c'a travers non poigna
> e no torne sa cartat vil. (IV, 9–16)

With difficulty can unbounded joy be found, for False Love twists and descends from so many sides that such joy is not to be found in the place where loyalty holds sway; for I do not find two ladies in a thousand who are free from false, delaying words, and who then do not hasten in the opposite direction and debase their self-esteem.

Arnaut praises his lady for the qualities that he expects from *Amors*, so that on occasion *Amors* and the *domna* merge. If *Amors* is the key to good reputation and the qualities that earn it (XI, 9), she is its stronghold (IX, 55). His lady excels in courtly qualities, upholds and guides *pretz* (X, 7) and is supreme through the *Jois* and *solatz* that she offers:

> Iois e solatz d'autra·m par fals e bortz,
> c'una de pretz ab lieis no·is pot egar,
> qe·l sieus solatz es dels autres sobriers.   (XV, 29–31)

Joy and conversation from any other lady appear false and spurious to me; none can equal her in reputation, for her company excels that of all others.

Joy is to be found in praise of the lady's excellence:

> Ben ai estat a maintas bonas cortz
> mas sai ab lieis trob pro mais que lauzar:
> mesur'e sen et autres bos mestiers,
> beutat, ioven, bos faitz e bels demors.[11]
> gen l'enseignet Cortesi'e la duois;
> tant a de si totz faitz desplazens rotz
> de lieis no cre rens de ben si'a dire.   (XV, 15–21)

I have been in many fine courts, but here with her do I find much more to praise: right judgment and wisdom and other good qualities, beauty, Youth, good deeds and fair delight. Courtesy taught and instructed her nobly, and she has banished from herself all displeasing deeds so that nothing good is lacking in her.

These good qualities are given by God:

> q'ieu no vau tant chams, vautz ni plans ni puois
> q'en un sol cors trob aissi bos aips totz:
> q'en lieis los volc Dieus triar et assire.   (XV, 12–14)

for however many fields, valleys, plains or hills I cross, I cannot find every good quality in this way in one single person: for God chose them and placed them in her.

Arnaut's lady is the paragon of *pretz, beutat, bos aips, saber e sen* (XVII, 5, 20, 23–4). Her courtly knowledge and deeds, her reputation and qualities of mind, her good and gentle learning and bright, perceptive and generous heart have led Arnaut

to the secure shelter where he most desires to be welcomed
(XI, 25–8).

Arnaut knows how swiftly the human heart can err and fall
into *faillirs*. The *domnas* are few who can offer unbounded happiness (*joi desliure*), and his idealised lady must be secure on all
sides against error, sin and *Fals'Amors*. Having chosen to be a
disciple of *Amors* and to aspire to such a lady, Arnaut sets his
face resolutely against inconstancy. Courtly doctrine and his
domna automatically demand loyalty, but Arnaut's frequent,
vehement protests that he will not turn away from *Amors*,
from *ben amar* or the *domna*, may be inspired by his fears of a
personal lapse from his ideal of courtly virtue. Only in *Lo ferm
voler* (XVIII) does Arnaut really appear to resolve the conflict
between the desire for harmony of mind which can be
granted by the *domna* and the impulse to find individual joy
come what may.

In his efforts to find shelter within the orthodox courtly
situation Arnaut attempts to control conflicting thoughts and
desires as rigorously as Guillaume de Lorris keeps the uncourtly vices out of the *vergier d'amour*. Although Arnaut excludes the problems that afflicted earlier troubadours and
cast doubt on the validity of the courtly ethic, such as the fears
of the after life, the relative happiness offered by God and
Amors and the search for the *mielhs*, these themes run as under-
currents beneath his protestations of courtly submission. In
his attempt at conscious self-absorption in the courtly ethic
Arnaut is practising a form of self-forgetfulness, the *s'oblidar*
of earlier troubadours. He turns his love inwards upon itself
and shrinks from the outward, sensual expression of love and
sorrow. Admiring the *bona doctrina, mesura, sen e saber* of his lady,
he sees the reflection of himself as he would wish to be, the
courtly lover whose heart is secretly afire:

> S'ieu dic pauc, inz el cor m'esta
> q'estar mi fai temen paors.   (VII, 12–13)

If I say little, the thought [of love] remains within my heart, for fear keeps
me timid.

and:

> Merces, Amors, c'aras m'acuoills!
> Tart mi fo, mas en grat m'o prenc,
> car, si m'art dinz la meola,
> lo fuocs non vuoill que s'escanta...   (VIII, 19–22)

Thanks be, Love, that you welcome me now. It has been long for me, but I accept this with gratitude, for although the fire burns in my marrow, I do not wish it to be put out...

Arnaut beneath his courtly stance is acutely aware of his sense of isolation:

> Sols sui qui sai lo sobrafan qe·m sortz
> al cor, d'amor sofren per sobramar,
> car mos volers es tant ferms et entiers
> c'anc no s'esduis de celliei ni s'estors
> cui encubic al prim vezer e puois;
> c'ades ses lieis dic a lieis cochos motz,
> puois qan la vei non sai, tant l'ai, que dire.   (xv, 1–7)

I alone know the too great sorrow that comes up in my heart, suffering from love through loving too much, for my desire is so constant and complete that it never turned aside or away from her whom I desired at first sight and afterwards; for constantly, absent from her, I say to her urgent words, then, when I see her, I know not what to say, so much do I have to say.

The sonorous opening of this stanza thins with -i- and -e-, until the harsh key-words *encubic* and *dic* create discord and introduce the jagged line (7) which is no longer a courtly commonplace but a personal admission.

In the same poem, Arnaut again uses a broken exclamatory line and two *braus* words, *lecs e glotz*, to signal the fire beneath courtly feeling:

> ...qe·l sieus solatz es dels autres sobriers.
> Hai! si no l'ai, las! tant mal m'a comors!
> Pero l'afans m'es deportz, ris e iois,
> car en pensan sui de lieis lecs e glotz:
> hai Dieus, si ia·n serai estiers gauzire!   (31–5)

...for her company excels that of all others. Alas! if I have her not, alas! in such evil plight am I possessed by her. Yet this sorrow is delight, laughter and joy to me, for in my thoughts I am lecherous and gluttonous for her. Ah God, if only I may rejoice in her in a different way.

Sensual desire breaks through in this poem as it does in *Lo ferm voler*. In *Doutz brais* Arnaut calls on God, who mercifully absolved the sins of Longinus, to allow:

> ...q'ieu e midonz iassam
> en la chambra on amdui nos mandem
> uns rics convens don tan gran ioi atendi,
> qe·l seu bel cors baisan rizen descobra
> e qe·l remir contra·l lum de la lampa.   (xii, 28–32)

...that I and my lady may lie in the room where we both pledged rich words of troth from which I await such great joy, when I may uncover, with kisses and laughter, her beautiful body and behold it in the light of the lamp.

This expression of sensual longing, which is a commonplace in earlier troubadours, is uncharacteristic of what remains of Arnaut's love lyrics and the explanation may be that Arnaut is imitating Raimbaut d'Aurenga:

> Quan la candela·m fetz vezer
> Vos baizan rizen, a! cal ser!   (XXII, 65–6)

When the candle made me see you as we kissed and laughed. Ah! what an evening!

Like Jaufre Rudel, Arnaut repents of sensual desire:

> doncs ben sui fols que quier tan qe·m rependi.   (XII, 46)

Then am I indeed a fool to desire so much that I repent.

Arnaut amplifies his fear of excessive desire by imitating Jaufre Rudel (II, 25):

> Tant l'am de cor e la queri
> c'ab trop voler cug la·m toli
> s'om ren per ben amar pert.   (X, 22–4)

I love and desire her so much from my heart that through too much longing I think that I rob myself of her, if one can lose anything through loving truly.

The struggle against desire within is exteriorised in a struggle against the forces of nature, as in Raimbaut d'Aurenga's *Ar resplan*. Arnaut is tireless in crossing bridges and fords for Love:

> S'ieu n'ai passatz pons ni planchas[12]
> per lieis, cuidatz q'ieu m'en duoilla?   (XVI, 29–30)

If I have crossed bridges and planks for her, do you think that I grieve because of this?

Courtly phrases and the fire within struggle in *Anc ieu non l'aic*:

> Tant sai son pretz fin e certa
> per q'ieu no·m puosc virar aillors;
> per so fatz ieu qe·l cors m'en dol,
> que qan sols clau ni s'aiorna
> eu non aus dir qui m'aflama;

lo cors m'abranda
e·ill huoill n'ant la vianda,
car solamen
vezen
m'estai aizida:
ve·us qe·m ten a vida!   (VII, 23–33)

I know that her virtues and reputation are so fine and assured that I cannot turn elsewhere. And for this reason I make my heart grieve, for when the sun is shut off or day brightens, I do not dare to name the one who sets me on fire. My heart is burning me, and my eyes are nourished. For only through what I can see, does pleasure remain with me. And that is what holds me to life.

The break in the rhyme-scheme at line 27 also marks the switch from courtly declamation to the short and sharp lines of personal feeling.

Love that is secret, shared and lasting can assuage his solitariness:

Pretz e Valors, vostre capduoills
es la bella c'ab si·m retenc,
qui m'a sol et ieu liei sola,
c'autr'el mon no m'atalanta;
    anz sui brus
    et estrus
ad autras e·l cor teing prems,
mas pel sieu ioi trep'e sauta:
no vuoill c'autra m'o comorda.   (VIII, 46–54)

Fine reputation and worth, your stronghold is the fair one who retained me for herself, who possesses me alone as I possess her alone, for no other woman in the world pleases me. On the contrary I am dark and refractory towards the others, and keep my heart closed, but it dances and leaps for the joy that comes from her. I want no other woman to take this from me.

Joy comes from love protected by the lady, who is the stronghold of *Pretz* and *Valor*. Such love must be secret: '*Bon'Amors* can decline, and that lover is a fool who thinks that, if he speaks out, his lady's reputation, and his own, will not suffer. The man who trembles with impatience to speak of his love, should rightly bite his tongue afterwards' (VIII, 28–36).

The identity of Arnaut's lady is secreted in his mind so that joy for him, as for Raimbaut d'Aurenga, comes from mental desire. Arnaut's secret love contrasts with that of Raimon de Miraval, who names his lady and describes her charms, and enters the social battle with accusation and defence, praise and abuse. For Arnaut, love that is declared openly can be

cortes ufaniers and he compares the assured joy he finds with his
lady to the changing happiness of fickle lovers (v, 36–42).

In a succinct form Arnaut is repeating Raimbaut d'Aurenga's
ideal of a sure, shared and secret love. He also rationalises
Raimbaut's conflict between inner tension and outward calm.
Raimbaut had said:

> Si que·l cor m'art, mas no·m rima
> Ren de foras, mas dinz rim;
> Q'Amors l'enclav'e l'escrinha
> — Si! pels sans qi son part Mila! —
> E·l ten pres dinz son escrinh. (II, 25–9)

So that my heart burns, but nothing outside of me burns, since it burns
within; for Love encloses and confines it — yes by the saints who are
beyond Milan! — and keeps it captive in his coffer.

For Raimbaut *Amors* was the dangerous, all-powerful oppo-
nent. Arnaut, who values his rational self-control, accepts
Amors as a friend and confidant. He cherishes the fire within
(VIII, 21–2).

Love leads Arnaut to its shelter (XI, 27–8) but reduces him
to timidity and confusion:

> Tant dopti que per non-aus
> devenc sovens niers e blancs;
> si m'a·l seus desirs forsduich
> no sap lo cors trep o·is duoilla. (XI, 33–6)

I am so afraid because of 'I dare not' that I often become black and white.
Desire for her has led me so greatly astray that I know not whether my
heart is dancing or grieving.

In *En cest sonet coind'e leri* reason looks at the courtly shell and
the inner fire and recognises the vanity of life. The opening is
smooth, polished, restrained:

> En cest sonet coind'e leri
> fauc motz e capuig e doli,
> que serant verai e cert
> qan n'aurai passat la lima;
> q'Amors marves plan'e daura
> mon chantar, que de liei mou
> qui pretz manten e governa. (X, 1–7)

To this gracious and gay tune I compose and plane and adze words so
that they are true and sure when I have passed the file across them; for
Love immediately smooths and gilds my song which comes from her who
upholds and protects fine reputation and worth.

Each day he improves and is purified because he adores the most gracious lady in the world; the love which flows like rain into his heart keeps him warm in the deepest winter (8–14). He hears and offers a thousand masses and burns wax and oil so that God may help him with the lady against whom he has no defence (15–18):

> e qan remir sa crin saura
> e·l cors q'es grailet e nou
> mais l'am que qi·m des Luserna.[13]   (19–21)

and when I see her golden hair and her body which is slim and fresh, I love her more than if I were to be given Luserna.

The poem pivots on the next stanza (IV) which begins in the traditional manner of *Fin'Amors* imitated from Jaufre Rudel. Arnaut fears that, if anything can be lost through loving well, he may lose his lady through excess of desire (22–4). Then language and imagery become harsh – his lady is a usurer who owns him lock, stock and barrel – and Arnaut intensifies the water image of the courtly rain of love (13):

> Q'el sieus cors sobretracima
> lo mieu tot e non s'eisaura;
> tant a de ver fait renou
> c'obrador n'a e taverna.   (25–8)

For her heart swamps mine with a wave which will not dry up: she has, in truth, exacted such great usury that she owns the workman and the shop.

Courtly harmony appears to be restored in the next stanza, but is once more destroyed by harsh words in the last line:

> No vuoill de Roma l'emperi
> ni c'om m'en fassa apostoli,
> q'en lieis non aia revert
> per cui m'art lo cors e·m rima;
> e si·l maltraich no·m restaura
> ab un baisar anz d'annou
> mi auci e si enferna.   (29–35)

I do not desire the Holy Roman Empire, or to be made Pope, if I may not return to her for whom my heart burns and splits; and if she does not heal my suffering with a kiss before New Year, she will give death to me and Hell-fire to herself.

In the next stanza, in which the key-words are *maltraich* from line 33, *desert* and *laura*, Arnaut looks with a cooler eye than Raimbaut at the waste land of joyless suffering:

Ges pel maltraich q'ieu soferi
de ben amar no·m destoli,
si tot me ten en desert,
c'aissi·n fatz los motz en rima.
Pieitz trac aman c'om que laura... (36–40)

Never because of the suffering I endure can I remove myself from true
loving, although I keep myself in a desert, for it is with such a mind that
I compose these words in rhyme. I suffer, loving, worse than a man who
ploughs the earth...

Arnaut sums up his plight in the famous *tornada*:

Ieu sui Arnautz q'amas l'aura,
e chatz la lebre ab lo bou
e nadi contra suberna. (43–5)

I am Arnaut who gathers the wind, and hunts the hare with the ox, and
swims against the rising tide.

Arnaut is not *cauz'enversa* or upside-down like Raimbaut, or
unsure whether he is black or white. He knows that he is
struggling against the impossible, and rational calm leads him
from confusion to a sense of barren isolation.

The image of gathering the wind is not new. Bernart Marti,
accepting that he must love because 'this is the thing to do',
'beats against the wind like a madman' (edn Hoepffner, 1),
and may have had in mind the *aerem verberans* of *Corinthians*, ix,
26. Raimbaut d'Aurenga had said:

Peire Rotgier, cum puosc sofrir
Qez eu am aissi solamens?
Meravill me! Si viu de vens! (VI, 29–31)

Peire Rogier, how can I endure to live in such solitude. I marvel at myself!
I am living on winds.

Hunting the hare with the ox continues the image of the
barren life in which Arnaut endures more than the plough-
man who tills the land (X, 38–40). Flushing the hare from its
hide and laboriously following its concentric run, Arnaut may
be hunting the apparently impossible, but he is also declaring
his intention to pursue fruitless love and the sterile suffering
of his existence.

Ovid had counselled the lover to persist with the lady who
is neither kindly nor courteous; the lover must gain his ends
by compliance:

Obsequio tranantur aquae: nec vincere possis
Flumina, si contra, quam rapit unda, nates.
Obsequium tigresque domat Numidasque leones;
Rustica paulatim taurus aratra subit.

(*Ars. am.*, II, 181–4)

By compliance are waters swum; nor can you conquer rivers if you swim against the current's flow. Compliance tames tigers and Numidian lions; little by little the bull submits to the rustic plough.[14]

Arnaut uses the imagery of the bull and the swimmer in reverse order to that of Ovid, and with an amplified meaning. The bull may be tamed to the ox-plough, but he will be used to chase the hare, symbol of elusive joy, and the swimmer, refusing to yield, will struggle against the rising tide. This is Arnaut's reaction to the increasing power of the Love that rains into his heart (13) and becomes a possessive and submerging wave of desire (25). For Arnaut as for Raimbaut the untamed power of nature represents the forces that bring frustration in love, and life. Arnaut's reply is not to drown, but to resist, as he would resist the four elements of wind, earth, water and fire.

The importance of this moment of passion and self-doubt which is symbolised by the wind-gatherer, the ox and the hare, and the swimmer, is made clear in *Amors e iois* (XIV), *Ans qe* (XVI) and *Lo ferm voler* (XVIII). In *Amors e iois* he says:

Amors e iois e liocs e tems
mi fan tornar lo sen e derc
d'aqel noi c'avia l'autr'an
can cassava·l lebr'ab lo bou;
era·m vai mieltz d'amor e pieis,
car ben am, d'aiso·m clam astrucs,
ma non amatz ioi gau en cers,
s'Amors no vens son dur cor e·l mieus precs.   (XIV, 1–8)

Love and joy and place and season bring my mind back to order after that folly I had the other year when I hunted the hare with the ox. Now I fare in love both better and worse; I call myself fortunate because I love truly, but I cannot enjoy sure joy as one who is loved, if Love and my entreaty do not win her hard heart.

Arnaut's mind is detached, but his situation is desperate:

Pauc pot hom valer de ioi sems:
per me·l sai que l'ai agut berc,
car per un sobrefais d'afan
don la dolor del cor no·s mou;

e s'ab ioi l'ira no·m for eis
tost m'auran miei paren faducs;
pero tals a mon cor convers
q'en liei amar volgra murir senecs. (17–24)

A man devoid of joy cannot be worth much. I know through my own
case when I had my joy broken, through an excess weight of sorrow which
stops grief from leaving my heart, and if this sadness will not come out
of me through joy, my kinsmen will soon have me as an idiot. Yet such
is the lady who has attracted my heart that I would wish to die an old
man while still loving her.

No hermit, monk or clerk is more constant to God than he
is to his lady; may he be blinded if he desires another. Long
doubts and fears make him improve and grow in stature; in
five or six years, when his head is white, he will perhaps enjoy
what now enslaves him (25–40).

Arnaut fares both worse in love because he sees the inevita-
bility of grief, and better because his love can remain controlled and steadfast for as long as he lives. Harmony for
Arnaut lies in the courage and hope of the mind:

De luencs suspirs e de grieus gems
mi pot trair cella cui m'aerc
c'ades sol per un bel semblan
n'ai mogut mon chantar tot nou.
Contra mon vauc e no m'encreis,
car gent mi fai pensar mos cucs.
Cor, vai sus: ben sai, si·t suffers,
sec tant q'en lieis, c'ai encubit, no·t pecs.

Ans er plus vils aurs non es fers
c'Arnautz desam lieis ont es fermanz necs. (41–50)

From long sighs and harsh moans can she save me, to whom I raise myself,
for at once, and only for a fair look she gave, have I begun a song that is
quite new. I go uphill and am not displeased, for my mind makes me
think fine thoughts. My heart, arise! I know well that, if you endure, you
will not then be deceived in her whom I have chosen to love.

Gold will become more common than iron before Arnaut ceases to love
the lady to whom he is secretly bound.

In *Sols sui* (xv) Arnaut accepts the service of Love and the
solitude this brings, and when he beholds his lady, the tor-
rents of love within become a smooth stretch of water.

In *Ans qe·l cim* he accepts Ovid's dictum: 'by compliance are
waters swum'. Peace of mind comes from the lessons of
Amors:

que gen m'a duoich de las artz de s'escola;
tant sai qe·l cors fatz restar de suberna
e mos bous es pro plus correns que lebres.   (XVI, 5–7)

for graciously has Love taught me the arts of its school. I know so much
that I stop the course of the mounting tide and my ox is much swifter
than a hare.

This sense of resolute purpose and the hope that desire will
be fulfilled through patience is the central theme of Lo ferm
voler (XVIII), which in technique and subject-matter is Arnaut's
masterpiece, the culmination of his ideas and the swan song
of the trobar clus. The poem, which owes much to Raimbaut's
Ar resplan, is constructed with six rhyme-words, intra, ongla,
arma, verga, oncle and cambra, which are rearranged, with relation
to the lines of the preceding stanza, in the order 6, 1, 5, 2, 4, 3.
In the tornada the rhyme-words are repeated with relation to
the preceding stanza, in the order 1, 4; 2, 5; 3, 6.

  I Lo ferm voler q'el cor m'intra
    no·m pot ies becs escoissendre ni ongla
    de lausengier, qui pert per mal dir s'arma;   3
    e car non l'aus batr'ab ram ni ab verga,
    sivals a frau, lai on non aurai oncle,
    iauzirai ioi, en vergier o dinz cambra.   6

  II Qan mi soven de la cambra
    on a mon dan sai que nuills hom non intra
    anz me son tuich plus que fraire ni oncle,   9
    non ai membre no·m fremisca, neis l'ongla,
    aissi cum fai l'enfas denant la verga:
    tal paor ai no·l sia trop de l'arma.   12

  III Del cors li fos, non de l'arma,
    e cossentis m'a celat dinz sa cambra!
    Que plus mi nafra·l cor que colps de verga   15
    car lo sieus sers lai on ill es non intra;
    totz temps serai ab lieis cum carns et ongla,
    e non creirai chastic d'amic ni d'oncle.   18

  IV Anc la seror de mon oncle
    non amei plus ni tant, per aqest'arma!
    C'aitant vezis cum es lo detz de l'ongla,   21
    s'a liei plagues, volgr'esser de sa cambra;
    de mi pot far l'amors q'inz el cor m'intra
    mieills a son vol c'om fortz de frevol verga.   24

  V Pois flori la seca verga
    ni d'en Adam mogron nebot ni oncle,
    tant fin'amors cum cella q'el cor m'intra   27
    non cuig fos anc en cors, ni eis en arma;

on q'ill estei, fors en plaz', o dins cambra,
mos cors no·is part de lieis tant cum ten l'ongla.   30

VI   C'aissi s'enpren e s'enongla
mos cors en lei cum l'escorss'en la verga:
q'ill m'es de ioi tors e palaitz e cambra,   33
e non am tant fraire, paren ni oncle:
q'en paradis n'aura doble ioi m'arma,
si ia nuills hom per ben amar lai intra.   36

VII Arnautz tramet sa chansson d'ongl'e d'oncle,
a grat de lieis que de sa verg'a l'arma,
son Desirat, cui pretz en cambra intra.   39

Neither beak nor nail of slanderer, who through evil speaking loses his soul's salvation, can tear from me the firm desire that enters my heart. And because I dare not beat him with stick or rod, at least in secret there where I have no witness, will I rejoice in joy, in orchard or in chamber.

When I remember that chamber where to my loss I know that no man enters, but where on the contrary all are more (watchful) than brother or uncle, I have no limb, even the nail, which does not tremble, just like the child before the rod, such fear do I have that I may belong to her too much with my soul.

Would that I might be hers with my body, not with my soul, and that she might admit me in secret to her room. For it wounds my heart more than a blow from a rod that her slave does not enter where she is. Always I shall be with her, like flesh and nail, and will not believe the reproach of friend or uncle.

I never loved the sister of my uncle, more or as much, by this soul of mine! For, if it pleased her, I would wish to be as close to her chamber as is the finger to the nail. The love which enters my heart can order me as it wills, better than a strong man with a weak rod.

Since the dry rod flowered and nephews and uncles were descended from Adam, I do not think that there existed in a body or even in a soul such perfect love as enters my heart. Wherever she is, outside in the square or in a room, my heart does not depart from her as far as the nail extends.

For my being fastens on her and clings to her with its nails like the bark on the branch, for to me she is the tower and palace and chamber of joy, and I do not love brother, parent or uncle as much, so that my soul will have double joy in Paradise if ever any man enters there through loving truly.

Arnaut sends his song of nail and uncle to please her who has the soul of her rod, his Desired one, into whose chamber reputation enters.

The following rules which apply to Dante's *Divine Comedy* can also be used for this poem by Arnaut Daniel in which we can see a literal sense, and a moral and Christian sense: 'To understand what is to follow you must know that this work has not one meaning but several meanings, for there is the meaning which one draws from the letters themselves and another meaning which we draw from the things signified by the letters. The first meaning is the literal, the second can be called allegorical, or moral or anagogical; that is why one must first examine the subject of this work literally and then according to its allegorical significance.'[15]

The literal interpretation of this poem is that of a profane *amor de lonh* which owes much to the poetry of Jaufre Rudel. In the first stanza Arnaut's desire for his lady is constant and immune to the gossip of the slanderers; rather than attack them, he will secretly rejoice in *Jois* with his lady, in orchard or chamber, the *locs aizis* of Jaufre Rudel (1–6). The thought of obstacles to his love makes him tremble; his love must not be too spiritual, without sensual pleasure (7–12). Would that he might belong to her in body and be admitted to her chamber. He will stay closer and more faithful than flesh to the nail. He will not obey the admonition of advisers, of friend or uncle (13–18). This love is greater than love for his family. It overpowers him; would that he were in her chamber (19–24). Such perfect love (*Fin'Amors*) as enters his heart was never found in body, or even in soul. His heart stays with her, wherever she is (25–30). His whole being is at one with her; she is the tower, palace and chamber of joy; he loves her more than his kinsfolk; because of this love his soul will have double joy in Paradise, if one wins salvation through loving well (31–6).

Arnaut's *Fin'Amors* is the balance of sensual and spiritual desire controlled by reason that Marcabru had advocated. Like Jaufre Rudel, Arnaut desires to 'rejoice in joy' for love of his lady, but whereas Jaufre, for security of mind and happiness, escapes from sensual 'close' love to mental 'distant' love, to 'Fin'Amors that never betrayed a man', Arnaut proceeds in the opposite direction. He believes that his love is too mental and spiritual and he wishes to move from a distant to a closer, and more sensual love, so that *Fin'Amors*, the highest form of profane love, may be a balance of sensual, mental and spiritual desire. Whereas Jaufre dreams of the moment when he will have seen and left his physical lady in order to win lasting joy in the reality of the world illuminated by her memory:

> Si qe la cambra e·l jardis
> Mi resembles totz temps palatz!
>
> (ed. Lejeune, V, 41–2)

Arnaut sees her already as the tower, palace and chamber of joy, and longs for the closeness of her physical reality. Arnaut, who uses Jaufre's imagery (*tors, palatz, cambra, fraire, seror*), is reversing the process of Fin'Amors in Jaufre's poems. Whereas Jaufre thanks his counsellors and his lady and God that he has triumphed over sensual love and is restored to a sense of self-esteem after the humiliation and moral confusion of 'close' love, Arnaut desires to achieve this closeness and refuses advice (*e non creirai chastic d'amic ni d'oncle*). In place of Jaufre's *auzelhs de lonh*, birds from afar, which in *Lanquan li jorn* bring present grief and the dream of spiritual happiness, Arnaut hears the beaks of the slanderers who will not destroy his unswerving desire. His whole being is rooted in his lady who to him is absolute joy (31–2). His soul and spirit are always with her; if his flesh were also there, his joy would be complete.

Behind this poem there lies the debate between *cors* and *arma*, body and soul. The dichotomy is resolved when Arnaut says: 'I do not think there existed in a body, or even in a soul, such perfect love [Fin'Amors] as enters my heart' (27–8). This affirmation of Fin'Amors as the perfect form of profane love is the high point of Arnaut's poem, as the line *Qu'anc fin'amors home non trays* was the key line to which Jaufre Rudel had been working in *Belhs m'es l'estius*. If *cors* in stanza VI of Arnaut's poem is translated not merely as 'my heart' but 'my whole being':

> C'aissi s'enpren e s'enongla
> mos cors en lei cum l'escorss'en la verga...   (31–2)

for my whole being fastens itself to her and clings to her with its nails like the bark on the branch...

it can be seen that Arnaut is exemplifying the strength of Fin'Amors as the balance of desire in body, mind and spirit, that he had praised in the previous stanza. Behind his poetry there is also the basic Augustinian debate of the struggle between carnal desire of the body and the soul's desire for God, and in the sixth and last stanza of his poem Arnaut affirms the excellence of Fin'Amors by equating it with love of God. Arnaut does this by a direct comparison, reminiscent of William of Saint Thierry (*De natura et dignitate Amoris*, III, chap. 2; PL, clxxxiv, col. 391–3), in which he asserts that his love is not only superior to love for one's kinsfolk but is equal in its good results to love of God. He imitates Rudel's use of words with rich overtones of meaning to strengthen this contrast between profane loves and Christian love of God. His intention is clear in the first lines of stanza v:

> Pois flori la seca verga
> ni d'en Adam mogron nebot ni oncle.   (25–6)

Oncle in medieval poetry is synonymous with kinsman, as in Bernier's defence of his family to Raoul de Cambrai:

> Or viex mon oncle et mon pere essillier!
> N'est pas mervelle s'or me vuel corecier:
> Il sont mi oncle, je lor volrai aidier.
>
> (ed. P. Meyer, 1648–50)

where the second *oncle* must mean 'kinsmen'. From Celtic days it was customary for an uncle to rear his nephew, and the bond between them might be stronger than that between the son and his parents.

With *seca verga* and *en Adam* Arnaut refers explicitly to the spirit and the flesh, the Virgin Mary and Adam, the New and the Old Testaments. His love is the *tors e palaitz e cambra* of joy, all words which could refer to the Virgin Mary, as *Desirat* in l. 39 may refer to Jesus,[16] and his soul will have double joy in Paradise, if one can enter there through loving well. Arnaut looks obliquely at the problem that troubled Peire d'Alvernhe and resolves it. The highest form of profane love, *Fin'Amors*, does not preclude the hope of happiness in the after-life. His own hope of such happiness binds up the song which began with the scandalmongers (*lauzengiers*) who lose their hope of salvation through their evil words. Arnaut is not convinced that the perfect pursuit of *Fin'Amors* can commend him positively to God, although he trusts that this is the case. In this he is more circumspect than the later Guilhem de Montanhagol.

Beneath the *trobar ric* overtones of his six rhyme-words[17] Arnaut unfolds his meaning in the style of the *trobar clus* and affirms his belief in *Fin'Amors* which not only allows a man to live *letz, cortes e sapiens*, but raises him to the moment of ultimate happiness, the *summum bonum* or *mielhs* of the early troubadours, in which moral, spiritual and Christian doubts are resolved, and the lover can hope for happiness in Paradise. Arnaut's triumphant affirmation of *Fin'Amors* is the high point of personal progress of the individual lover towards the abstract vision of *Fin'Amors* which Marcabru had seen. It resolves the conflict between carnal and mental desire, close and distant love, that had tormented Jaufre Rudel, and it reconciles the highest form of profane love with love of family and love of God.

8

Raimon de Miraval and the
Joy of the Court

THE MONK OF MONTAUDON, reviewing the poets of his day, jests at Miraval's generosity in giving to his lady a castle in which he never entertains:

> E lo tertz es de Carcases
> Miravals que·s fai molt cortes
> Que dona son castel soven,
> E no·i esta l'an ges u mes
> Ni anc mais calendas no·i pres,
> Per que no·il te dan qu'il se pren.
>
> (ed. Klein, I, 19–24)

And the third comes from Carcases, Miraval who makes himself out very courtly and often gives his castle away. He does not stay in it for more than one month in the year, and he never spent the calends there, so it is no loss to him if his gift is accepted.[1]

Miraval's castle, bounded on three sides by the river Orbiel, was an outpost of Carcassonne on the road leading North through the Black Mountains. Raimon's *vida*[2] says that he was a poor knight who owned only the fourth part of the castle in which there were less than forty men. The Miraval family had lost wealth and power in the twelfth century; they had given up lands in Rouergue and Larzac, and in 1174 their immediate overlord Viscount Rogier II of Béziers and Carcassonne demanded from Guilhem de Miraval the surrender of lands that he held at Castres 'as recompense for the war he had waged and the acts of brigandage of which he was guilty'.[3] Miraval's castle was in the focal area of the Cathar heresy and was captured by Simon de Montfort's crusaders soon after the fall of Carcassonne, in 1209, or 1211 at the latest.

To give away his castle in his poetry was Miraval's way of affirming his nobility and the authorship of his songs.

Although he composed between 1185 and 1213, which was the richest and most courtly period of troubadour poetry, his fame was outstanding. About 1191 Elias de Barjols chooses Miraval's songs for the composite picture of his imaginary courtly knight[4] and in the early thirteenth century the Catalan troubadour Raimon Vidal de Bezaudun in his verse romance of love casuistry *So fo el tems qu'om era gais,* praised Miraval as the supreme authority on Love:

> E si non voletz creire mi,
> aujatz d'en Miravalh qu'en dis,
> qui saup mai d'amor que Paris
> ni hom de c'auzissetz parlar![5]

And if you do not wish to believe me, hear what lord Miraval says about this, for he knew more about Love than Paris or any man of whom you might hear tell.

Matfre Ermengaud quotes him seven times in his *Breviari d'amor,* and the large number of manuscripts which contain his songs and the long and fanciful accounts of his amorous exploits in the Provençal biographies, show that as a courtly lover and troubadour he was as famous as the warrior poet Bertran de Born.

As Bertran de Born was the friend of the Young King, the eldest son of Henry II, so Miraval was the acknowledged companion of Count Raimon VI of Toulouse, the most powerful patron of troubadours in the South, with whom he exchanged the reciprocal pseudonym *Audiart.*[6] Miraval's fame is bound up with his success as a courtier who composed to entertain his companions (*per solatz dels compaignos*) as well as to please himself and his lady (XXXII, 1–8). He was welcomed at many courts in Languedoc and Spain and sent his jongleur Bajona to them, after he had complained about the thin rewards from an earlier song at the courts of Carcassonne and Narbonne:

> A Dieu me coman, Bajona,
> Cal diable t'an tengut!
> Cant est sirventesc no·t sona,
> Ben t'en deus clamar perdut,
> Qu'ieu t'agra dat caval maucut
> Ab sela de Carcassona
> Et entressenh et escut
> De la cort de Narbona.   (XXXIX, 1–8)

God keep me, Bajona, what devils have taken hold of you! If this *sirventes* does not please you, you must indeed consider yourself a lost cause, for I should have given you a fat-bellied horse with a saddle of Carcassonne and an ensign and shield from the court of Narbonne.

Miraval directs Bajona through the courts of Carcasses to Bertran de Saissac, tutor and guardian of the young viscount Trencavel of Carcassonne:

> A·n Bertran de Saissac chanta
> Sirventes e mais chansos,
> E di·l que no·s tenh'az anta,
> Car premier non l'ai somos;
> Et ja de luy no·t partras blos,
> C'un caval c'a col de ganta
> No·t don per amor de nos
> Si dars non l'atalanta.   (41–8)

Sing some *sirventes* to lord Bertran de Saissac and, preferably, songs, and tell him not to be offended because I did not address him first. You will never leave him empty handed, without his giving you for love of me a horse with a neck like a swan – although giving gives him no pleasure.

Bertran de Born achieved notoriety by throwing his brother Constantin out of the family castle at Autafort. Miraval threw out his wife Gaudairenca and was admonished for this by the Catalan nobleman and poet Uc de Mataplana:

> Car per sos bels captenemens
> e per son bel trobar parti
> sa cortesa moiller de si.
> (ed. Miraval, 19–21, p. 334)

for it was because of her fine manners and her fine poems that he removed his courtly wife from himself.

And he rubs salt in the wound. Let the husband accept his wife's admirers as she accepts his courtly wooing of *domnas*:

> E pois er sos albercs gauzens,
> qand ab lieis aura faita fi,
> ab que ia mais non la chasti
> de trobar ni de motz plazens,
> ni de lieis no·is don doptanssa,
> ni non s'o teign'a grevanssa
> si sos albercs es soven corteiatz:
> c'assi er d'agradatge
> a nos cortes, et als gelos salvatge.   (37–45)

And then when he has made peace with her, his dwelling will be filled with joy, if he does not chide her for her poetry and her words that are pleasing to her suitors. Let him not be worried about her, nor grieved if his dwelling is frequented by courtly wooers, for in this way he will be pleasing to us who are courtly and repulsive to those who are jealous.

Miraval was riled to the point of composing a defence (*Grans mestiers*) with the same rhyme scheme and the same rhyme words: I am in no way a jealous husband; I have put so much effort into courtly behaviour that I am recognised as supreme in this matter. A wife cannot expect the same devotion as the *domna* who accepts a knight's homage and advances his reputation.

> Que cavalliers q'en pretz se fi
> Deu laissar, so·ns mostra Jovens,
> Moiller que pren per enfanssa;
> Mas si sa dompna l'enanssa
> Tant qe·l prenda, estre deu estacatz
> D'un certan homenatge,
> Qe ja nuill temps non seg'autre viatge.   (XLII, 21–7)

For a knight whose trust is in courtly renown must leave, as 'Youth' tells us, a wife whom he marries lightly. But if his lady does him such honour that she accepts him, he must be bound by such constant homage that he will never at any time take another path.

Jovens here is no longer the generosity of spirit of the early troubadours, but the courtly code which sets the *domna* on a separate and higher social plane than that of the wife. Let Uc be shamed; through loving his wife too much he neglects fame:

> Que de lui dizon siei vezi
> Q'en aisso es desconoissens,
> Qe per amor de na Sanssa
> Estai, c'aillors no·is bobanssa;
> E puois q'el vol estre totz moilleratz,
> Ja no·i aiam dampnatge
> Nos autre drut que seguem dreich viatge.   (30–6)

For his neighbours say of him that he lacks courtly judgment in loving my lady Sancha and seeking no praise elsewhere. Since he wishes to be tied to his wife completely, let us, the true lovers who follow the right path, suffer no harm from him.

The lady must tread a careful path between her social duty to increase the happiness of the court and her wifely task of adding lustre to her husband's reputation:

> La dompna q'es bell'e plazens
> Lais Dieus venir lai on hom ri,
> Et el nostr'alberc atressi
> Nos don cortejadors plazens

Ab moiller qe·ns fass'honranssa;
Et ieu non ai d'als fianssa,
Mas dels bels digz ab avinen solatz
E l'amoros visatge
Qe son dels huoils al cor privat messatge.   (37–45)

May God let the lady who is beautiful and pleasing be present there where there is laughter, and let Him give us, in our dwelling likewise, pleasing suitors with a wife who may do us honour. And I have no trust in anything except fair words with pleasing companionship and the loving looks which are the trusted messengers of the eyes to the heart.

Raimon is affirming the Joy of the Court against the isolationist contentment of the love of husband for wife, one of the themes, in a slightly different form, of *Erec et Enide* by Chrétien de Troyes. The kind of love that Raimon advocates should rightly be called courtly love. It depends on fair words, loving looks, the delights of company, and the desire for the happiness of the court in which the lover subordinates desire and passion to the needs, manners and rules of the community. This type of love demanded a display of the qualities of *jois*, *jovens* and *cortesia* which in earlier troubadours were accepted naturally as the requisite inner virtues of the truly courtly man. *Cortesia* is now ostentatious outward appearance, *bobanssa* and *ufana*, a social courtoisie comparable to that promulgated at the court of Eleanor of Aquitaine and parodied gently by Andreas Capellanus. Such a mannered love had bored Guilhem IX, scared Raimbaut d'Aurenga and tormented Arnaut Daniel, who were all seeking individual rather than social happiness. For Miraval, as for scores of contemporary troubadours, this social Joy of the Court is all-important; it is the inspiration and the reward for the correct observance of the courtly code. *Jois* inspires Raimon to repent of his uncourtly behaviour, to turn from deceit and sin and become a *fis amaire* (I, 12–16). The envious man who lacks courtly aspiration sins against the code of *Jois* (XII, 4–8). Feeble-hearted *domnas*, afraid of scandal, leave *Jois* in the lurch (XII, 13–16).

It is with the lady Azalais de Boissezon de Lombers, whom Miraval praises towards the end of his career, between 1203 and 1207, that Raimon achieves his most successful courtly relationship. Lady and troubadour engage themselves in a reciprocal partnership, the lady to grant her protection, companionship and possibly her favour to the troubadour, and the troubadour to increase her fame by all means in his power:

> Vers es q'en autres cavalliers
> Pot chausir e q'ieu no·il sui pars,
> Tant es sos pretz valens e cars.
> Mas tant a d'avinens mestiers
> C'obs es q'el sieu seignoratge
> Ai'un dels adreitz trobadors,
> Que sapch'enanssar sas lauzors
> E·il serva de bon coratge. (xxv, 25–32)

It is true that she can make her choice among other knights and that I am not her equal, so noble and precious is her reputation. But she has so many gracious qualities that she needs to have in her retinue a skilful troubadour who may increase her praise and serve her with a loyal heart.

The *Jois* that the lady Azalais radiates is a summons to happiness at her court. She inspires the courtier to rejoice in courtly display:

> E s'anc nuill jorn fui esforcius
> D'esser adreitz, cortes e gais,
> Eras coven que m'i eslais
> Ab ditz et ab faitz agradius,
> Q'en tal dompn'ai sospeisso
> Qe·l sieu ric, car guizerdo
> Non pot servir nuills hom desavinens,
> Si tot s'es rics e poderos e gens. (xxvi, 9–16)

And if I have ever made an effort to be witty, courtly and gay, I must now throw myself into this with words and deeds that please, for I have set my hopes on a lady whose noble and cherished reward is not to be won by any unaccomplished man, however rich and powerful and handsome he is.

He loves everything and every person at her court:

> Per lieis am fontanas e rius,
> Bos e vergiers e plans e plais,
> Las dompnas e·ls pros e·ls savais,
> E·ls savis e·ls fols e·ls badius
> De la francha regio
> Don ill es e de viro;
> Que tant es lai viratz mos pessamens,
> Qe mais non cuig sia terra ni gens. (41–8)

She makes me love springs and streams, woods, orchards, market gardens and hedges, the ladies and the excellent and despicable men, the wise and the foolish men, and the simpletons, of the noble region where she lives, and the country around: for my thoughts are turned so much in that direction that I do not think that any other land or people exist.

Love that inspires universal benevolence is a courtly commonplace, but joy for Raimon lies in being accepted and
respected at a court where he plays his courtly role and feels
at one with those around him. *Cortesia* that is free from deceit
is the highest virtue and *cortez'ufana*, the splendid gloss of
courtly illusion, is preferable to churlish truth, the ailments
and vices of real life that Guillaume de Lorris was to exclude
from his garden of Love.

The Joy of the Court of Azalais will rejoice and improve no
less a ruler and lover than Pedro II of Aragon:

> S'a Lombers corteja·l reys,
> Tostemps mais er joys ab luy;
> E, si tot s'es sobradreys,
> Per un pretz li·n venran duy:
> Que la cortezi'e·l guays
> De la belha n'Alazais,
> E·l fresca colors ab pel blon
> Fan tot lo segle jauzion.   (XXVII, 41–8)

If the king pays court at Lombers, joy will be with him ever more, and,
although he excels in courtly skills, for one courtly quality that he has,
two will come to him, for the courtly and joyous ways of the beautiful
lady Azalais and her fresh complexion with fair hair make the whole
world rejoice.

The troubadour is not at court merely to compose poetry.
He must uphold this system of praise, courtly splendour and
reputation:

> S'es larcs, cortes et arditz
> E sap servir d'avinen,
> Sos chans qual dona·l defen?
> Vers es que trobars ses als
> Non es proeza cabals
> Ni sol us mestiers valors;
> Pero corteza lauzors,
> Bendigz et onratz bobans
> Es de totz bos pretz enans.   (X, 19–27)

If he is generous, courtly and bold, and knows how to offer pleasing service, what lady can forbid him to sing? It is true that composing in itself
is not excellent prowess and that worth is not a matter of one quality; but
courtly praise, and words of praise and the splendour that brings honour
increase all fine reputations.

Azalais de Boissezon has beauty, skilled conversation and
manners, desire for courtly reputation and understanding of
the *art de plaire* by which this can be won. She is Miraval's ideal

of the *domna*. She offers respite from desire for other women, and from the harshness of life:

> La grans beutatz que pareys
> En·la belha cui homs suj,
> E·l rics pretz q'a totz jorns creys,
> M'a tout domneyar d'autruj;
> Mas us dous esgartz m'atrays
> Vas la belha, don jamais
> Non temsera fam, freg ni son,
> S'agues cor del dig que·m respon.   (xxvii, 25–32)

The great beauty that is apparent in the fair one whose liege man I am, and the noble reputation that increases every day, have taken from me the desire to woo anyone else. But a sweet glance drew me so strongly to this fair lady that I would never fear hunger, cold or care, if I had courage from the reply she gives me.

His feudal submission is complete and he accepts the blame for his lady's sins:

> S'ieu de midons aic ren d'arrap,
> No·ilh vuelh tort ni dreg contendre,
> C'adobatz li sui del rendre,
> Mas juntas e de genolhos,
> Pero, s'ilh plagues que fos dos,
> Molt feira gran cortezia,
> E s'a lieys non platz, estia,
> Qu'eu·n sui batutz plus fort c'ab un vergil!
>
> Menar me pot ab un prim fil
> E·l sieu mezeis tort car vendre,
> Qu'ieu no·m vuelh a lieys defendre,
> Si tot m'en era poderos:
> Que tant sui sieus per qu'es razos
> Que s'elha en ren falhia,
> Que·il colpa deu esser mia,
> Et es ben dreg qe·m torne sus el cap.   (xxviii, 33–48)

If I have taken anything from my lady by force, I will not dispute the rights or wrongs of the case, for I am ready to give it back to her, on my knees with my hands together. Yet if she were pleased to consider this a gift she would act with great courtesy. And if this does not please her, let me be tormented by her more harshly than if I were beaten with a rod.

She can lead me with a fine thread and increase the cost of the wrong she does me, for I do not wish to defend myself against her, even if I had the power to do so. For I am hers so completely that if she sinned in any way, the blame must rightfully be mine and should fall with justice on my head.

With Azalais de Boissezon Raimon is looking for calm waters after his tempestuous affair with *Mais d'amic* who, according to one of his biographies (*razo* C), was Loba de Pennautier. This famous *domna* was also courted by Peire Vidal, who for the *foudatz* of his love for her took the name of wolf (*Lop*), dressed himself in a wolfskin and was hunted on the hills of Cabaret by shepherds and dogs until (half dead) he was carried home, and received with joy and medicaments by Loba and her husband. At least, this is the story in Peire's biographies.[7] Historically Loba may have been Auda de Pennautier, wife of Arnaud d'Aragon, who was probably a knight of the castle of Cabaret a few miles from Miraval.[8]

Whether she was Loba de Pennautier or not, the turbulent, unpredictable *Mais d'amic* enslaved Miraval: 'My lady, you are my guide in everything, for I have folly or wisdom only at your command. My desire is so heartfelt that a year seems like a day, yet long waiting makes me fear, and my song seems senseless to me, for when one woos without deceit, a fixed term of service of three years is a great hardship' (x, 46–54).

When *Mais d'amic* is slandered he offers her encouragement, for reason and truth must triumph over false repute (XII, 25–38), and like an Ovidian lover he will fight courageously in her defence. His service is that of the feudal vassal to his overlord:

> Per q'ieu justa ley m'abric
> Quar no falh en re qu'enprenda,
> Ni a poder que dissenda
> Per se ni per enemic;
> Per so·m ten pres cum soudadier d'Espanha,
> Que qora·s vol m'emprenh en la mesclanha,
> A tot lo sieu voler ai sen
> E non am nulh son malvolen. (XIII, 9–16)

I seek protection with her for she fails in nothing that she undertakes and her power cannot be lessened by herself or by her enemy. So she holds me captive like a mercenary from Spain so that as soon as she wishes I throw myself into the fight, I agree with all that she desires and I love no enemy of hers.

Miraval offers unswerving loyalty only as long as it is matched by that of his lady, whom he watches as closely as he would his feudal lord. Self-seeking hypocrisy is rife:

> Que dompna promet et estrai
> E ditz mainz plazers avinens
> Per tal q'entre las bonas gens
> Vuoill'om totz sos pretz enantir. (xx, 21–4)

227

For a lady makes promises and retracts them and pays charming and pleasing compliments in order that a man will want to praise all her courtly qualities and reputation among good and noble people.

And if his lady gives pleasure and joy to men of excellent reputation, this is her courtly role, and he must endure any grief this causes him (XXII, 17–24).

Miraval welcomes the artificiality of courtly life, the rust and film that for Raimbaut d'Aurenga tarnished the quick brightness of joy. It is better, he says, to live with courtly pretence than churlish truth, and this applies to conversation and song (XXXI, 43–5). Fine dress and appearance is all: 'And the least important gatekeeper who might feel gay and presumptuous enough to dare to wear scarlet cloth would have such a rich reward that he would lie in his cabin in linen from Rheims' (XXXI, 49–54).

The Joy of the Court demands that personal sorrow and uncertainties should be disciplined and concealed:

> Ben aia·l cortes essiens,
> Que tostemps m'aond'enaissi
> Qu'iratz chan e·m deport e·m ri
> Et atressi quan sui jauzens;
> Mas ara·m torn en balansa
> Quan perc sa gran benanansa,
> Adoncs say ieu mostrar de mon solatz
> Qu'ab semblan d'agradatge
> Sai de perda gen cobrir mon dampnatge. (VII, 1–9)

Blessed be courtly knowledge which always helps me so that I sing and delight and laugh when I am sad, just as I do when I rejoice. But now that I fall into uncertainty since I lose the great happiness she gives, I know how to show in my conversation that by affecting pleasure I can gracefully conceal my hurt at this loss.

Amors and *Jovens* are Raimon's guiding principles, but they have both become sober, well-conducted characters. Together they reaffirm courtly gaiety and restore all that moderation and sense (*mesur'e sens*) take away (XXVI, 7–8), but *Jovens* is the allegory of the courtly way of life (XXIV, 31) and *Amors* is the code of courtly behaviour, of wooing, pleasing and rewarding:

> Que d'amor ven gaugz e ven bes,
> E per amor es hom cortes,
> Et amors dona l'art e·l geing
> Per que bos pretz troba manteing. (XXXII, 21–4)

For from love comes enjoyment and happiness, and because of love a man is courtly, and love gives the art and the skill through which true reputation finds support.

The self-conscious gaiety of folly is a part of Raimon's *cortesia*. He instructs Forniers, a former mercenary, in the art of courtliness: 'Be a jongleur and mix wisdom with folly, for a man who is too wise is worth little among men of high reputation' (XLI, 51–6). And Raimon follows his own advice: he desires to possess and lie with his lady before accepting love tokens and wooing her (XXXII, 9–16); he praises jealousy that teaches devotion (XXXII, 32–43); he chooses a lady of little beauty or wealth in order to escape rival suitors (XXXIII, 9–16). Behind the courtly jesting, which has none of the mercurial and melancholy quality of Raimbaut d'Aurenga, Miraval realises that the suitor, wooing and loving within a disciplined convention, must know how to act, like Peire Vidal, with grand folly, and assert some semblance of personal feeling:

> Ben es savis a lei de tos
> Qui drut blasma de follejar;
> C'om, des qe·is vol amesurar,
> Non es puois adreich amoros,
> Mas cel q'en sap far necies,
> Aquel sap d'amor tot qant n'es:
> Eu no·n sai trop ni no m'en feing,
> Ni ja no vuoill c'om m'en esseing.   (XXXII, 25–32)

That man has the wisdom of a boy who blames a lover for acting foolishly, for a lover, as soon as he wants to act moderately, is no longer a skilful lover; but the man who knows how to act like an uncourtly fool knows all that there is in love. For my part, I do not know very much about love, and do not pretend to do so and I do not wish to be taught about it.

When Miraval is faced with betrayal by his lady he can react in a detached, courtly fashion or with violent anger. He can decide to deceive her, and remain at peace with her (XIV, 11–30), or to destroy her reputation. In *Chansoneta farai, Vencut* he attacks his recreant lady for 'selling' her love; he would refuse the Greek Empire if this meant having the reputation of a *cocu*; any man who defends such false love is betraying himself:

> Avol soudad'a midons resseubuda,
> Quar per aver s'es de bon pretz moguda,
> Que, s'ieu saupes per aver fos venguda,
> Ma soudada ne pogr'aver avuda.   (VIII, 21–4)

My lady has received a base payment since she has abandoned fine reputation for the sake of money, for if I had known that she came here for money she could have had payment from me as well.

He reaches a climax of fury:

> Ai! fals escutz, tan leu vos laissatz fendre
> Qu'om de part vos non auza colp atendre,
> Et ai vos o ben en cor a carvendre;
> S'ie·us pugei aut, bas vos farai dissendre (37–40)

Ah! false shield, so easily do you let yourself be split that no one dares to await a blow behind you, and I have it in mind to make you pay dearly for this; if I raised you high, I will cast you down low.

This brutal language has led to equally harsh criticism of Miraval: 'Un troubadour, et un troubadour célèbre pour sa courtoisie, se conduisant comme un goujat! quelle que soit la femme malmenée par lui, ce poète, qui met son art au service de ses rancunes d'amant, joue un rôle odieux.'[9] And A. Jeanroy calls him a 'cynique qui n'a aucunement conscience de sa bassesse'.[10] However, Miraval makes it clear that he attacks his lady because she has sinned against the rules of courtly love, in fact against courtly society. In the poem *Ben aia·l cortes essiens*, which appears to be concerned with the same incident, he says:

> Adoncs muri totz jauzimens
> E tornet Amors en decli,
> Pus domna pres pels ni rossi. (VII, 10–12)

All enjoyment died and Love fell into decline when a lady accepted furs and a horse.

and:

> Falhimens es e vas domnas peccatz,
> Quan domna met uzatge
> Que per aver trameta son messatge. (VII, 16–18)

It is a crime and a sin against ladies, if a lady begins the fashion of sending her message of love for gain.

Raimon sees himself as the *mantenedor* of *pretz* and courtly love:

> Eu no chan per autre sen
> Mas per so qu'amors no bays,
> E que domnas valhan mais
> Per lo mieu essenhamen. (XXIII, 9–12)

I sing for no other reason but that Love may not decline and that ladies may grow in courtly worth through my teaching.

For Miraval, the courtly code of love, *Amors* as a rule of life, is more important than his lady, but nothing is so important as his reputation as undisputed master of the courtly art. Of the moral standards required by the courtly code, the most important is faithfulness and it is this quality by which Miraval recommends himself to his lady. His fidelity, however, lasts only as long as she obeys what he conceives to be the rules of courtly behaviour. If she errs from the courtly path she must be corrected, and she must be willing to listen to advice and to obey a just admonition. Miraval reproaches his lady for insufficient care in the choice of her suitor:

> Dona no pot aver estiers
> Si non ama, pretz e valor;
> Qu'atressi qom li amador
> An mais de totz bos aips sobriers,
> Selha que trop no s'en tria
> En val mais qui la·n castia,
> Adoncs fai mal si mielhs no s'i enpren
> Mas creire deu adreg castiamen.   (XXIV, 17–24)

If she does not love, a lady cannot have reputation or courtly worth. Just as lovers have more good and excellent qualities than other men, so does that lady who does not make her choice among them with sufficient care, increase in worth if she is corrected about this. She acts wrongly if she does not improve in this matter, since she ought to obey a just reproof.

Although his criticisms may bring him accusations of talking too much, he considers it the duty of a true counsellor to keep his lady or his lord from suffering dishonour. He will not cease to blame and fight the uncourtly and unwise actions of which ladies are guilty:

> E s'ieu sui tengutz per parliers,
> Quar a dona ni a senhor
> Non deu cossentir dezonor
> Neguns sos fizels cosselliers,
> Non laissarai q'ieu non dia –
> Q'ieu tostemps non contradia –
> So que faran domnas contra Joven
> Ni·m semblara de mal captenemen.   (XXIV, 25–32)

And even if I am considered a gossip – because no faithful counsellor ought to allow his lady or his lord to suffer dishonour, I will not cease to blame and contest without respite those things which are done by ladies in contravention of 'Youth' and which in my view are acts of evil behaviour.

This attitude exposed Miraval to the charge of being what Raimbaut d'Aurenga had called *cortes ufaniers*. The gibe uttered by the Monk of Montaudon about Miraval (*que·s fai molt cortes*) would indicate as much, and Miraval himself makes frequent reference to the attacks that his attitude draws upon him. He replies by saying that he is not interested in receiving praise from the *domnas de mals talans* or the *desconoissedors* who surround them (x, 6–10). He desires only to be accepted by the best ladies and by those people who are most accomplished in the art of courtly love.

Miraval's *pretz*, his prestige and reputation as a *conoisedor*, were of vital importance to him. If his lady is guilty of uncourtly conduct he will try to correct her, and if this fails he must leave her. The moment of separation has great dangers for the troubadour and he must ensure that his reputation does not suffer unjustly. It is best to part from one's lady on amicable terms. In the poem *S'ieu en chantar soven* (xiv) Miraval has discovered the deception his lady practised on him but will preserve peace with her and seek a lady who will do him more honour. Raimon's attitude at parting from his lady is not out of place in his conception of courtly behaviour. If the final separation from his lady seems likely to lead to recriminations, the troubadour must beware. In the poem *Pueis onguan* he declares his fears: Do you know why I have become the enemy of deceitful women? It is because I am exiled from my lady and know of no guilt except hers? He continues:

> Et en aiso tem n'esser encolpatz
> Que·l tortz sieus sembla vertatz,
> C'als sieus bels digz lo mieus dregz par niens;
> Tant es gaillartz sos bels razonamens! (xxi, 21–4)

And I fear to be blamed about this, for her wrongdoing has the appearance of truth and in the presence of her fine words the rightness of my cause seems not to exist, so clever is the fine defence that she offers.

Since he cannot defend himself against what his lady may say about him, he desires to make some agreement with her by which he will not be unjustly accused:

> Totz acordiers m'en seria onratz;
> Mas no vueill que pueis digatz
> Mieus es lo tortz, quan venra·l partimens,
> C'a las autras en penri'espavens. (37–40)

Any agreement with you would bring me honour, but I do not want you to say afterwards, when it comes to parting, that the blame is mine, for this would frighten the other ladies.

The absence of any Provençal treatise comparable to the *De amore* of Andreas Capellanus must increase interest in the system of courtly behaviour which Miraval can be seen to be advocating in his poems. In any case, Miraval's ideas cannot be lightly dismissed in view of Raimon Vidal's contention that he knew more about love than any other. A general similarity may be seen between Miraval's ideas and those expressed by Andreas Capellanus, and many of the generalisations on love and courtly behaviour which he intersperses in his poems have their counterparts in Books I and II of the *De amore*. There is obviously room to mention only a few of these similarities. Both writers stress the importance of a carefully reasoned approach by the lover to the lady and of the care she must show both in delaying sufficiently and in choosing a true lover: the lady must not be over-praised, else praise becomes worthless, the lady must shun the use of harsh words, must not deceive with false promises and she must not grant her love in exchange for rich gifts. She must desire above all to be renowned as one who does what is worthy of praise.

If a woman should prove unfaithful to her lover, says Andreas, her error should not be tolerated. If she goes back to her former lover after she has enjoyed the embraces of someone else, he will be disgraced. Most pertinent of all, if any woman has mistakenly accepted an unworthy lover, she must strive by all means to correct and improve him. If all her efforts are in vain, she may send him away without fear of blame and never embrace him again. This rule, and it is enlightening in view of Miraval's attitude to his ladies, applies also to the man: *Idem credimus in amatore dicendum, qui erroris umbra deceptus improbo se minus provide obligavit amori.*[11]

It is impossible to know whether Miraval knew of the treatise by Andreas Capellanus or of any other similar treatise which has not survived. His interest in the court affairs of Northern France is shown by the story he wrote, based presumably on the famous history of the Count of Flanders, who had a knight, possibly Walter of Fontaines, put to death, because of the encouragement shown to him by the Count's wife.[12] Miraval may be referring to this incident in his sardonic *sirventes, Aras no m'en puosc plus tardar.*

> Mas eu no·m vuoill far entestar,
> Q'ieu sui tant fis dompnejaire
> E sai ma dompna tant honrar,
> Que si mos seigner ditz que plou
> Eu dic q'aital temps deu faire,
> C'a midonz auria faillit
> Si·n ren desdizia·l marit.   (XXXVIII, 22–8)

But I do not want to have my head beaten, for I am so loyal in my service to my lady and know how to do her such honour that if my lord says that it is raining, I say that the weather must be just like that, for I should have failed my lady if I contradicted her husband in any way at all.

Earlier troubadours were tested by the personal tussle between lust and ideal love (Marcabru and Jaufre Rudel), between courtly joy and the eternal bliss of salvation (Peire d'Alvernhe), and between the desire to find joy as an individual and the social pressure of the 'Joy of the Court' (Raimbaut d'Aurenga and Arnaut Daniel). For Raimon de Miraval the moral battle between lust and Fin'*Amors* and the conflict between the individual and society are resolved by his unquestioning acceptance of *Amors* as a great moral and social law, a straight road (*dreih viatge*) of courtly convention from which any deviation means social ostracism. He woos and battles in the courtly *champ de Mars* to secure happiness and reputation and the survival of *Amors* as a courtly way of life. Miraval is bounded by the walls of the courtly world. He has an idea of the unity of the poet, the external world and feelings of love, which earlier troubadours thought of as *Jois*, but his personal happiness and sense of harmony depend on a secure awareness of his own courtly status in the eyes of his lady and society. Happiness comes when:

> Ma domna et eu et Amors
> Eram pro d'un voler tuich trei...   (XXXV, 10–11)

My lady and I and Love were agreed all three about one desire...

Raimon has no true inner joy of the heart like Bernart de Ventadorn. Although he is given to fits of despair and anger, especially in his earlier poems, he is not *jauzens* or *joyos*, but *gais*, socially happy, rational, detached and wary, with a wry humour about his courtly struggles. Fin'*Amors* is no fount of moral or spiritual goodness, or *fons de bontat*, but the faithful and correct courtly wooing of one *domna* (XVII, 25–32),

> Vas fin'amor fatz esmenda
> Tot al sieu plazer,
> E s'anc passiei son voler,
> Chantan vais autra fazenda,
> A lieys, que de pretz es guitz,
> Me sui juratz e plevitz
> Sos homs litges, marves, de ginolhos,
> Ab cor leyal e de totz enjans blos.　　　(XXII, 9–16)

Towards true Love do I make amends entirely as it may require, and if I have ever transgressed against its desire in singing of other themes, it is to her who is the guide to fine reputation that I have sworn and pledged myself, making absolute submission, as her liege man, on my knees, with a loyal heart and free from all deceit.

When Miraval says in *Bel m'es*, which is his last datable poem:

> Eu non sui drutz mas dompnei,
> Ni non tem pena ni fais,
> Ni·m rancur leu ni m'irais,
> Ni per orguoill no m'esfrei.　　　(XXXVII, 10–13)

I am not a lover but I woo, and I do not fear pain or burden, and I do not easily grow bitter or angry and I am not dismayed by arrogance.

he is rejecting Rudel's qualms about the 'foolish burden' of sensual love, Bernart's desire for escape and 'death', and his own earlier violent feelings about *Mais d'amic*. The poet has become a player on the scene of social love, and courtly values, reason, Ovidian tactics and the search for *pretz* provide the part. In this final courtly role he does not love the physical lady but the ideal image in his mind of her *pretz* and the skill with which she justifies this in society.

As the poetry of Arnaut Daniel is the ultimate expression of the Fin'*Amors* formulated by Marcabru, the songs of Raimon de Miraval are the culmination of the poetic tradition of Bernart de Ventadorn from whom Miraval borrows themes, poetic imagery and rhyme words. Miraval's success represents the triumph of a purely courtly poetry that a 'clus' troubadour would have called 'fragmented'. He represents the victory of the *trobar leu* or clear style of composition and attacks the *clus* style as dark and 'untamed' in its mixture of smooth and harsh sounds and its levels and nuances of meaning:

> Anc trobars clus ni braus
> Non dec aver pretz ni laus,
> Pus fon faitz per vendre
> Contra·ls sonetz suaus
> Conhdetz, aissi cum ieu·ls paus,
> E leus ad aprendre,
> Ab bels ditz clars e gen claus,[13]
> Que per far entendre
> Non cal trop contendre.   (XXXI, 1–9)

Never has dark and untamed poetry deserved to have reputation or praise, since it was composed to be sold, compared to the sweet and graceful melodies such as I compose, which are easy to learn with their fine, clear and well turned words, for to make oneself understood, one should not dispute too much.

The *clus* style depended on a sense of moral or religious conflict within the poet who was aspiring to the highest individual happiness, and on an awareness of deeper levels of meaning to life than the courtly convention. It was an attempt to compose 'integrated' rather than 'fragmented' poetry. In choosing the clear and well-turned phrases of the *trobar leu* Miraval is rejecting the disturbing, unexpected nuances of meaning which we find in Arnaut Daniel, and is attuned to the importance of communal *Jois*, the well-being and happiness of courtly society, rather than to any quest for individual happiness. Miraval's smooth conventional nature imagery, his meadows, gardens and rose trees, reflects this desire for social harmony in contrast to the harsh natural obstacles, rocks, floods, marshes, mountains, in the poetry of Arnaut Daniel. Raimon's poetry accords with the tastes of a noble society which in its splendour and luxury walled itself in from contact with the rough reality of life outside. Even when Béziers, Carcassonne, Beaucaire, and Miraval itself, had fallen to the Crusading army of Simon de Montfort, Raimon's appeal for help to Pedro II of Aragon, sent shortly before the fateful battle of Muret, is added almost as an afterthought to a love song which is both Raimon's swan song and that of the courts of Southern France:

> Chanssos, vai me dir al rei
> Cui jois guid'e vest e pais,
> Q'en lui non a ren biais,
> C'aital cum ieu vuoill lo vei;

Ab que cobre Montagut
E Carcasson'el repaire,
Pois er de pretz emperaire,
E doptaran son escut
Sai Frances e lai Masmut.

Dompn'ades m'avetz valgut
Tant que per vos sui chantaire;
E no·n cuiei chanson faire
Tro·l fieu vos agues rendut
De Miraval q'ai perdut.

Mas lo reis m'a covengut
Que·l cobrarai anz de gaire,
E mos Audiartz Belcaire:
Puois poiran dompnas e drut
Tornar el joi q'ant perdut. (XXXVII, 55–73)

Song, go on my behalf and tell the king whom joy guides and clothes and nourishes, that in him there is nothing awry, for I see him as I desire to see him. Provided that he recovers Montégut and returns to Carcassonne, he will then be the emperor of fine reputation, and the French will fear his shield over here, and the Moslems likewise over there.

My lady, you have always helped me so much that it is for you that I still sing, even though I did not expect to compose a song about you until I had given back to you the fief of Miraval which I have lost.

But the king had promised me that I will recover it shortly, and that my Audiart will recover Beaucaire. Then ladies and lovers will be able to return to the joy that they have lost.

But the Joy of the Court was not to be found again.

Late Troubadours

9

Guilhem de Montanhagol,
Peire Cardenal and Guiraut Riquier

ABOUT 1230 THE TROUBADOUR Bernart Sicart de Marvéjols grieved for the defeated South: 'All day I live in
sadness and sorrow. At night I sigh, awake and asleep.
Wherever I turn I hear courtly people crying out "My lord",
humbly, to the Frenchman.'

> Ai! Toloza e Proensa
> E la terra d'Argensa,
> Bezers e Carcassey
> Quo vos vi e quo·us vey![1]

Alas! Toulouse and Provence and the land of Argence, Béziers and
Carcasses, how I saw you and how I see you!

What Bernart Sicart 'saw' was the splendid, worldly, easy-
going, courtly society that was shattered by the Albigensian
Crusade. What he 'sees' and laments is the South after the
Treaty of Paris of 1229, with its native aristocracy largely dis-
possessed, its courtly society almost destroyed, its independence destined to disappear at the death of the reigning count
of Toulouse and the Inquisition established to root out the
Cathar heresy which saw all existence as divided between the
world of matter, the creation of a God of evil, and the world
of the Spirit created by the true, infinitely good and perfect
God.

By 1230 the French king and the Pope were reclaiming the
lands and minds which had almost slipped from their grasp.
In 1100 the king of France had ruled with difficulty a thin
strip of territory from the Seine to the Loire, and his nominal
vassal the count of Toulouse had been rich in lands from the
Garonne to the Rhône, the Pyrenees to Cahors, and Narbonne
to Le Puy. For some seventy years papal legates and mission-

aries, including St Bernard and St Dominic, had visited, admonished and cajoled the heretical towns, villages and castles of the South, but in 1209, after the assassination of his legate Raimon de Castelnau, the Pope preached a Crusade against Southern heresy. The once powerful house of Toulouse lost its land and wealth to a handful of knights from the North who were supported by the mighty influence of the French king, and after bitter and sporadic fighting for forty years, the South was finally 'annexed' to the North and the political and geographical pattern of Renaissance and modern France began to evolve.

The Crusading armies were hastening the fall of a society in decline. The sophisticated and worldly civilisation of the South was inspired by a passive spirit of political, social and spiritual anarchy, a refusal to be bound absolutely by one set of rules or conventions, and a general inclination towards an equable existence on several planes of thought and behaviour. A mosque, synagogue, place of heretical worship and a Christian church could exist in the same town. Moors could teach as professors in the universities and Jews could hold high administrative office. A knight might live on the plane of feudal fighting, of robbery and the abduction of rich heiresses, on the mannered courtly plane of respect for the *domna*, or on the conjugal plane, and only rarely, as with the tragic Eudoxia of Constantinople[2] or Miraval's comic opera rejection of Gaudairenca, do we see these different codes of behaviour in conflict.

The readiness of the South to accept new ideas and to fashion new conventions of courtly or religious thinking, to encourage troubadours of all social classes at court and Cathar and Waldensian priests in the towns and villages, had its reverse side. The South was choosing to be divided, politically, socially and religiously, into many segments. In the North the French king, backed by the Church and the abbey of St Denis, ruled as a feudal monarch. In the South, with its remnants of Roman law and wide trade in the Mediterranean, the feudal oath was held so lightly that a vassal would support the enemy of his overlord rather than the overlord himself. The feudal dependencies of Toulouse were a patchwork of 'enclaves', which owed allegiance to foreign rulers. The lords of Miraval about 1200 did homage for their lands to the viscount of Carcassonne, then to the King of Aragon, and then finally to the count of Toulouse. The King of Aragon, whom Miraval called 'our king', ruled most of Provence and frequently visited his vassals in Languedoc. The Church was concerned more with temporal pleasure and aggrandisement than with pastoral care or support for the house of Toulouse.

Raimon VI of Toulouse drifted in a society which ignored the idea of political order. He could subdue neither his vassals nor the city of Toulouse. He allowed his rival and subordinate, the young viscount of Béziers and Carcassonne, to be murdered and his lands to be usurped by the Crusaders, and at the critical battle of Muret in 1213 he hung back when his allies the Aragonese were overrun by de Montfort's swiftly manœuvring cavalry. The South was disrupted by the strife of the feudal barons, by the disputes of the towns against the barons, and of the laity against the clergy. An attempt to destroy brigandage and reform the social order in favour of the poorer classes was made by the *Confréries de la Paix*. These were societies of hooded men or *capuciés* which spread rapidly through all the provinces of Central and Southern France from December 1182 to April 1183, until the Church and the nobility grew alarmed and had them hunted down and destroyed.[3]

This internal sickness of the South is apparent to our eyes, but to the contemporary it could rarely have suggested the destruction to come. War for pillage and booty, as we see from Bertran de Born,[4] was a recognised function of feudal life, and was balanced by the prosperity and stability of the great cities in which feudal distinctions were blurred. The urban knight would fight in the town army and unite with the patrician burghers to govern the city. He might be absorbed into the class of wealthy merchants, who, for their part, might attend at court and, in rare cases, be knighted.

The count of Toulouse had little power in the city in which he held court. Toulouse had a long tradition of government by Consuls and in the elections of 1202 the popular party of burghers and artisans came to power and started a war of aggression in the Toulousain. Neighbouring lords and towns were forced to accept the taxes imposed by Toulouse and the transformation of the Toulousain, which the Consuls began to call the Fatherland of Toulouse, 'in tolosana patria', into a form of city state was only prevented by the onset of the

Albigensian Crusade. This accession to power of the popular party in Toulouse is symptomatic of the rise of the 'new rich' who, unlike the feudal knights, profited vastly from inflation and speculation in town property.

Economic evolution in the second half of the twelfth century had outdated the political and judicial system of the South. The great trading towns, such as Montpellier and Marseille, broke their feudal ties by 1150, and grew immensely wealthy from trade with Aragon and with the Middle East, where their merchants enjoyed concessional areas, streets and churches in Jerusalem, Acre and other cities.[5]

The Albigensian Crusade was a disaster for the troubadours, but their art was poised for decline. Their poetic technique and ideas had been fully developed by Arnaut Daniel within the constraints of the courtly convention, and the weighty tradition of the *canso* as the highest genre, set to music on the highest subject in the highest style, discouraged poetic innovation which might have rejuvenated their art. Troubadour poetry was stifling in its fame; its language was recognised as supreme for cultivated lyric poetry in the vernacular,[6] but its terminology had lost its pristine shine. The troubadours still sang of *pretz*, *valors* and *Jois*, but to an audience which no longer prized these values actively as a way of life. The rational, scholastic and didactic mentality of the thirteenth century, influenced by Aristotelian and Averroist thinking in the North and the strict discipline of the Inquisition in the South, touched and petrified their art, and their patrons, increasingly from the merchant class, looked to them for moral instruction. Joy is displaced by *Mesura*. Wisdom throws off the cap and bells and the joyous melancholy that had shone through the 'folly' of Raimbaut d'Aurenga's upside-down world and Arnaut Daniel's tussles with air, water, earth and the fire within. Many troubadours sought patronage in the courts of Spain and Italy. Those who remained clutched at the hope of an ordered life.

The troubadour Guilhem de Montanhagol, a knight of Toulouse, was a last-ditch fighter for the courtly virtues, and attempted to recreate his own world according to his vision of the golden past, *lai el tems qu'era gais*, before the Crusade. He fought in Spain in 1238 for James I of Aragon and gave his ardent support to Raimon VII of Toulouse as the last hope of

Southern independence, lamenting his unsuccessful attempts
to remarry and sire a male heir and the failure of the 1242
uprising against the French.

In Montanhagol's poetry the courtly virtues move out
from behind the walls which had been demolished by social
and political change and become the essential virtues of
everyday life. The delectable anarchy of living on separate
planes is replaced by a rational vision of an integrated and
stable life which gives peace and contentment to the individual and society. The key to this life is *mesura*. Through
mesura, the estates of society, clergy, nobles and peasants, must
recognise and fulfil their duty to one another. Through *mesura*
the individual finds self-knowledge, rejects pretence, hypocrisy and illusion, and lives harmoniously with himself and
others: 'let the man who wishes to please others, honour each
man according to his due, in word and deed. Let him not be
arrogant or captious, but let him have moderation and
restraint within himself, and let him be the same in his heart
as in his appearance' (XIII, 1–6).[7]

Courtly excellence and Christian virtue go hand in hand.
Since God Himself was made man, He must desire that man,
made in His image, should see his true dignity and aspire to
excellence, praise and renown.

> Quar Dieus vol pretz e vol lauzor,
> e Dieus fo vers hom, qu'ieu o sai,
> e hom que vas Dieu res desfai,
> e Dieus l'a fait aitan d'onor
> qu'al sieu semblan l'a fag ric e maior
> e pres de si mais de neguna re,
> doncx ben es fols totz hom que car no·s te:
> e que fassa en aquest segle tan
> que sai e lai n'aya grat, on que·s n'an.   (I, 10–18)

For God desires reputation and praise and God was, in truth, a man, as I
well know; any man who goes against God in anything, when God has
done him such honour that He has made him in His likeness noble and
greater and closer to Him than any other creature...any such man who
does not hold himself dear is indeed a fool and sinner. Let every man act
in this world so that, wherever he may go, he may be rewarded here, or
there, in the other world.

Since the worldly life that is disciplined by courtly virtue
is pleasing to God, let the Dominican Inquisitors, observing
mesura, bring the strays back to the fold with fair and just

words, free from anger, but let them not attack the finery with which the *domna* asserts her quality as *domna*. No man or woman who is free from pride will lose God's grace through elegant dress, nor will priests win salvation merely with black habits and white smocks (I, 21–36).

> A! per que vol clercx belha vestidura
> ni per que vol viure tan ricamen,
> ni per que vol belha cavalgadura
> qu'el sap que Dieus volc viure paubramen?
> Ni per que vol tan l'autrui n'i enten?
> Qu'el sap que tot quan met ni quan despen,
> part son manjar e son vestir vilmen,
> tolh als paubres, si no men la Scriptura.   (XIV, 17–24)

Alas, why does a cleric desire fine raiment and why does he want to live so richly, and why does he desire fine horses when he knows that God wished to live in poverty? And why does he desire so much what others own, and strive to get this when he knows that all that he spends or fritters away, beyond his food and lowly garments, is stolen from the poor, if the Scriptures do not lie.

God gives the fruits of the earth to men to use properly, to live in elegant style and provide wealth and food for others, and He will punish the man who fails in this duty (V, 35–6).

Love brings honour and joy and demands that a man should live up to the virtue within him (XI, 1–9). Montan-hagol is conventionally ardent – he will die if his lady delays too long – but Love for him is no quest for joy for its own sake as a bastion against the deceit and tarnish of life. He is not escaping from the world into Love. The Joy of the Court has become the Joy of the society in which he moves. Happiness lies in playing one's part in a social order established by God, and showing virtue and kindness to others. The courtly man must woo a lady, but must seek to advance her honour a hundred times more than his own (XI, 26–7). The true lover must show *benevolentia*, in Cicero's sense:

> qu'amors non es res mas aysso qu'enansa
> so que ama e vol ben lialmen,
> e qui·n quier als lo nom d'amor desmen.   (XI, 16–18)

for love is nothing else than the wish to advance and benefit that which it loves and for which it truly feels affection; and anyone who seeks anything different from this, denies the name of love.

In a casuistical debate whether the lover should know his

lady's mind or *vice versa* Montanhagol attacks Sordello for his cardboard image of his lady for whom he languishes night and day. Both lady and lover, he says, should be sincere and independent and honest according to the virtue or deceit they see in others. He abjures courtly pretence...'it is more important for you, Sordello, to know the heart and all the thoughts of the lady for whom you sing' (III, 49–60). In any case, he adds, any lady will be a fool to trust you.[8]

The true lover who is guided by *mesura* will be rewarded by God in this world and the next (XI, 35–6), for God desires that each man should seek reputation, praise and honour — and these, in the view of Montanhagol, must be won through *Amors*. *Mesura*, the rational control of desire by which innate virtue flowers, had inspired Marcabru's ideal of *Fin'Amors*, but Montanhagol declares openly that 'from love chastity comes forth':

> Ben devon li amador
> de bon cor servir amor,
> qar amors non es peccatz,
> anz es vertutz qe·ls malvatz
> fai bons, e·ll bo·n son meillor,
> e met hom'en via
> de ben far tot dia;
> e d'amor mou castitatz,
> qar qi·n amor ben s'enten
> non pot far qe pueis mal renh.   (XII, 11–20)

Lovers ought indeed to serve love with a good heart, for love is no sin but the virtue which makes the wicked good, and the good better, and it sets a man on the path of good deeds every day. And from love chastity comes forth, for if a man aspires entirely to love he cannot then act badly.

What does Montanhagol mean by *castitatz*? Probably not 'chastity' in its modern sense, but the control and ordering of sexual desire. Such an idea was not new in the poetry of profane love. Both in Ibn Hazm's *Tawq* and the didactic work of his predecessors such as Ibn Dâwûd, and in the eleventh-century Arab poets in Spain, the practice of a chaste love (*al-hawa al-'udri*), implying a self-imposed renunciation, is a sign of a man's good character and breeding. A similar idea is defined by Andreas Capellanus in his treatise *De amore*, which was written about 1186 at the behest of Marie de Champagne. Speaking of *amor purus*, in contrast to *amor mixtus*, he says: 'it [pure love] consists in the contemplation of the mind and the affection of the heart; it goes as far as the kiss and the embrace and the modest contact with the nude lover ...This love is distinguished by being of such virtue that from it arises all excellence of character, and no injury comes from it, and God sees very little offense in it. No maiden can ever be corrupted by such a love, nor can a widow or a wife receive any harm or suffer any injury to her reputation.'[9]

Montanhagol's idea of *castitatz* is probably very close to that of Thomas Aquinas in his *Summa Theologica* where he defines *castitas* as a virtue to which belongs the moderated exercise of the bodily organs according to the judgment of reason and the choice of the will. *Castitas* for Thomas Aquinas does not mean the Christian idea of complete sexual abstinence which he calls *perfecta abstinentia*, the suppression of sexual pleasures.[10]

Montanhagol's lady, although fashioned by God:

> Pero be·us dic que mielhs creire deuria
> que sa beutatz desus del cel partis,
> que tan sembla obra de paradis
> qu'a penas par terrenals sa conhdia.　(VIII, 27–30)

But I tell you that I am persuaded and convinced that her beauty came down from Heaven, for she seems so clearly the creation of Paradise that her grace scarcely appears to be of this world.

must also practise rational control and judgment in love.

> Trop fai son dan dona que·s do ricor,
> 　　quant hom d'amor
> 　la comet, ni·s n'irays,
> que plus bel li es que sofra preyador
> 　　que si d'alhor
> 　　era·l peccatz savais.
> Que tals n'i a, quays qu'om non o creiria
> ab que fos dig, qu'en fan assais fraydis,
> per qu'amors falh entr'elas e vilsis,
> quar tenon mal en car lor carestia.[11]　(VIII, 41–50)

A lady harms herself greatly by angry or arrogant behaviour when she is entreated in love, for it is better for her to be patient with a humble suitor than that base sin should come to her from elsewhere. For there are ladies, although this were unbelievable even if it were spoken aloud, who behave like tramps. And to love is destroyed and cheapened in their company because they fail to cherish their true worth.

The lady, recognising her role as *domna*, must guard her integrity and sense of dearness to herself (*carestia*). Love must be confined within the discipline of courtly *castitatz*, for the alternative is churlish conduct worthy of vagabonds, the sexual promiscuousness against which Marcabru had fulminated exactly a century before.

Beneath his contemplative and lightly scholastic attitudes Montanhagol reveals a selfless good will which rejects self-indulgence and seeks a happiness that is integrated in Christian belief and social and political order. His merits were evident to his contemporaries, and his brother-in-law, Pons Santolh of Toulouse, laments his death: 'pure and good, tempered by your sense of moderation, pleasing to all. . .like a wise and upright man, devoted entirely to righteousness, doing all the wise things that you taught, did you live in this world. . .and gave us an example of saintly living with. . .your noble, constant and sure knowledge. Your sense of what is right made you the head and the father of the troubadours. . .' (edn Ricketts, Appendix II, 17–26).

Although he composed without adornment, in the *leu* style, Montanhagol was attempting to be a 'whole' poet, to reconcile the present disorder of life with his vision of the past, to condemn injustice and immoderation and gain happiness on earth and salvation in Heaven. His verse gives practical expression to the ideal of the good life[12] based on *Fin'Amors* that Marcabru had visualised, and brings into the open Marcabru's enigmatic analogies between this way of life and the Christian ethos (XI, 28–36).

Two other leading troubadours of the thirteenth century, however, pay little heed to Montanhagol's equation of courtly and Christian values, and reject profane love in favour of love of God, Christ and the Virgin Mary. The first of these poets is Peire Cardenal, who lived from about 1180 to 1278, 'was of noble birth and was destined to be a canon at Le Puy, but feeling gay, handsome and young, left the clerical life and composed many fine songs'. Although he spent many years at the court of Toulouse and was probably secretary (or *scriba*) to count Raimon VI,[13] he rejected *Amors* and courtly values humorously and decisively: 'Now I can praise myself, for Love does not stop me from eating or sleeping, I do not feel cold or heat, do not yawn, sigh or go a-roaming in the night. . .I am not thrown upside-down, nor robbed by it. . . and my heart is not stolen from me' (I, 1–20). 'The man who defeats disloyal desire wins a greater victory than the conquest of a hundred cities' (I, 31–40). Peire has loved once, 'and would know how to love again' (III), but he turns his back on Love with its deceits and false values.

Peire offers his whole devotion to God who keeps his bow bent to the task of punishing or rewarding vice or virtue (LXIX, 46–50). In a series of brilliant poems he chastises hypocrisy and social injustice, and in *Jhesus Cristz, nostre salvaire* (LV) shows compassion for the poor. He preaches love of God that demands all the strength of one's body and soul (*Predicator*, LXV) and expressed this in a remarkable song to the Virgin, *Vera vergena, Maria* (XXXVIII).

The other great troubadour who sang to the Virgin Mary was Guiraut Riquier, who was born in Narbonne about 1230, probably of humble origins, and died in 1292. He composed for the king of Castile from 1270 to 1279 and for Henry II of Rodez, an enlightened patron of contemporary poetry, from 1280 to 1285, but he complained of the dearth of patronage in a society which preferred the 'classic' songs of earlier troubadours or the scabrous effusions of *joglars*.

In his songs to *Belh Deport*, who may have been an imaginary *domna* or the viscountess of Narbonne, he sees *Fin'Amors* as the way to positive moral health, noble virtues and desires, and the furtherance of his lady's reputation. The greatest sin for both lady and lover is self-pride. Troubadours, he says, are favoured by God and the mark of this favour is the wisdom and knowledge (*saber*) which they display in their divine mission as poets. His lament for the death of *Belh Deport* (*vers* XIV, 40) may be an allegory of the end of courtly loving,[14] or the final personal stroke which convinced him that as a poet he had come too late to a world which was no longer interested in *Fin'Amors*.

Riquier shares the belief of Montanhagol and Sordello[15] that the true courtly man must be equally pleasing in the sight of God and the world, but he does not attempt to reconcile *Fin'Amors* with religious love. He sees *Amors* as an autonomous profane ethic and rejects it in favour of Christian love of God. The occasion of this rejection was a contest arranged in 1280 at the court of Rodez. Four troubadours were asked for an interpretation of Guiraut de Calanson's poem *Celeis cui am de cor e de saber* on the theme of the three parts of love.[16] Riquier's commentary (Epistle VIII) was adjudged the winning contribution and gained him the award of a diploma. He defines three sorts of love:

heavenly love, natural love of kinsfolk, and carnal love which is the lowest third of love. This love has irresistible power over kings, princes and marquesses. It is unbridled, devoid of clear judgment, listening only to desire and not to reason. In the beginning lovers find it pleasing, afterwards come torments, cares, sorrows. This love disappears once it has been fulfilled. Of the five doors which a man must pass to reach it, the first four are desire, the humble entreaty, service and the kiss. If one stayed there, love would not die. But the lover goes on to the fifth door which is the act, through which love dies.

The highest love is love of God which Riquier desires most of all, 'peace without end, love without restriction, perfect bliss without harm, pleasure without sadness and joy without desire'. May God deliver him from the lowest third of Love.[17]

Riquier's rejection of profane love as sensual *Amors* probably reflects the state of mind of the courtly elite at Rodez who awarded him their prize. The fine nuances and gradations of early Fin'*Amors*, the joy of the imagination and the spirit, are coldly bypassed by the ageing Riquier and a society which prefers the clear Augustinian choice between the sensual and the spiritual life. Not so did Peire d'Alvernhe choose love of God, and feel the wrench at losing the joy of the court. Riquier's rejection of *Amors* is the stern and absolute renunciation of Folquet de Marseille, who as Bishop of Toulouse did penance when he heard the verse of his earlier days sung at table.[18] Riquier, having lost *Belh Deport*, denies the ideal of the *domna* together with all the temptations of Eve, and turns his song to praise of the Virgin Mary, a genre which was to become supreme in the poetic contest of the *Jocs Florals* founded at Toulouse in 1323 by the seven bourgeois members of the consistory of *Gai Saber*.[19]

Troubadour song was born and nurtured in a noble society which believed optimistically in the capacity of man as an individual to seek and find happiness on all the levels of experience. It had the misfortune to decline in France in an age when didactic moralising, scholastic influences, and rigorous religious dogma grasped and moulded it into a lifeless existence. In Riquier's day the hope of a return to *cortesia*, which had sustained Montanhagol, had vanished. Fin'*Amors* as a rationalisation of the conflict between sensual desire and spiritual aspiration had previously been related, though enigmatically, to the Christian rejection of the carnal in favour of the spiritual. Once Christian teaching, supported by the Inquisition, had defeated heresy in the South of France, and war and economic and social change had destroyed the function of *cortesia* as a high moral code of behaviour based on profane love, Fin'*Amors* had no possible chance of survival in troubadour poetry. Already in the society for which Miraval composed it had lost much of its exalted status as a guide to moral happiness. Both Fin'*Amors* and Christian teaching, the *domna* and the Virgin Mary, had offered a refuge and security to the reflective troubadours of the twelfth century whose imagination and 'coloured' imagery lightly embraced both the profane and the religious ideal. After the fall from courtly favour, soon after 1 200, of their evocative poetry, and the decay, during and after the Albigensian Crusade, of the courtly society itself, the choice for the late thirteenth-century troubadour in France was simple. The sole refuge for the spirit must lie in love of God and the Virgin Mary. Fin'*Amors* and the moral values of *cortesia* were confined to the didactic treatises;[20] *Jovens*, which in the late twelfth century, in Bertran de Born and Miraval, referred to social behaviour rather than innate virtue, vanished; *Jois*, which had begun as the limitless soaring aspiration to the *summum bonum* of personal happiness and by 1 200 had been thinned down in the *trobar leu* to the communal Joy of the Court, disappeared in its secular form from troubadour poetry. It was left to the poet of *Flamenca*, about 1 270,[21] and to the great Italians such as Guittone d'Arezzo, to see troubadour ideas on love in the round, from the highest *sen* of exalted, mystical love to the mannered wooing of the exalted lady, and the *foudatz* of the sensual romp, the burlesque that would lead to Cervantes.

Appendix 1

Chronological table

711 Invasion of Spain by N. African Berbers.
732 Charles Martel defeats Moors at Old Poitiers (Tours).
793 Narbonne finally freed from Moslem domination.
929–1031 Great era of Moslem rule in Spain under the Khalifs.
967–70 Gerbert of Aurillac studies arithmetic, music, astronomy and geometry in Spain, and teaches at Rheims from 972 to 982.
993–1030 Guilhem the Great, III Count of Poitou, V Duke of Aquitaine.
994–1040 Odilon Abbot of Cluny.
c. 1000 Surviving verse fragment of a Provençal life of Boethius.
1006–28 Fulbert, Bishop of Chartres.
1017–35 Canute the Great of Denmark, King of England.
1019 Marriage of Guilhem the Great, III Count of Poitou, to Agnes of Burgundy.
1022 Ibn Hazm summarises Hispano-Arabic theories of love in his *Tawq al-Hamama*, 'The Dove's Neck-ring'.
1043 Marriage of Ala (Agnes), daughter of Agnes of Burgundy, to the Emperor Henry III.
c. 1076–1154 Gilbert de la Porrée, Platonist pupil of Bernard of Chartres, Chancellor of Chartres 1124–41, Bishop of Poitiers 1142–54.
1080–1145 William of Conches, pupil of Bernard of Chartres, tutor to Henry of Anjou, later Henry II of England.
1086–1127 Guilhem IX Duke of Aquitaine VII Count of Poitou b. 1071.
1086 Compilation of Domesday Book.
c. 1090 Oxford version of *La Chanson de Roland*.
1099 The Crusaders establish the kingdom of Jerusalem.
1101 Guilhem IX Duke of Aquitaine takes the cross.
1115–53 St Bernard (b. 1091), first Abbot of Clairvaux.
1121 Condemnation of Abelard at Soissons.
c. 1138–c. 1150 Marcabru fl.
c. 1140 Cercamon fl.
1144 Rebuilding of Chartres Cathedral, dedicated to the Virgin, begins.

c. 1145–80 Bernart de Ventadorn fl.
1147–8 The Second Crusade.
c. 1147 Jaufre Rudel fl.
1148 Death of William of Saint Thierry.
1150–80 Peire d'Alvernhe fl.
1152 Marriage of Henry of Anjou to Eleanor of Aquitaine.
1152–90 Reign of Frederick Barbarossa.
1154–89 Henry II King of England.
1160–c. 1180 Peire Rogier fl.
1160–70 Beroul composes the first half of the extant fragment of his *Roman de Tristran*.
1160–70 Thomas composes his *Roman de Tristan*.
c. 1160–c. 1190 Marie de France fl.
1170 Murder of Thomas Becket.
1170 Peter Waldo begins to preach at Lyons.
c. 1165–c. 1200 Guiraut de Bornelh fl.
1170–c. 1181 Chrétien de Troyes fl.
1173 Death of Raimbaut d'Aurenga, Count of Orange (b. c. 1146).
1175–80 Andreas Capellanus fl.
1179–95 Folquet de Marseille fl., Abbot of Toronet 1201, Bishop of Toulouse 1205, friend and protector of St Dominic. d. 1231.
1180–c. 1206 Peire Vidal fl.
1181–97 Bertran de Born fl.
1183 Death of Henry the Young King, eldest son of Henry II.
c. 1185–1213 Raimon de Miraval fl.
1189–92 The Third Crusade.
1189–99 Richard I King of England.
1194–1222 Raimon VI Count of Toulouse.
c. 1200 Arnaut Daniel fl.
c. 1200–78 Peire Cardenal (b. c. 1180) fl.
1204 The Fourth Crusade sacks Constantinople.
1206 Esclarmonda of Foix becomes a Cathar in public ceremony at Fanjeaux.
1206 St Dominic and Diego of Osma begin to preach against heresy at Montpellier. In Nov. 1206 Innocent III orders groups of preaching friars to do likewise.
1209 The Albigensian Crusade begins. Massacre of Béziers. Capture of Carcassonne. Election of Simon IV de Montfort as leader of the Crusade.
1213 Battle of Muret. Defeat of Toulouse and Aragon by Simon de Montfort's Crusading army. Death of Pedro II of Aragon.
1215 Fourth Lateran Council. Simon de Montfort is confirmed in his possession of 'territory conquered from the heretics'.
1218 Simon IV de Montfort is killed besieging Toulouse.
1222–49 Raimon VII Count of Toulouse.

1229 Treaty of Paris; Count Raimon VII of Toulouse does penitence at Notre Dame de Paris.

c. 1230 Guillaume de Lorris composes *Le Roman de la Rose*.

c. 1230–
after 1292 Guiraut Riquier.

1233–c. 1258 Guilhem de Montanhagol fl.

1234 Inquisition (inaugurated in 1233) becomes active in Toulouse.

c. 1235–94 Guittone d'Arezzo.

1237–41 Mongol invasion of Europe.

1242 Raimon VII of Toulouse campaigns unsuccessfully against French forces in the South.

1244 Capture of Montségur and mass burning of Cathar 'Perfects' of both sexes.

1249 Alphonse de Poitiers, brother of Louis IX king of France and husband of Jeanne, sole heir of Raimon VII of Toulouse, becomes Count of Toulouse. Effective political union of South with French crown.

1265–1321 Dante Alighieri.

c. 1270 Jean de Meung composes his continuation of *Le Roman de la Rose*.

c. 1270 The romance of *Flamenca* written.

1274 Death of St Thomas Aquinas.

1304–74 Petrarch.

1305–14 Clement V Pope. Papacy transferred to Avignon.

1323 Institution of poetic concourse of the *Jocs Florals* by the Consistory of *Gai Saber* at Toulouse.

1324 First *Jocs Florals* held at Toulouse.

1337 Hundred Years' War begins.

c. 1337–
after 1404 Jean Froissart.

c. 1340–1400 Geoffrey Chaucer.

1353 Boccaccio finishes the *Decameron*.

1356 *Leys d'Amors*, compendium of rules of grammar and composition of poetry in Provençal, promulgated by Consistory of *Gai Saber*.

A short glossary of poetic and courtly terms

Chansons de toile (sewing songs). Sometimes called *chansons d'histoire*. Short Northern French love-songs in *langue d'oïl*, usually in assonance. Popular in origin, they are influenced by courtly terms and motifs. The characters, usually noblewomen, long for the return of their absent or disdainful lover.

Congé. A poem of leave-taking, from one's native town, from Love, or from life. More common in the North of France than in troubadour poetry.

Conoissensa. The power of discrimination.

Coq-à-l'âne. Nonsense verse concealing satire beneath apparent incoherence, which flourished in France in the sixteenth century.

Cortesia. The sum of all the courtly virtues and their expression in social behaviour.

Devinalh. A riddle poem which might be solved by another poem, or 'key', possibly with a religious interpretation.

Fatrasie. A Northern French rhymed nonsense poem with humorous and sometimes satirical intention.

Foudatz. Folly; mockery of convention; surrender to emotion and refusal to obey *mesura*.

Gap. A poem, sometimes in bawdy style, of self-praise, challenge or confrontation. The word derives from Old Norse *gabb* 'mockery'. *Gabar* in Old Provençal has the meaning of 'self-mockery', 'vain boasting', 'exaggeration' and 'excessive praise'.

Joc partit or *partimen.* A poem in the form of a debate, in which an adversary is offered a choice of argument and the proposer accepts the choice that is rejected.

Jovens. Youthfulness and generosity of spirit; behaviour epitomised by this.

Mesura. The rational faculty of being able to follow the course of action most suited to the demands of social and courtly convention and to the talents, aspiration and quality of the individual (as revealed through *conoissensa*); moderation, the mean between too much and too little.

Pastorela. A poem about the attempted seduction of a shepherdess by praise, gifts and promises. Related to Virgil's *Bucolics*, it provided light relief to the courtly *canso* and flourished in the North and South of France in the twelfth and thirteenth centuries. In a different type of poetry, composed frequently at Arras, the poet describes the rustic merrymaking of shepherds and shepherdesses, or of artisans on a picnic.

Pretz. Courtly social reputation.

Razo. The theme or subject-matter of a song.

Sirventes. A moralising poem, usually of blame, or a poem concerned with impending war or deeds of war, or incidents of everyday life. Probably of pre-courtly origin, it could use the rhyme-scheme and melody of a *canso*, and a less exalted vocabulary than that of the love-song.

Tenso. A poem in the form of a debate, usually on a topic of love casuistry.

Trobar. The art of composing words and music.

Trobar clus, or 'closed style'. A term applied to troubadour poetry which contained different levels of meaning and words which evoked extra nuances of meaning. This term was also applied in the later twelfth century to a debased form of this style which was intentionally obscure and possibly void of meaning.

Trobar leu, or 'clear, easy style of composition' which was generally used for courtly songs.

Trobar ric, or 'rich style' in which emphasis was laid on the evocative sound and meanings of individual words, intricate rhyme-schemes, and concise use of language.

Trouvère. Northern French counterparts of the troubadours. They composed in the *langue d'oïl*, and in ideas and the technique of lyric composition they were often deeply influenced by the troubadours.

Valors. Innate moral worth, usually in a courtly and not a Christian sense.

Abbreviations

AMid	Annales du Midi
ASNSL	Archiv für das Studium der neueren Sprachen und Literaturen
CCMed	Cahiers de civilisation médiévale
CN	Cultura Neolatina
DVE	De Vulgari Eloquentia
FiR	Filologia romanza now Filologia e letteratura
FS	French Studies
GRM	Germanisch-Romanische Monatsschrift
MA	Moyen Age
MAe	Medium Aevum
MedS	Mediaeval Studies
MLR	Modern Language Review
NMi	Neuphilologische Mitteilungen
PL	Patrologia Latina
R	Romania
RF	Romanische Forschungen
RLLO	Revue de langue et littérature d'oc
RLR	Revue des langues romanes
SM	Studi medievali
SMV	Studi mediolatini volgari
Sp	Speculum
SP	Studies in Philology
ZFSL	Zeitschrift für französische Sprache und Literatur
ZRP	Zeitschrift für romanische Philologie

NOTES

INTRODUCTION

1 Information about the lives of troubadours comes almost entirely from historical sources, and is usually limited to poets of noble birth. Prose biographies of the troubadours were composed in Provençal from the thirteenth century, and are of two kinds, *vidas* and *razos*. A *razo* of 'theme of a song' described incidents from a poet's life which had 'inspired' the song which it introduced. The information given by the *razos* is largely invented, drawn from the song itself and embroidered by fantasy. In many cases the *vidas* or 'lives' appear to give reliable information about the place of birth and death and social status of a troubadour. In other matters they are probably fictitious except occasionally as in the *vida* of Guillem de Berguedà (cf. edn M. de Riquer (Abadia de Poblet, 1971, 2 vols.) I, pp. 28–32). For text and discussion of the biographies see J. Boutière and A. H. Schutz, *Biographies des troubadours* (Paris, 1964).

2 These MSS. date mostly from the thirteenth and fourteenth centuries and are located in Paris, in the Bibliothèque Nationale, and in Italian libraries, and in Barcelona, Saragossa, New York and Oxford. Cf. A. Pillet and H. Carstens, *Bibliographie der Troubadours* (Halle/Saale, 1933), from which references to the MSS. have been taken.

3 At the first concourse on 1 May 1324 a golden violet was awarded as the prize for a poem to the Virgin. The *Jocs Florals* is still held at Toulouse at the beginning of May.

4 A reading of Plato's *Symposium* (which was not directly available in the early twelfth century), Cicero's *De amicitia*, Boethius' *De consolatione philosophiae* and Ovid's *Ars amatoria* and *Amores*, is valuable for an understanding of courtly ideas on love. H. Davenson, *Les troubadours* (Paris, 1961), gives a brief and sensible introduction to the problem of 'sources'. Cf. also R. Briffault, *Les troubadours et le sentiment romanesque* (Paris, 1945), and *The Troubadours* (Bloomington, 1965); A. R. Nykl, *Hispano-Arabic Poetry and its Relations with the Old Provençal Troubadours* (Baltimore, 1946); A. J. Denomy, 'Concerning the accessibility of Arabic influences to the earliest Provençal troubadours', *MedS*, XV (1953), pp. 147–58; D. Scheludko, 'Ovid und die Trobadors', *ZRP*, LIV (1934), pp. 128–74. P. Dronke, *Medieval Latin and the Rise of the European Love-Lyric* (Oxford, 1965); H. Kolb, *Der Begriff der Minne und das Entstehen der höfischen*

Lyrik (Tübingen, 1958); L. Pollmann, *Die Liebe in der hochmit-telalterlichen Literatur Frankreichs* (Frankfurt a. Main, 1966). For music and versification cf. J. Chailley, 'Les premiers troubadours et les versus de l'école d'Aquitaine', R, LXXVI (1955), pp. 212–39, and *Histoire musicale du moyen âge* (Paris, 1950); A. Roncaglia, 'Laisat estar lo gazel (Contributo alla discussione sul rapporti fra lo zagial e la ritmica romanza)', CN, IX (1949), pp. 67–99. Some music by later courtly troubadours such as Raimon de Miraval resembles folk melodies (see p. 272).

5 Cf. A. Richard, *Histoire des comtes de Poitou* (Paris, 1903), I, and R. R. Bezzola, *Les origines et la formation de la littérature courtoise en Occident* (Paris, 1960), Pt II, pp. 255–62.

6 Cf. Hildegarius, favourite pupil of Fulbert, who was sent by him to establish the famous episcopal school at Poitiers. Cf. also the probable influence of Gilbert de la Porrée, Platonist thinker and pupil of Bernard of Chartres. He was born c. 1076, was Chancellor of Chartres from 1124 to 1141 and Bishop of Poitiers from 1142 to 1154. William of Conches (1080–1145), another pupil of Bernard of Chartres, was tutor of the young prince who became Henry II of England, husband of Eleanor of Poitou and Aquitaine.

7 For *invenire* and *inventio* used in this sense by Quintilian and Cicero, cf. H. Lausberg, *Handbuch der literarischen Rhetorik* (Munich, 1960), p. 139, and further examples pp. 728–9. *Trobar* may derive from Vulgar Latin *tropare* from Low Latin *contropare*, attested in Cassiodorus (and Visigothic laws) meaning 'to compare, examine comparatively', and possibly 'to say with tropes' from Greek *tropos*. Cf. L. Spitzer, 'Trouver', R, LXVI (1940–1), pp. 1–11. J. Chailley, R, LXXVI (1955), pp. 212–39, derives *trobador* from *tropatorem* 'a composer of tropes'.

8 For a complete catalogue and analysis of metrical schemes, cf. I. Frank, *Répertoire métrique de la poésie des troubadours*, 2 vols. (Paris, 1953 and 1957).

9 Cf. J. Chailley, R, LXXVI (1955), pp. 212–39.

10 The origin of the word *sirventes* is obscure. The word may have meant 'a poem possessing the style and characteristics of a hired man', or 'a poem composed by a *sirven* for his master', or 'a poem which was an inferior "servant" to the *canso* from which it could borrow its music and rhyme scheme'. The first of these explanations seems to be the most likely.

11 Raimon Vidal, *Razos de trobar*, ed. J. H. Marshall (Oxford, 1972), p. 6: 'La parladura francesca val mais et [es] plus avinenz a far romanz et pasturellas, mas cella de Lemosin val mais per far vers et cansons et serventes. Et per totas las terras de nostre lengage son de maior autoritat li cantar de la lenga lemosina qe de neguna autra parladura...' *La lenga lemosina* almost certainly refers to the standard language of troubadour poetry which we call Provençal, and its association here with 'Limousin' may have derived from the large number of early troubadours who came from that region. The Provençal area covered very roughly the area south of the mouth of the Gironde, La Roche-foucauld, Confolens, Montluçon, Clermont-Ferrand and Saint-Sauveur near Annonay. The term Provençal is used in this work for the literary

language which was common to the South of France and not for the dialect of the marquisate of Provence. Raimon Vidal may have written the *Razos de trobar* between 1190 and 1213 (edn Marshall, p. lxx).

12 This number, which is approximate, is based on the listing of troubadours in A. Pillet and H. Carstens, *Bibliographie*.

13 Cf. I. Frank, 'Du rôle des troubadours dans la formation de la poésie lyrique moderne', *Mélanges Roques* (Paris, 1951), I, pp. 63–81.

14 For a fuller discussion of the pronunciation of Old Provençal, cf. J. Anglade, *Grammaire de l'ancien provençal* (Paris, 1921); Å. Grafström, *Etude sur la graphie des plus anciennes chartes languedociennes, avec un essai d'interprétation phonétique* (Uppsala, 1958); C. H. Grandgent, *An Outline of the Phonology and Morphology of Old Provençal* (Boston, 1905); A. Roncaglia, *La lingua dei trovatori* (Rome, 1965).

15 Cf. H. J. Chaytor, *From Script to Print; an Introduction to Medieval Literature* (Cambridge, 1945; London, 1966) for a discussion of this matter.

I GUILHEM IX OF AQUITAINE

1 J. Boutière and A. H. Schutz, *Biographies des troubadours* (Paris, 1964), p. 7 (*Biographies*).

2 Orderic Vitalis, *Hist. Eccl. lib. x*, ed. Prévost, IV, p. 132: *captivitas* may mean here 'wretched state'; cf. OFr. *chetif < captivus*.

3 Migne, PL, CLXXIX, col. 1384.

4 P. Labbe, *Novae bibl. man.* II, p. 297, and *Rec. des hist. de France*, XIV, p. 169.

5 Cf. A. Richard, *Histoire des comtes de Poitou* (Paris, 1903), I, pp. 498–9.

6 Cf. R. R. Bezzola, *Les origines et la formation de la littérature courtoise en Occident*, IIe partie (Paris, 1960), pp. 275–92.

7 The numbering of the poems and quotations is taken from A. Jeanroy, *Les chansons de Guillaume IX Duc d'Aquitaine* (Paris, 1927).

8 Cf. M. Dumitrescu, *CCMed*, XI (1968), pp. 379–412; her attribution of poems VII–X to Eble II of Ventadorn, however, lacks any authority.

9 For the relationship between *trobar clus* and the classical and medieval rhetorical tradition cf. E. Köhler in *Trobadorlyrik und höfischer Roman* (Berlin, 1962), pp. 133–52, also publ. in *RF*, LXIV (1952), pp. 71–101; L. Pollmann, *Trobar Clus, Bibelexegese und Hispano-Arabische Literatur* (Münster, 1965); U. Mölk, *Trobar clus–trobar leu* (Munich, 1968); and L. M. Paterson, *Troubadours and Eloquence* (Oxford, 1974). For the use of a 'lay' rhetoric in Guilhem's love lyrics cf. p. 26.

10 Such self-praise became a commonplace in troubadour poetry. For the genre of the *gap*, which was essentially a poem of boasting, see J. U. Fechner, *GRM* n.s. XIV (1964), pp. 15–34.

11 *Color* can mean 'manner, kind, quality, brilliance, deception', but refers here to the images used by Guilhem and to the nuances of meaning given to them. Cf. *Lex. rom.* II, p. 440; *SWB*, I, pp. 283–4, and H. Lausberg, *Handbuch der literarischen Rhetorik* (Munich, 1960), p. 664.

12 The *humilis* style was the lowest in the medieval ordering of styles: *gravis, mediocris, humilis*. Cf. H. J. Chaytor, *From Script to Print*, p. 62.

13 Edn A. Jeanroy has a semi-colon after *escient*.

Notes

14 Rita Lejeune in 'L'extraordinaire insolence du troubadour Guillaume IX d'Aquitaine', *Mélanges Pierre Le Gentil* (Paris, 1973), pp. 485–503, suggests that in this poem Guilhem IX is mocking the spiritual friendship which his aunts, Agnes, Empress of Germany, and Ermesent, Duchess of Aquitaine, enjoyed with the monk Peter Damian who preached the virtues of chastisement of the flesh and was visited by these noble ladies at Rome. (See also R. R. Bezzola, *Origines*, Pt II, p. 260.)

15 L. Pollmann, 'Dichtung und Liebe bei Wilhelm von Aquitanien', ZRP, LXXVIII (1962), p. 332.

16 Quotations and the numbering of Marcabru's poems are from the edn by J. M. L. Dejeanne (Toulouse, 1909).

17 On Joy cf. C. Camproux, 'A propos de "joi"', *Mel. I.* Frank (Saarbrücken, 1957), and *Le joy d'amor* (Montpellier, 1965); on *Jovens* cf. A. J. Denomy, MedS, XI (1949), pp. 1–22.

18 Ironical in view of his amorous reputation. L. Pollmann, *Trobar Clus*, p. 12, takes poems II and III, however, as serious examples of a genre called *casteis* and poem III as a possible forerunner of the *trobar clus* (p. 19) which may have influenced Marcabru (p. 22).

19 A. Jeanroy, *La poésie lyrique des troubadours* (Paris/Toulouse, 1934) II, p. 6. Martial, who was widely studied in the eleventh and twelfth centuries, may have provided a model for this genre of poetry. Cf. Epigrams, VII, xviii, *Cum tibi sit facies*.

20 H. Spanke, *Untersuchungen über die Ursprünge des romanischen Minnesangs*, Marcabrustudien, Abh. der Ges. der Wiss. zu Göttingen, 3e Folge, nr. XXIV (Göttingen, 1940), p. 51.

21 In *Neophilologus*, XLVII (1963), p. 28 and p. 33, n. 16. The translation of *cons* by 'cunt', with its limited range of meaning, would destroy much of the sophisticated humour in this poem.

22 Edn A. Jeanroy, R, XXXIV (1905); poem IV, 46–7, p. 515.

23 Edn L. T. Topsfield, NMi, LXIX (1968), pp. 289–91; other recent edns by L. Pollmann, *Neophilologus*, XLVII (1963), pp. 24–34; N. Pasero, CN, XXVII (1967), pp. 19–29; U. Mölk, *Trobar Clus*, pp. 46–50.

24 *Conres* gives a pun on *con* and a variety of other meanings; 'equipment, provisioning, hospitality, feast, a course in a meal'. Cf. E. Levy, SWB, I, pp. 330–2, and *Pet. Dict.* p. 91.

25 Possibly a slighting reference to poetry of *nien*, the illusion of imaginary love which inspired Guilhem's *Farai un vers de dreyt nien* (IV).

26 Edn L. T. Topsfield (Paris, 1971), XLI, 51–6, p. 327.

27 Edn C. Appel, *Chres* 6 edn, p. 122.

28 Edn O. Klein (Marburg, 1885), *Autra vetz* (III) and *Fort m'envia* (IV).

29 Edn G. Toja (Florence, 1960), pp. 173–91.

30 Cf. M. Lazar, *Bernard de Ventadour* (Paris, 1966): 'la vulgarité et les expressions grossières et soldatesques d'un Guillaume IX'. Marcabru and Peire Cardenal use similarly outspoken expressions in their moralising poetry.

31 Cf. L. Pollmann, ZRP, LXXVIII (1962), p. 356: 'Die Bedeutung Wilhelms von Aquitanien lag darin, die Welt des Ritters über Schalk und ritterlich männliches Denken hinzuführen zum Phänomen der Liebe.'

32 Cf. F. Schlösser, *Andreas Capellanus seine Minnelehre und das christliche Weltbild um 1200* (Bonn, 1960), p. 298: 'denn gerade in den Liedern Wilhelms IX, bei ein und demselben Troubadour, stehen sich zwei Liebesauffassungen gegenüber, von denen die zweite (Lieder 7–10) die geistige Überwindung der ersten (1–6) darstellt'. L. Pollmann, *Trobar Clus*, p. 79, quoting R. Menéndez Pidal, *Poesia árabe y poesia europea*, suggests that in poem IV Guilhem is progressing beyond the monotonous rhyme sequence of poems I–III. The poet changes intention and style, however, to suit the genre, and the simpler rhyme scheme of poems I–III might reflect their lower literary status. Poem VI was probably composed in a consciously elevated style for the purpose of literary burlesque.

33 Several of Guilhem's images and expressions have parallels in Ovid: fish imagery (III, 15), *Ars am.* I, 48, 393; the theme of *non begues enanz de l'aiga* (II, 21), *Amores*, II, xix, 31–2; the horse as sex symbol, *Ars am.* III, 785, and protests against the husband who curtails his wife's freedom, *Amores*, II, ii, especially lines 11–12:

> Vir quoque non sapiens; quid enim servare laboret,
> unde nihil, quamvis non tueare, perit?

which comes close in idea to III, 16–19.

34 J. Frappier, 'Vues sur les conceptions courtoises', *CCMed*, II (1959), pp. 135–56, stresses the part played by clerks trained in the classical humanities in parodying the affectations of courtly behaviour, but sees only rare traces of the influence of 'clergie' in the work of the troubadours (p. 146). The influence of clerical and learned thought on the court of Poitou has been indicated by R. R. Bezzola *Origines*, IIe partie, pp. 253ff) and such influence which, however indirect, appears inescapably evident in the case of Guilhem IX in the light of his mockery of debating topics and his use of and mockery of the uses of rhetoric, is clearly apparent in the poetry of Marcabru and Jaufre Rudel. So far as poetic technique is concerned, H. Spanke, *Marcabrustudien*, p. 37, quotes poems I–III, IV, V and VII as imitations of the versification of the medieval *conductus*, and in *Beziehungen zwischen romanischer und mittellateinischer Lyrik* (Berlin, 1936), p. 19, relates the versification of *Companho, faray un vers . . . covinen* (1) to that of the *versus Promat chorus hodie, o contio*. Cf. also J. Chailley, 'Les premiers troubadours et les versus de l'école d'Aquitaine', *R*, LXXVI (1955), pp. 212–39. Such imitation, especially if extended to the music, would heighten the burlesque quality of poems I–III and V. E. Hoepffner, *Les troubadours* (Paris, 1955), p. 21, suggests that the three *Companho* poems 'd'un type archaïque en vers monorimes de onze et de quatorze syllabes, peuvent être considérées comme à peu près les derniers représentants d'une ancienne poésie joglaresque'. For possible Hispano-Arabic influence on the versification and structure of Guilhem's poetry, cf. L. Pollmann, *Trobar Clus*, pp. 55–92.

35 The *Lai dou lecheor*, ed. G. Paris, *R*, VIII (1879), pp. 64–6, offers an elegant parody on the conventional attitude of courtly society to tales of adventure, love and chivalry. Eight of the noblest *dames* of the court:

Franches, cortoises et proisies,
. . . de Bretaigne la flors
Et la proesce et la valors (58–60)

decide that many men for all their fame

. . . ne vausissent un bouton
Se par l'entente du con non (91–2)

and end the *lai* with a parody of the opening lines:

Faisons du con le lai novel
Si l'orront tel cui ert molt bel.

36 C. H. Livingston, *Le jongleur Gautier le Leu* (Cambridge, Mass., 1951), sees *le dit du C.* (VIII) as a parody on the 'lives of the saints' (p. 237) and relates the paradoxical mingling of obscene subject matter and courtly tone to the *Lai dou lecheor* (p. 235). Cf. also *Seinor, qui les bons cons savez* (IX), p. 251.

37 Courtly attitudes are mocked in *Le Roman de Renart, Ière branche*, ed. M. Roques (Paris, 1948), pp. 51–2, 62–3, 66–8, when Renart ravishes the Queen in view of the 'court' after she has engaged him with ring and kiss as her courtly suitor. This episode, although composed in a style which parodies the 'chanson de geste' (ll. 1853–8), is not unlike the outcome of Guilhem's adventure with lady Agnes and Ermessen (poem V). The satire is heightened when the Queen none the less wishes to retain Renart as her 'soupirant'.

38 Cf. A. Monteverdi in *Studi in onore di Salvatore Santangelo, Siculorum Gymnasium*, 1955, pp. 6–15, and L. Pollmann, ZRP, LXXVIII (1962), p. 350, n. 1.

39 Cf. L. Pollmann, *Trobar Clus*, part II, pp. 61 ff.

40 Edn A. Jeanroy (IV, 24, n. p. 33): 'j'adopte pour ce vers le texte et le sens proposés par Levy (s.v. *amalir*) et Appel: *Mas non, si amau*.' The MS. readings are: *Mor non si mau* (E) and *Mas ia non sia mau* (C). There is no reason why *ia* should not be preferred to *mas*, thus giving a better sense to the line. Cf. *Mél. . . Boutière* (Liège, 1971), p. 577.

41 D. Scheludko, *Archivum Romanicum*, XV (1931), p. 167.

42 L. Spitzer, *L'amour lointain de Jaufre Rudel* (Chapel Hill, 1944), pp. 51–3.

43 A. Jeanroy, edn *Guillaume IX*, p. 32.

44 I. Cluzel, *Rev. de lang. et litt. prov.* III (1961), p. 30, and R, LXXXI (1960), p. 549.

45 P. Dronke, RF, LXXII (1961), p. 328.

46 R. R. Bezzola, R, LXVI (1940–1), p. 214, and *Les origines et la formation de la littérature courtoise en Occident*, part II (Paris, 1960), p. 298.

47 A. del Monte, FiR, II (1955), p. 140.

48 M. Casella, *Archivio storico italiano*, LCVI (1938), II, pp. 3–63.

49 L. Pollmann, ZRP, LXXVIII (1962), p. 356.

50 E. Köhler, *Esprit und arkadische Freiheit* (Frankfurt a. Main/Bonn, 1966), pp. 46–66.

51 Cf. E. Köhler, ibid. p. 51, and PL, XXXII, col. 885.

52 Cf. R. R. Bezzola, *Origines*, II, p. 257.

53 Cf. H. Kolb, *Der Begriff der Minne* (Tübingen, 1958), pp. 48–51, and also D. R. Sutherland, *Studies... Alfred Ewert* (Oxford, 1961), pp. 165–93.

54 Since MS. C gives *ornam* and E *ornan*, A. Jeanroy's emendation to *onra·m* appears to be unjustified. Bartsch (*Lesebuch*, p. 45) reads *or n'am*. *Ornam* appears to be acceptable in the sense of 'to adorn, to equip', cf. ll. 22–30 and 34–6.

2 JAUFRE RUDEL

1 Edn J. Boutière and A. H. Schutz, *Biographies des troubadours* (Paris, 1964) (MSS. IK), p. 17.

2 Cf. P. Cravayat, 'Les origines du troubadour Jaufre Rudel', R, LXXI (1950), pp. 166–79.

3 Cf. A. Jeanroy, *Les chansons de Jaufre Rudel* (Paris, 1924), p. IV: 'Elles [les poésies] se divisent assez naturellement en deux groupes: l'un est formé des pièces II, V, VI, qui chantent un amour idéal et "lointain"; l'autre des pièces I, III, IV, relatives à des amours plus reélles, semble-t-il, et dont l'objet était plus rapproché du poète.' Cf. also I. Cluzel, 'Jaufre Rudel et l'*amor de lonh*: essai d'une nouvelle classification des pièces du troubadour', R, LXXVIII (1957), pp. 86–97.

4 *Color* had several meanings in troubadour poetry (see p. 261, n. 11). In this discussion words are referred to as 'coloured' which possess, in themselves or in the context in which they are used, extra levels and nuances of meaning. Guilhem IX and Marcabru appear to have used *color* in this sense. For the so-called colours of rhetoric in medieval vernacular poetry, cf. H. J. Chaytor, *From Script to Print*, p. 63.

5 Edn Dejeanne (Toulouse, 1909), from which quotations from Marcabru are taken, gives (XVI, 49) *De pluzors sens* (CE), but *Dels plus torsens* (AIK), in which *sens* (rhyming with *prens*=*prenhs*) = *senhs* meaning 'rhetorical colours', gives a better meaning. Cf. L. M. Paterson, *Troubadours and Eloquence*, and A. Roncaglia, 'Il *gap* di Marcabruno', SM, XVII (1951), pp. 46–70.

6 *Desideratus* was a name for Christ. Cf. F. J. E. Raby, *The Oxford Book of Medieval Latin Verse* (Oxford, 1959), no. 59: *desideratus gentibus*: Marcabru (V, 49–54) appears to refer with the image of the *hortus conclusus* to his love for the Virgin Mary. In the following line he uses *Desirat* (55), with a possible Christian meaning.

7 Y. Lefèvre, AMid, LXXVIII (1966), pp. 415–22, sees *espina* as the thorn which St Paul says was planted in his flesh to humiliate him and cause him suffering (Corinthians, II, xii, 7).

8 For the use of the *topos* or commonplace in classical rhetoric and medieval poetry, cf. E. R. Curtius, *European Literature and the Latin Middle Ages* (London, 1953), pp. 70 and 79–105.

9 Cf. D. W. Robertson Jr, SP, XLIX (1952), p. 576.

10 D. Stone Jr, 'Rudel's *Belhs m'es l'estius*: a new reading', NMi, LXVII (1966), pp. 137–44.

11 *Foudatz* and *fols* in Marcabru's poetry have the connotation of 'wanton, indiscriminate, sinful behaviour'. Cf. *folie* in Old French and 'folly' in Middle English.

12 It is possible that Jaufre Rudel's *Plus savis hom* may refer to Marcabru. Cf. pp. 95–6.

13 Cf. D. W. Robertson Jr, *SP*, XLIX, p. 579 (*seror*=Mary, *fraire*=Christ); L. Pollmann, *Die Liebe in der hochmittelalterlichen Literatur Frankreichs* (Frankfurt a. Main, 1966), p. 177 (*fraire*=*amor de cavalier*, *seror*=höfische Liebe); M. Lazar, *Amour courtois et Fin'Amors* (Paris, 1964), p. 93 (*seror* =une jeune fille, an unmarried girl who has replaced the *domna* as the new conquest of the troubadour, *fraire*=her brother).

14 R. Lejeune, 'La chanson de l'''amour de loin'' de Jaufré Rudel', *Studi in onore di Angelo Monteverdi* (Modena, 1959), pp. 403–42. Quotations are taken from this edition of the poem (pp. 416–18).

15 *Ibid.*, p. 435.

16 Cf. *ibid.*, p. 425.

17 Marcabru, XL, 9.

18 Cf. E. Gilson, *La théologie mystique de Saint Bernard* (Paris, 1934).

19 *No sap chantar qui so non di*, poem VI in Jeanroy's edition, has not been discussed in this chapter. It has the appearance of a literary exercise composed in imitation of *Farai un vers de dreyt nien* and *Ben vuelh* by Guilhem IX. As a disquisition on the themes of *amor de lonh* and dream love it provides a sequence of commonplaces and says little about *Jois, Amors* and *Fin'Amors* that is not better expressed in Rudel's other poems.

3 MARCABRU

1 *Biographies*, p. 10.

2 *Ibid.*, p. 11, n. 1.

3 Quotations and numbering of poems are taken from *Poésies complètes du troubadour Marcabru* (Toulouse, 1909). For studies on Marcabru see F. Pirot, 'Bibliographie commentée du troubadour Marcabru', *Moyen Age*, XXII (1967), pp. 87–126.

4 Cf. A. Roncaglia, *CN*, XI (1951), pp. 25–7.

5 Cf. St Bernard, *Epistola*, CCXLI: 'The churches are empty, the people are without priests; the priests do not have the respect due to them. Christians deny Christ, and their churches are like synagogues. The sacred character of God's sanctuaries is ignored, and the sacraments are no longer considered holy...men die with their sins upon them ...children do not learn to know Christ and they are not afforded the grace of baptism.' *PL*, CLXXXII, col. 434.

6 See L. M. Paterson, *Troubadours and Eloquence*, for Marcabru's knowledge of classical and medieval rhetoric.

7 *deum* is given by all three MSS. *AIK* and is preferable to Dejeanne's emendation 'devin'.

8 A. Del Monte, *Peire d'Alvernha, Liriche* (Turin, 1955) – from which quotations and numbering of poems are taken – reads *no conoissa natura* and suggests, p. 142, n. 41, that the subjunctive *membre* in l. 42 demands the subjunctive *conoissa*. But *membre* can be indicative: cf. J. Anglade, *Grammaire de l'ancien provençal* (Toulouse, 1921), p. 270, Bernart von Ventadorn, ed. C. Appel, XXX, 1, p. 181; *Lo tems vai e ven e vire*, and below p. 269, chap. 5, n. 15.

9 There is an excellent discussion of *trobars naturaus* in Marcabru by A. Roncaglia in '"Trobar clus": discussione aperta', CN, XXIX (1969), pp. 41–51.

10 D. Scheludko, 'Zur Geschichte des Natureingangs bei den Trobadors', ZFSL, LX (1935–7), p. 282, suggests a close Medieval Latin source for this stanza.

11 For the image of the lover who burns like damp hay with slow fires, cf. Ovid, *Ars am.* III, 573–5.

12 In classical rhetoric the *genus demonstrativum* was the genre of works devoted to Praise and Blame: *haec causa dividitur in laudem et vituperationem* (*Ad. C. Herennium*, III, 10 (edn Loeb, 1954)), p. 172.

13 H. Spanke, *Marcabrustudien, Abh. der Gesellschaft der Wissenschaften zu Göttingen* (Göttingen, 1940), p. 101, and J. H. Marshall, *Actes. . .IIIᵉ Congrès*, II, p. 56, have questioned the attribution of this poem to Marcabru.

14 A. Roncaglia, '"Trobar clus": discussione aperta', CN, XXIX (1969), pp. 20–2, however, sees *Desirat* as Sancho III of Castile.

15 This reading (CEIK) offers a better meaning than edn Dejeanne *Que per art cuid'esser peritz* (A).

16 Cf. A. Roncaglia, '"Trobar clus"', CN, XXIX (1969), p. 14.

17 Edn Dejeanne: *fons de bontat,/C'a[s] tot. . .*

18 Cf. the obscene use of dice imagery in Guilhem IX, *Ben vuelh*.

19 Cf. A. Roncaglia's edn of this poem, with notes, in SM, XVII (1951), pp. 46–70.

20 Cf. p. 265, n. 5.

21 Text by R. Lejeune, 'Pour le commentaire du troubadour Marcabru: une allusion à Waïfre, roi d'Aquitaine', AMid, LXXVI (1964), pp. 363–70, who first recognised the meaning of *baus Gaifier*.

22 *Sola* in all MSS. Dejeanne emends unnecessarily to *folla*.

23 Cf. J. M. Déchanet, *Oeuvres choisies de Guillaume de Saint-Thierry* (Paris, 1944), pp. 151–62.

24 Eble II of Ventadorn, probably *Ebolus cantator*, who was a rival of Guilhem IX. In *Lo tems vai e ven e vire* Bernart de Ventadorn renounces the *escola* 'school, ways of thinking' of Lord Eble (see p. 134).

25 Cf. *De amicitia* (edn Loeb), pp. 138–41, 174–7, 186–9 and 190–1.

26 For further discussion of these virtues cf. A. J. Denomy, MedS, XI (1949), pp. 1–22 (*Jovens*), MedS, XIII (1951), pp. 177–217 (*Jois*), and Sp, XXVIII (1953), pp. 44–63 (*Cortesia*); M. Lazar, SMV, 6/7 (1959), pp. 66–96 (*Cortesia*); A. H. Schutz, Sp, XIX (1944), pp. 488–93 (*pretz e valor*), and Sp, XXXIII (1958), pp. 508–14 (*sabers, sciensa, sen and connoissensa*); E. Köhler, *Mél.* Crozet (Poitiers, 1966), pp. 569–83 (*Jovens*).

27 For references to studies on *Fin'Amors* see F. Pirot's valuable bibliography on Marcabru in *Moyen Age*, XXII (1967), pp. 87–117.

4 BERNART DE VENTADORN

1 Cf. R. Lejeune, 'La "Galerie Littéraire" du troubadour Peire d'Alvernhe', *Actes et mém. du IIIᵉ congrès international de langue et litt. d'oc* (Bordeaux, 1965), II, pp. 35–54, and RLLO, 12/13 (1965), pp. 35–54.

2 Edn A. del Monte (Turin, 1955), p. 121; reads *nanal* in l. 22.

3 *Biographies,* pp. 20–1.
4 Quotations and numbering of poems from C. Appel, *Bernart von Ventadorn* (Halle a. S., 1915). See also M. Lazar, *Bernard de Ventadour, chansons d'amour* (Paris, 1966). In ll. 21–2 Appel has a comma after *mes,* and none after *pren.*
5 In this contrast between the merciful restraint of the courtly world and the ferocity of nature, Bernart may be mocking Marcabru's idea of the ordered balance of the natural world.
6 *Sen per un efan.* Cf. Marcabru's attack on the *trobador ab sen d'enfanssa* who inflame lovers with sensual desires.
7 Cf. *Mélanges. . . Rostaing* (Liège, 1974), and above, p. 266, n. 8.
8 *De amore libri tres,* ed. E. Trojel (Copenhagen, 1892), transl. J. J. Parry, *Andreas Capellanus, The Art of Courtly Love* (New York, 1959).
9 *Ponto,* 4, 10, 5, and *Ars am.* I, 475. Cf. C. Appel, edn, pp. 96–7, n. 38.
10 A possible parody of Marcabru XLI, *Mos sens foilla sul vergan* (AIK). . . Qui *que paus, ieu pes e cossir. . . Segon natura et estiers.* Bernart bursts into leaf with song and delight, Marcabru with meditation.
11 Cf. p. 205, for the skill with which Arnaut Daniel develops the technique of lightening courtly phrases with expression of personal feeling in simple, direct language.

5 RAIMBAUT D'AURENGA

1 Cf. W. T. Pattison, *The Life and Works of the Troubadour Raimbaut d'Orange* (Minnesota, 1952), pp. 14–15. Quotations and numbering of poems are taken from this edn.
2 Cf. A. del Monte, edn *Peire d'Alvernha,* p. 132, n. 56.
3 Cf. also the edition of this text by J. H. Marshall, *MAe,* XXXVII (1968), pp. 12–36, with *a* as base MS. in place of D.
4 St John's day was the medieval feast of midsummer sensuality, in contrast to the teaching of his Gospel. Cf. *Flamenca,* ed. R. Lavaud and R. Nelli, *Les troubadours* (Bruges, 1960), ll. 471–575.
5 *Joglar* is also a pun on Raimbaut's reciprocal pseudonym with a lady, cf. edn W. T. Pattison, XXIV, 34, note, and A. Sakari, 'Azalais de Porcairagues, le Joglar de Raimbaut d'Orange', NMi, L (1949), pp. 23–43, 56–87, 174–98.
6 Raimbaut's jest about the perfect joy (*gaug entier*) of impotence may be a parody of Peire d'Alvernhe's idea of perfect, integrated joy (*jois entiers*) and 'growing fat from desiring and seeing' (ll. 46–8) may parody Peire's XIII, 32–5, see p. 179.
7 Cf. '"Cortez'ufana" chez Raimon de Miraval', *Actes et mém. du IIIᵉ congrès international de langue et litt. d'oc* (Bordeaux, 1965), II, pp. 102–10, and RLLO, 12/13 (1965), pp. 102–10.
8 Cf. A. Roncaglia, 'Carestia', CN, XVIII (1958), pp. 121–37.
9 *mes* could also be translated as 'since'.
10 Text and translation, revised edn Loeb (1968), pp. 158–9.
11 In *Ans que venha,* edn A. Kolsen (Halle a.S., 1910) III, Guiraut de Bornelh 'darkens his style' with wisdom, and refuses to be 'mean' (*escas*) in his language. Cf. L. M. Paterson, *Troubadours and Eloquence,* for

text and discussion of this poem, and also for the suggestion that Guiraut de Bornelh invented the term *trobar leu*.

12 Cf. edn Pattison, p. 154, n. 1, and p. 42, for the controversial invention of new forms and terminology, current in Raimbaut's day.

13 For this reference to a lewd story, known also to Arnaut Daniel, cf. W. T. Pattison, edn, p. 155, n. 35.

14 Cf. W. T. Pattison, edn, pp. 44–5.

15 *Trenque* may be 3rd Pers. Sing. Pres. Indic. as in Peire d'Alvernhe *membre* (XIII, 42) and Bernart de Ventadorn *vire* (XXX, 1). Cf. above, p. 266, n. 8. *Trenque* might be 3rd Pers. Sing. Pres. Subj., indicating possibility. In this case the translation could be: 'But I discover that powerlessness may keep me from it.' The MS. variant for IKN² in edn W. T. Pattison reads: *par quem trenca*.

6 PEIRE D'ALVERNHE

1 Quotations and numbering of poems from A. del Monte, *Peire d'Alvernha, Liriche* (Turin, 1955). See also R. Zenker (ed.), *Die Lieder Peires von Auvergne* (Erlangen, 1900).

2 *Biographies*, pp. 263–6.

3 Cf. R. Zenker, edn, pp. 16–40, for a discussion of Peire's poetic career.

4 *si fraysses*; a pun on the dispute about song that is *entiers* or *frach*. See below, p. 184.

5 Edn A. del Monte gives *qe· retrai*.

6 This staccato effect in the last line of the stanza was also used by Arnaut Daniel. Peire is translating into social reality the imaginary scene with his distant love that delighted Jaufre Rudel:

> Iratz e gauzens m'en partrai
> Qan veirai cest amor de loing.
>
> (ed. Lejeune, 15–16)

The line *tan tem qe·l mieils lais e prenda·l sordeis* states the conflict that Peire fears to undergo between *Fin'Amors* and *Amors*.

7 Edn A. del Monte gives *fau*.

8 D. W. Robertson Jr, SP, XLIX (1952), pp. 566–82.

9 D. Scheludko, ZRP, LX (1940), p. 221.

10 A. Jeanroy, *Poésies de Uc de Saint-Circ* (Toulouse, 1913), VIII, 65, note, p. 185.

11 A. del Monte, edn, p. 95.

12 *agensar* also has the meaning 'to adorn', 'make more beautiful'.

13 With his compasses the medieval master-mason could transfer a small working-drawing to actual size, just as God with His compasses could trace out his plan of the universe.

14 See A. del Monte, edn, p. 83, note, for a discussion of the interpretations proposed for this poem, and his own suggestion.

15 Marcabru: *D'aut chai em bas*; *fols, fays, follejar*; *ort serrat*; *dels antics . . . lo ric al ric*; *me totz d'amor lonhar*: *un amic/vas cui m'abric*. Jaufre Rudel: *totz crestias*, the rejection of *autrui conquistz, amor de lonh* and Guilhem IX: *m'amigua*

qu'eu tenc plus car, De tot can suelh/amar, me tuelh and apres ma mort/no·m fass'om
tort.

16 Cf. R. Zenker, edn, pp. 24–6.

17 For ll. 31–3 I have followed the text of R. Zenker, edn, and M. de
Riquer, *La Lírica de los Trovadores* (Barcelona, 1948), p. 202, with the
exception of *c'a longias* given by MS. E. Speaking of the joy inspired by
his lady's look, Bernart de Ventadorn sings:

> e si·m durava lonjamen,
> sobre sainz li juraria
> qu'el mon mais nulhs jois no sia;
> mais al partir art et encem.
>
> (edn Appel, XVII, 45–8)

18 See p. 266, n. 8.

19 For a more detailed discussion of this question cf. 'The "natural fool"
in Peire d'Alvernhe, Marcabru and Bernart de Ventadorn', *Mél...
Rostaing* (Liège, 1974).

20 Cf. *MAe*, XXXVI (1967), pp. 119–33.

21 *Biographies*, p. 263.

22 A. del Monte, edn, gives mi but translates 'si mostra'. Cf. edn, p. 114,
notes 9–11, for his emendation and translation of the corrupt text.

23 *aic*, the MS. reading, gives an impure internal rhyme but better sense
than *dic*, the emendation suggested by Zenker and followed by A. del
Monte (cf. edn, pp. 116–17, notes to ll. 33–6 and 33). For *aver* 'to
learn' see E. Levy, *SWB*, I, p. 112, and for *lur anar environ* 'to circulate in
their company' cf. *SWB*, I, p. 62b (*anar entorn ad alcun*) and Raynouard,
Lex. rom., V, 550 (*viron lor*). A. del Monte, edn, gives *iovens* (32).

24 A. del Monte, edn, gives que·l t., and in 6, al b.s. cuma [cuma] p.

7 ARNAUT DANIEL

1 *Biographies*, p. 59. The phrase *et fetz se joglars* may mean that he sang his
own songs on his travels or that like Raimbaut d'Aurenga he mingled
folly with wisdom and became a *fols cantayre cortes*. Cf. also G. Toja,
Arnaut Daniel Canzoni (Florence, 1960), p. 12. Texts and numbering of
poems are taken from this edn, with minor changes in punctuation.
Other edns by U. A. Canello, *La vita e le opere del trovatore Arnaldo Daniello*
(Halle, 1883) and R. Lavaud, *Les poésies d'Arnaut Daniel* (Toulouse, 1910,
and *AMid*, XXII (1910) and XXIII (1911)).

2 Ed. G. Contini, *SM*, n.s. IX (1936), p. 231.

3 Edn Lacaita, p. 134. Cf. edn G. Toja, p. 19, n. 1.

4 Cf. song XII, 57–8; Canello, p. 8, and Toja, p. 15.

5 Cf. Toja, p. 11.

6 References in this form are to A. Pillett and H. Carstens, *Bibliographie der
Troubadours* (Halle a.S., 1933). See also Canello, p. 41.

7 No prose work by Arnaut has survived. Luigi Pulci (1432–84) attri-
butes to Arnaut a story, which he says he used in his *Morgante Maggiore*,
about Renaud in Egypt and his fight at Roncesvalles. Torquato Tasso,
Discorsi del poema eroico, edn L. Poma (Bari, 1964), p. 106, names Arnaut

as the author of the romance of Lancelot, cf. Lavaud, edn, pp. 129–32, and Toja, pp. 25–34. Quotations from Purgatorio from Temple edn (London, 1941).

8 Biographies, p. 39.

9 Edn E. Chiòrboli (Bari, 1930), Trionfo d'Amore, IV, 40–2, p. 321. Cf. edn Toja, p. 106.

10 Edn Toja gives sentim.

11 Edn Toja has a comma after demors.

12 Cf. Raimbaut d'Aurenga XXXIV, 21, for the same expression.

13 For Luserna, legendary Spanish city named in the chansons de geste, cf. Toja, edn, pp. 278–80.

14 Edn Loeb (London/Cambridge, Mass., 1957), transl. J. H. Mozley.

15 For Dante's discussion of these levels of understanding, cf. Convivio II, 1.

16 Cf. p. 265, n. 6; Toja, edn, pp. 382–4, discusses possible meanings for Desirat.

17 Cf. Toja, edn, pp. 379–82, and L. M. Paterson, Troubadours and Eloquence.

8 RAIMON DE MIRAVAL

1 The owner of a castle was expected to provide festivities on the first days of each month. For calendas cf. also Peire Cardenal, edn R. Lavaud, LXVII, 25.

2 Biographies, p. 375.

3 Cf. L. T. Topsfield, Les poésies du troubadour Raimon de Miraval (Paris, 1971), pp. 17 and 379. Texts and numbering of poems are taken from this edn.

4 Cf. S. Stronski, Le troubadour Elias de Barjols (Toulouse, 1906), p. 41.

5 Ed. M. Cornicelius (Berlin, 1888), ll. 108–11. Raimon Vidal quotes Miraval nine times in So fo and names him in ll. 1143 and 1724 of Abrils issi e mays intrava (ed. W. Bohs, RF, XV (1904)), pp. 270 and 294.

6 Biographies, p. 375. A. Kolsen, Archivum Romanicum, XXI (1937), p. 309, denies that the senhal was reciprocal. Miraval names Audiart as lo comte Raimon in XXVII, 53–6.

7 Biographies, p. 369.

8 Cf. edn L. T. Topsfield, pp. 33–6, for a discussion of Loba de Pennautier.

9 P. Andraud, La vie et l'œuvre du troubadour Raimon de Miraval (Paris, 1902), p. 125.

10 A. Jeanroy, La poésie lyrique des troubadours (Toulouse, 1934), II, p. 161.

11 Andreas Capellanus, De amore, II, chap. VI, p. 308. For comparative references to the poems of Raimon de Miraval and the De amore of Andreas Capellanus (ed. S. Battaglia (Rome, 1947)), cf. MLR, LI (1956), p. 40, notes 1–8.

12 This romance by Miraval is known to us only through a reference by Francesco da Barberino, who says that it was the source of one of the stories in his Fiori di novelle. Cf. Francesco Egidi, I Documenti d'Amore di Francesco da Barberino (Rome, 1905), I, p. 270.

13 ditz gen claus may refer to the rhetorical principle of rounding off a sentence appropriately in order to give an effect of finality. For this, see

D. L. Clark, *Rhetoric in Greco-Roman Education* (Columbia, U.P. 1957), pp. 97–9.

For *sonetz suaus* (l. 4), cf. H. Anglès, *La música a Catalunya fins al segle XIII* (Barcelona, 1935), pp. 400–3, who considers that some of Miraval's melodies (twenty-two of which have survived) resemble the traditions of Catalan folklore. J.-P. Lallemend, *Le troubadour Raimon de Miraval, contribution à l'étude de la musique des troubadours* (Univ. of Liège, 1973, thesis), 2 vols., has produced a detailed and valuable study of Miraval's music.

9 GUILHEM DE MONTANHAGOL, PEIRE CARDENAL AND GUIRAUT RIQUIER

1 Ed. J. Audiau and R. Lavaud, *Nouvelle anthologie des troubadours* (Paris, 1928), p. 170.

2 See S. Stronski, *Le troubadour Folquet de Marseille* (Cracow, 1910), pp. 13*–15* and index. Eudoxia, daughter of the Emperor of Constantinople, was promised in marriage to Alphonso II of Aragon, but, as he had already married Sancha of Castile, she was passed on as wife to Guilhem of Montpellier, and bore him a daughter Marie. He repudiated her after twelve years and imprisoned her in the monastery at Aniane. Marie, heiress of Montpellier, suffered even worse. She was married to the aged Barral of Marseille in 1191, was widowed in 1192, forced to renounce her rights to Montpellier, married to the profligate count of Comminges in 1197, repudiated by him in 1201, restored to her rights in Montpellier by the people of the city in 1202, married to Pedro II of Aragon in 1204, bore a son who became James the Conqueror, was unhappy in her marriage from 1206, was repudiated in 1213, and died shortly afterwards at Rome.

3 For this complicated social and political background see P. Belperron, *La croisade contre les Albigeois et l'union du Languedoc à la France* (Paris, 1948); R. Limouzin-Lamothe, *La commune de Toulouse et les sources de son histoire (1120–1249)* (Toulouse/Paris, 1932); J. H. Mundy, *Liberty and Political Power in Toulouse 1050–1230* (New York, 1954 – useful bibliography); Devic Dom (Cl.) and Dom (J.) Vaissette, *Histoire générale de Languedoc* (Toulouse, 1872–92), 15 vols.

4 Ed. C. Appel, *Die Lieder Bertrans von Born* (Halle, 1932); A. Thomas, *Poésies complètes de Bertran de Born* (Toulouse, 1888), and A. Stimming, *Bertran de Born. Sein Leben und seine Werke* (Halle, 1879).

5 Cf. V. L. Bourrilly and R. Busquet, *La Provence au moyen âge* (Paris, 1924), pp. 436–44.

6 Cf. p. 5, and n. 11.

7 Quotations and the numbering of poems are taken from P. T. Ricketts, *Les poésies de Guilhem de Montanhagol* (Toronto, 1964). See also J. Coulet, *Le troubadour Guilhem Montanhagol* (Toulouse, 1898).

8 Cf. Bertran d'Alamanon in a *tenso* with Granet, 'Since Sordel has changed a good hundred ladies, I can change one if she is not kind to me' (Appel, *Chres*, 86, 44–5).

9 Translation from J. J. Parry, *The Art of Courtly Love by Andreas Capellanus*

(New York, 1941), p. 122. The passage occurs in *De amore*, vol. I, chap. VI H, ed. S. Battaglia (Rome, 1947), p. 212. For this question, cf. 'The theme of courtly love in the poems of Guilhem Montanhagol, *FS*, XI (1957), pp. 127–34.

10 Cf. P. T. Ricketts, 'Castitatz chez Guilhem de Montanhagol', *RLR*, LXXVII (1966), pp. 147–50.

11 The text and translation of this stanza differs from that of P. T. Ricketts; *sofra* (44) is given by base MS. C, *suefra* by J and *suefrun* (emended to *sofr'un* by Coulet) by R. Edn Ricketts gives *sofran*. Cf. *MAe*, XXXV (1966), pp. 258–9. *assais* was probably a courtly term for the test of sensual temptation inflicted by the lady on her suitor; cf. R. Nelli, *L'Erotique des troubadours* (Toulouse, 1963), pp. 199–209. *carestia*; for this cardinal virtue of the *domna* cf. A. Roncaglia, 'Carestia', *CN*, XVIII (1958), pp. 121–37.

12 This ideal of the good life was intended, of course, for the nobility and patrician burghers for whom he was singing. He defended the poor against the greedy clerics (XIV, 22–4) and against feudal injustice (XIV, 25–32), but in an abstract, theorising fashion, and he advised them to keep their place as the third estate in the feudal hierarchy, if they wanted peace and happiness.

13 Cf. R. Lavaud, *Poésies complètes du troubadour Peire Cardenal* (1180–1278) (Toulouse, 1957), p. 618. The numbering of poems is taken from this edn.

14 Cf. U. Mölk, 'Belh Deport. Über das Ende des provenzalischen Minnesangs', *ZRP*, LXXVIII (1962), pp. 358–74.

15 *Sordello, Le Poesie*, ed. M. Boni (Bologna, 1954), XLIII (Ensenhamens d'onor), pp. 89–92.

16 Ed. C. Appel, *Chres*, XXXIV, p. 75.

17 Cf. J. Anglade, *Le troubadour Guiraut Riquier, étude sur la décadence de l'ancienne poésie provençale* (Bordeaux, 1905), pp. 254–6, and C. A. F. Mahn, *Die Werke der Troubadours*, vol. IV (Berlin, 1853), LXXXIV, 909–15, p. 231.

18 Robert de Sorbon in one of his sermons, possibly preached in Paris about 1260: 'Folquetus, espiscopus Tolosanus, cum audiebat cantare aliquam cantilenam quam ipse existens in saeculo composuerat, in illa die, in prima hora, non comedebat nisi panem et aquam...' Quoted by S. Stronski, edn F. de M., p. 112*.

19 Cf. J. Anglade, *Les origines du Gai Savoir* (Paris, 1920); A. Jeanroy, *La poésie lyrique des troubadours* (Toulouse/Paris, 1934), II, pp. 300–8. One of the seven founder members belonged to the minor nobility.

20 The most famous is the *Breviari d'Amor*, written by Matfre Ermengaud of Béziers between 1288 and 1292. Out of 34,600 lines, mostly on theology and religious history, the last 6800, the *Perilhos tractat d'amor de donas*, are concerned with profane love and include 266 quotations from 85 troubadours. Ed. G. Azais, *Le Breviari d'Amor de Matfre Ermengaud suivi de sa lettre à sa sœur* (Béziers/Paris, 1862–81), 2 vols. There were also many *ensenhamen* or treatises on courtly behaviour, cf. n. 15, above.

21 For the ability of the poet of *Flamenca* to view *Amors* and *cortesia* from different angles cf. 'Intention and ideas in *Flamenca*', *MAe*, XXXVI (1967), pp. 119–33.

BIBLIOGRAPHY

This bibliography of books and articles also includes some recent anthologies of troubadour poetry and a few works on the stylistic, musical and historical background to which reference has not been made in the text.

Actes et mémoires du Ier congrès international de langue et littérature du Midi de la France (Avignon, 1957) (*Actes . . . Ier Congrès*).

Actes et mémoires du IIIe congrès de langue et littérature d'oc (Bordeaux, 1965) (*Actes . . . IIIe Congrès*).

Ageno Franca (ed.) *Luigi Pulci. Morgante* (Milan, 1955).

Andraud, P., *La vie et l'œuvre du troubadour Raimon de Miraval* (Paris, 1902).

Anglade, J. *Le troubadour Guiraut Riquier, étude sur la décadence de l'ancienne poésie provençale* (Bordeaux, 1905).

Les origines du Gai Savoir (Paris, 1920).

Grammaire de l'ancien provençal (Paris, 1921).

Anglès, H. *La música a Catalunya fins al segle XIII* (Barcelona, 1935).

Appel, C. 'Wiederum zu Jaufre Rudel', *ASNSL*, CVII (1901), pp. 338–49.

(ed.) *Bernart von Ventadorn* (Halle, 1926).

Provenzalische Chrestomathie, 6th edn (Leipzig, 1930) (*Chres*).

(ed.) *Die Lieder Bertrans von Born* (Halle, 1932).

Aston, S. C. 'The troubadours and the concept of style', *Stil- und Formprobleme in der Literatur. Vorträge des VII. Kongresses der Internationalen Vereinigung für moderne Sprachen und Literaturen* (Heidelberg, 1959).

Audiau, J. and Lavaud, R. *Nouvelle anthologie des troubadours* (Paris, 1928).

Avalle, D'A. S. (ed.) *Peire Vidal, Poesie* (Milan/Naples, 1960), 2 vols.

Azais, G. (ed.) *Le Breviari d'Amor de Matfre Ermengaud suivi de sa lettre à sa sœur* (Béziers/Paris, 1862–81), 2 vols.

Baehr, R. (ed.) *Der provenzalische Minnesang. Ein Querschnitt durch die neuere Forschungsdiscussion* (Darmstadt, 1967).

Baratier, E. *Histoire de la Provence* (Toulouse, 1969).

Documents de l'histoire de la Provence (Toulouse, 1971).

Bartsch, K. *Provenzalisches Lesebuch. Mit einer literarischen Einleitung und einem Wörterbuche* (Elberfeld, 1855).

Chrestomathie de l'ancien français, 10th edn (Leipzig, 1910) (*Chres*).

Battaglia, S. (ed.) *Trattato d'amore Andreae Capellani regii francorum 'De Amore' Libri Tres testo latino del sec. XII con due traduzioni toscane inedite del sec. XIV* (Rome, 1947).

Bibliography

Bédier, J. Le roman de Tristan par Thomas, poème du XIIe siècle (Paris, 1902–5), 2 vols.

Belperron, P. La croisade contre les Albigeois et l'union du Languedoc à la France (Paris, 1948).

La joie d'Amour. Contribution à l'étude des troubadours et de l'amour courtois (Paris, 1948).

Bergin, T. G. see Hill, R. T.

Bezzola, R. R. 'Guillaume IX et les origines de l'amour courtois', R, LXVI (1940–1), pp. 145–237.

Les origines et la formation de la littérature courtoise en Occident (Paris, 1960), 3 parts (Origines).

Boethius Tractates, de consolatione Philosophiae (Loeb Classical Library, London/Cambridge, Mass., 1962).

Bohs, W. (ed.) 'Abrils issi'e mays intrava. Lehrgedicht von Raimon Vidal von Bezaudun', RF, XV (1904), pp. 204–313.

Boni, M. (ed.) Sordello, Le Poesie (Bologna, 1954).

Bourrilly, V. L. and Busquet, R. La Provence au moyen âge (Paris, 1924).

Boutière, J. and Schutz, A. H. Biographies des troubadours 2nd revised edn (Paris, 1964) (Biographies).

Briffault, R. Les troubadours et le sentiment romanesque (Paris, 1945); and The Troubadours (Bloomington, 1965).

Camproux, C. Histoire de la littérature occitane (Toulouse, 1945).

'A propos de "joi"', Mélanges de linguistique et de littérature romanes à la mémoire d'I. Frank (Saarbrücken, 1957), pp. 100–17.

Le joy d'amor (Montpellier, 1965).

Canello, U. A. (ed.) La vita e le opere del trovatore Arnaldo Daniello (Halle, 1883).

Casella, M. 'Il più antico trovatore', Archivio storico italiano, LCVI (1938), II, pp. 3–63.

'Poesia e storia II Gaufredo Rudel', Archivio storico italiano, XCVI (1938), pp. 153–99.

Chailley, J. Histoire musicale du moyen âge (Paris, 1950).

'Les premiers troubadours et les versus de l'école d'Aquitaine', R, LXXVI (1955), pp. 212–39.

Chaytor, H. J. From Script to Print: an introduction to medieval literature (Cambridge, 1945; London, 1966).

Chiòrboli, E. see Petrarch.

Cicero De Senectute, De Amicitia, De Divinatione (Loeb Classical Library, London/Cambridge, Mass., 1964).

Clark, D. L. Rhetoric in Greco-Roman Education (Columbia U.P., 1957).

Cluzel, I. 'Jaufre Rudel et l'amor de lonh: essai d'une nouvelle classification des pièces du troubadour', R, LXXVIII (1957), pp. 86–97.

'A propos des origines de la littérature courtoise en occident', R, LXXXI (1960), pp. 538–55.

Contini, G. 'Per la conoscenza di un sirventese di Arnaut Daniel', SM, IX (1936), pp. 223–31.

Cornicelius, M. (ed.) So fo el temps c'om era jays, nouvelle de Raimon Vidal de Bezaudun (Diss. Berlin, 1888).

Coulet, J. (ed.) Le troubadour Guilhem Montanhagol (Toulouse, 1898).

Bibliography

Cravayat, P. 'Les origines du troubadour Jaufre Rudel', R, LXXI (1950), pp. 166–79.

Curtius, E. R. European Literature and the Latin Middle Ages (London, 1953).

Dante De Vulgari Eloquentia ridotto a miglior lezione, commentato e tradotto da A. Marigo (Florence, 1957) (DVE).

Il Convivio, ed. M. Simonelli (Bologna, 1966).

Purgatorio, Temple edn (London, 1941).

Davenson, H. Les troubadours (Paris, 1961).

Déchanet, J. M. Œuvres choisies de Guillaume de Saint-Thierry (Paris, 1944).

Dejeanne, J. M. L. (ed.) Poésies complètes du troubadour Marcabru (Toulouse, 1909).

Del Monte, A. (ed.) Peire d'Alvernha, Liriche (Turin, 1955).

'En durmen sobre chevau', FiR, II (1955), pp. 140–7.

Denomy, A. J. 'Jovens: the notion of Youth among the troubadours, its meaning and source', MedS, XI (1949), pp. 1–22.

'Jois among the early troubadours: its meaning and possible source', MedS, XIII (1951), pp. 177–217.

'Concerning the accessibility of Arabic influences to the earliest Provençal troubadours', MedS, XV (1953), pp. 147–58.

'Courtly love and courtliness', Sp, XXVIII (1953), pp. 44–63.

Devic Dom (Cl.) and Dom (J.) Vaissette. Histoire générale de Languedoc (Toulouse, 1872–92), 15 vols.

Dronke, P. 'Guillaume IX and Courtoisie', RF, LXXIII (1961), pp. 327–38.

Medieval Latin and the Rise of the European Love-Lyric (Oxford, 1965), 2 vols.

Dumitrescu, M. 'Eble II de Ventadorn et Guillaume IX d'Aquitaine', CCMed, XI (1968), pp. 379–412.

Egidi, F. I Documenti d'Amore di Francesco da Barberino (Rome, 1905).

Fechner, J. U. 'Zum gap in der altprovenzalischen Lyrik', GRM n.s., XIV (1964), pp. 15–34.

Frank, Grace. 'The distant love of Jaufré Rudel', MLN, LVII (1942), pp. 528–34.

'Jaufré Rudel, Casella and Spitzer', MLN, LIX (1944), pp. 526–31.

Frank, I. 'Du rôle des troubadours dans la formation de la poésie lyrique moderne', Mélanges de linquistique et de littérature romanes offerts à Mario Roques (Paris, 1950–3), 3 vols., I, pp. 63–81.

Répertoire métrique de la poésie des troubadours (Paris, 1953 and 1957), 2 vols.

Frappier, J. 'Vues sur les conceptions courtoises dans les littératures d'oc et d'oïl au XIIe siècle', CCMed (1959), pp. 135–56.

Gennrich, F. Der musikalische Nachlass der Troubadours (Darmstadt, 1958–65), 3 vols.

Gérold, T. La musique au Moyen Age (Paris, 1932).

Gilson, E. H. The Mystical Theology of St Bernard; transl. A. H. C. Downes (London, 1940).

Goldin, F. Lyrics of the Troubadours and Trouvères (New York, 1973) – anthology.

Grafström, Å. Etude sur la graphie des plus anciennes chartes languedociennes, avec un essai d'interprétation phonétique (Uppsala, 1958).

Grandgent, C. H. An Outline of the Phonology and Morphology of Old Provençal (Boston, 1905).

Bibliography

Hamlin, F. R., Ricketts, P. T. and Hathaway, J. *Introduction à l'étude de l'ancien provençal; textes d'étude* (Geneva, 1967).

Hill, R. T. and Bergin, T. G. *Anthology of the Provençal Troubadours*, 2nd revised edn (Yale U.P., 1973).

Hoepffner, E. *Les troubadours* (Paris, 1955). (ed.) *Bernart Marti* (Paris, 1929).

Jeanroy, A. (ed.) 'Poésies du troubadour Gavaudan', R, XXXIV (1905), pp. 497–539.

(ed.) *Poésies de Uc de Saint-Circ* (Toulouse, 1913).

Les Chansons de Jaufré Rudel, 2nd revised edn (Paris, 1924).

Les chansons de Guillaume IX Duc d'Aquitaine, 2nd edn (Paris, 1927).

La poésie lyrique des troubadours (Toulouse/Paris, 1934), 2 vols.

Klein, O. *Die Dichtungen des Mönchs von Montaudon* (Marburg, 1885).

Köhler, E. *Trobadorlyrik und höfischer Roman* (Berlin, 1962).

'Sens et fonction du terme "jeunesse" dans la poésie des troubadours', *Mélanges offerts à R. Crozet à l'occasion de son soixante-dixième anniversaire* (Poitiers, 1966), pp. 569–83.

Esprit und arkadische Freiheit (Frankfurt a. Main/Bonn, 1966).

Kolb, H. *Der Begriff der Minne und das Entstehen der höfischen Lyrik* (Tübingen, 1958).

Kolsen, A. (ed.) *Sämtliche Lieder des Trobadors Giraut de Bornelh*, vol. 1 (Halle, 1910) text and translation; vol. 2 (Halle, 1935) notes, introduction and glossary.

'Vier Lieder des Trobadors Raimon de Miraval', *Archivum Romanicum*, XXI (1937), pp. 299–319.

Labbe, P. *Novae bibliothecae manuscript. librorum tomus primus (-secundus)* (Paris, 1657).

Lacaita, Sir J. P. (ed.) *Benvenuto da Imola* (Florence, 1887).

Lallemend, J.-P. 'Le troubadour Raimon de Miraval. Contribution à l'étude de la musique des troubadours' (Univ. of Liège, 1973, diss.).

Lausberg, H. *Handbuch der literarischen Rhetorik* (Munich, 1960).

Lavaud, R. (ed.) *Les poésies d'Arnaut Daniel* (Toulouse, 1910), also publ. in *AMid*, XXII (1910) and XXIII (1911).

(ed.) *Poésies complètes du troubadour Peire Cardenal* (1180–1278) (Toulouse, 1957).

Lavaud, R. and Nelli, R. *Les troubadours; Jaufre, Flamenca, Barlaam et Josaphat* (Bruges, 1960).

Lavaud, R. *see* Audiau, J.

Lazar, M. 'Les éléments constitutifs de la "cortezia" dans la lyrique des troubadours', *SMV*, VI–VII (1959), pp. 66–96.

Amour courtois et Fin'Amors (Paris, 1964).

(ed.) *Bernard de Ventadour. Chansons d'amour* (Paris, 1966).

Lefèvre, Y. 'Jaufre Rudel, professeur de morale', *AMid*, LXXVIII (1966), pp. 415–22.

Le Goff, J. *La civilisation de l'occident médiéval* (Paris, 1964).

Lejeune, R. 'La chanson de l'"amour de loin" de Jaufré Rudel', *Studi in onore di Angelo Monteverdi* (Modena, 1959), 2 vols., I, pp. 403–42.

'Pour le commentaire du troubadour Marcabru: une allusion à Waïfre, roi d'Aquitaine', *AMid*, LXXVI (1964), pp. 363–70.

Bibliography

'La "Galerie Littéraire" du troubadour Peire d'Alvernhe', *Actes*. . . III⁰
Congrès, II, pp. 35–54, and RLLO, 12/13 (1965), pp. 35–54.

'L'extraordinaire insolence du troubadour Guillaume IX d'Aquitaine',
*Mélanges Pierre Le Gentil. Mélanges de langue et littérature médiévales. Espagne,
France, Portugal* (Paris, 1973), pp. 485–503.

Levy, E. *Petit dictionnaire Provençal–Français* (Heidelberg, 1909) (*Pet. Dict.*).
Provenzalisches Supplement-Wörterbuch (Leipzig, 1894–1924) (*SWB*).

Lewent, K. *Zum Text der Lieder des Giraut de Bornelh* (Florence, 1938).

Linskill, J. *The Poems of the Troubadour Raimbaut de Vaqueiras* (The Hague, 1964).

Limouzin-Lamothe, R. *La commune de Toulouse et les sources de son histoire
(1120–1249)* (Toulouse/Paris, 1932).

Livingston, C. H. *Le jongleur Gautier le Leu* (Cambridge, Mass., 1951).

Mahn, C. A. F. *Die Werke der Troubadours*, IV (Berlin, 1853).

Marigo, A. *see* Dante.

Marshall, J. H. 'Le *Vers* au XII⁰ siècle : genre poétique', *Actes*. . . III⁰ *Congrès*, II,
pp. 55–63.

'On the text and interpretation of a poem by Raimbaut d'Orange (*Cars
douz*; ed. Pattison, I)', *MAe*, XXXVII (1968), pp. 12–36.

(ed.) *The 'Razos de Trobar' of Raimon Vidal and Associated Texts* (Oxford,
1972).

Martial. *Epigrams; with an English translation by Walter C. A. Ker*, revised edn
(Loeb Classical Library, London/Cambridge, Mass., 1968).

Menéndez Pidal, R. *Poesía árabe y poesía europea, con otros estudios de literatura
medieval* (Buenos Aires, 1941).

Migne, J. P. *Patrologia cursus completus. Series latina* (Paris, 1844–64) (*PL*).

Mölk, U. (ed.) *Guiraut Riquier, Las cansos* (Heidelberg, 1962).

'Belh Deport. Über das Ende des provenzalischen Minnesangs', *ZRP*,
LXXVIII (1962), pp. 358–74.

Trobar clus–trobar leu (Munich, 1968).

Monteverdi, A. '"Chansoneta Nueva" attribuita a Guglielmo d'Aquitania',
Studi in onore di Salvatore Santangelo, Siculorum Gymnasium (1955), pp. 6–15.

Mouzat, J. *Les poèmes de Gaucelm Faidit* (Paris, 1965).

Mundy, J. H. *Liberty and Political Power in Toulouse (1050–1230)* (New York,
1954).

Nelli, R. *L'Erotique des troubadours* (Toulouse, 1963).
see Lavaud, R.

Nykl, A. R. *Hispano-Arabic Poetry and its Relations with the Old Provençal Troubadours*
(Baltimore, 1946).

Ordericus Vitalis. *Historiae ecclesiasticae libri tredecim*, ed. A. le Prévost (Paris,
1838–55).

Ortiz, R. 'Intorno a Jaufre Rudel', *ZRP*, XXXV (1911), pp. 543–54.

Ovid. *Heroides and Amores* (Loeb Classical Library, London/Cambridge,
Mass., 1958).

The Art of Love and other poems (Loeb Classical Library, London/Cambridge,
Mass., 1962) (*Ars am.*).

Tristia. Ex Ponto (Loeb Classical Library, London/Cambridge, Mass.,
1965).

Paris, G. (ed.) 'Lais inédits de Tyolet, de Guingamor, de Doon, du
Lecheor et de Tydorel', *R*, VIII (1879), pp. 29–72.

'Jaufré Rudel', *Mélanges de littérature française du Moyen Age*, II (Paris, 1912), pp. 498–538.

Parry, J. J. (transl.) *Andreas Capellanus, The Art of Courtly Love* (New York, 1959).

Pasero, N. '*Companho, tant ai agutz d'avols conres* di Guglielmo IX d'Aquitania e il tema dell'amore invincibile', CN, XXVII (1967), pp. 19–29.

'Devinalh, "non-senso" e "interiorizzazione testuale"', CN, XXVIII (1968), pp. 113–46.

Paterson, L. M. *Troubadours and Eloquence* (Oxford, 1974).

Patrologia Latina (PL) see Migne.

Pattison, W. T. *The Life and Works of the Troubadour Raimbaut d'Orange* (Minnesota, 1952).

Petrarch. *Le Rime sparse e i Trionfi*, ed. E. Chiòrboli (Bari, 1930).

Pillet, A. and Carstens, H. *Bibliographie der Troubadours* (Halle/Saale, 1933) (PC).

Pirot, F. 'Bibliographie commentée du troubadour Marcabru', MA, LXXIII (1967), pp. 87–126.

Plato. *The Symposium*, transl. W. Hamilton (Penguin Classics, Harmondsworth, 1952).

Pollmann, L. 'Dichtung und Liebe bei Wilhelm von Aquitanien', ZRP, LXXVIII (1962), pp. 326–57.

'*Companho, tant ai agutz d'avols conres*', *Neophilologus*, XLVII (1963), pp. 24–34.

Trobar Clus, Bibelexegese und Hispano-Arabische Literatur (Münster, 1965).

Die Liebe in der hochmittelalterlichen Literatur Frankreichs (Frankfurt a. Main, 1966).

Press, A. R. *Anthology of Troubadour Lyric Poetry* (Edinburgh U.P., 1971).

Raby, F. J. E. *The Oxford Book of Medieval Latin Verse* (Oxford, 1959).

Raynouard, F. *Lexique romane ou dictionnaire de la langue des troubadours* (Paris, 1838–44), 6 vols. (Lex. rom.).

Recueil des historiens des Gaules et de la France (Paris, 1738 to present day).

Reese, G. *Music in the Middle Ages* (New York, 1940).

Rhetorica ad Herennium (Loeb Classical Library, London/Cambridge, Mass., 1964).

Richard, A. *Histoire des comtes de Poitou* (Paris, 1903), 2 vols.

Ricketts, P. T. (ed.) *Les poésies de Guilhem de Montanhagol* (Toronto, 1964).

'Castitatz chez Guilhem de Montanhagol', RLR, LXXVII (1966), pp. 147–50.

Riquer, M. de. *La Lírica de los Trovadores* (Barcelona, 1948) – anthology.

(ed.) *Guillem de Berguedà* (Abadia de Poblet, 1971), 2 vols.

Robertson, D. W. '*Amors de terra lonhdana*', SP, XLIX (1952), pp. 566–82.

Roncaglia, A. 'Laisat estar lo gazel (contributo alla discussione sul rapporti fra lo zagial e la ritmica romanza)', CN, IX (1949), pp. 67–99.

'Per un'edizione e per l'interpretazione dei testi del trovatore Marcabruno', Actes. . .Ier Congrès, pp. 47–55.

'Lo vers comens quan vei del fau', CN, XI (1951), pp. 25–48.

'Il gap di Marcabruno', SM, XVII (1951), pp. 46–70.

'Al departir del brau tempier', CN, XIII (1953), pp. 5–33.

'Aujatz de chan', CN, XVII (1957), pp. 20–48.

Carestia', CN, XVIII (1958), pp. 121–37.

'Cortesamen voill comensar', *Rivista di cultura classica e medioevale*, VII (1965), pp. 948–61.

La lingua dei trovatori (Rome, 1965).

'"Trobar clus"; discussione aperta', CN, XXIX (1969), pp. 1–51 ('Trobar Clus').

Roques, M. (ed.) *Le Roman de Renart, Ière branche* (Paris, 1948).

Sakari, A. 'Azalais de Porcairagues, le joglar de Raimbaut d'Orange', NMi, L (1949), pp. 23–43, 56–87, 174–98.

Scheludko, D. 'Beiträge zur Entstehungsgeschichte der altprovenzalischen Lyrik', *Archivum Romanicum*, XI (1927), pp. 273–312; XII (1928), pp. 30–127; XV (1931), pp. 132–206.

'Ovid und die Trobadors', ZRP, LIV (1934), pp. 128–74.

'Zur Geschichte des Natureingangs bei den Trobadors', ZFSL, LX (1935–7), pp. 257–334.

'Über die Theorien der Liebe bei den Trobadors', ZRP, LX (1940), pp. 191–234.

Schlösser, F. *Andreas Capellanus seine Minnelehre und das christliche Weltbild um 1200* (Bonn, 1960).

Schutz, A. H. 'The Provençal expressions *Pretz e Valor*', Sp, XIX (1944), pp. 488–93.

'Some Provençal words indicative of knowledge', Sp, XXXIII (1958), pp. 508–14.

see Boutière, J.

Spanke, H. *Beziehungen zwischen romanischer und mittellateinischer Lyrik* (Berlin, 1936).

Untersuchungen über die Ursprünge des romanischen Minnesangs, Marcabrustudien. Abh. der Ges. der Wiss. zu Göttingen, 3e Folge, XXIV (Göttingen, 1940).

Spitzer, L. 'Trouver', R, LXVI (1940–1), pp. 1–11.

L'amour lointain de Jaufré Rudel et le sens de la poésie des troubadours (Chapel Hill, N. Carolina, 1944).

Stimming, A. (ed.) *Bertran de Born. Sein Leben und seine Werke* (Halle, 1879).

Stone, D., Jr. 'Rudel's *Belhs m'es l'estius*: a new reading', NMi, LXVII (1966), pp. 137–44.

Stroński, S. (ed.) *Le troubadour Elias de Barjols* (Toulouse, 1906).

(ed.) *Le troubadour Folquet de Marseille* (Cracow, 1910).

Sutherland, D. R. 'The love meditation in courtly literature', *Studies in Medieval French Presented to Alfred Ewert* (Oxford, 1961), pp. 165–93.

Tasso Torquato. *Discorsi dell'arte poetica e del poema eroico*, ed. L. Poma (Bari, 1964).

Thomas, A. (ed.) *Poésies complètes de Bertran de Born* (Toulouse, 1888).

Toja, G. (ed.) *Arnaut Daniel, Canzoni* (Florence, 1960).

Topsfield, L. T. 'Raimon de Miraval and the art of courtly love', MLR, LI (1956), pp. 33–41.

'The theme of courtly love in the poems of Guilhem Montanhagol', FS, XI (1957), pp. 127–34.

'"Cortez'ufana" chez Raimon de Miraval', *Actes*. . .IIIe *Congrès*, II, pp. 102–10, and RLLO, 12/13 (1965), pp. 102–10.

'Intention and ideas in *Flamenca*', MAe, XXXVI (1967), pp. 119–33.

Bibliography

'The burlesque poetry of Guilhem IX of Aquitaine', NMi, LXIX (1968), pp. 280–302.

'Jois, Amors and Fin'Amors in the poetry of Jaufre Rudel', NMi, LXXI (1970), pp. 277–305.

'Three levels of love in the poetry of the early troubadours, Guilhem IX, Marcarbru and Jaufre Rudel', *Mélanges de philologie romane dédiés à la mémoire de Jean Boutière* (Liège, 1971), pp. 571–87 (Mel. Boutière).

(ed.) *Les poésies du troubadour Raimon de Miraval* (Paris, 1971).

'The "natural fool" in Peire d'Alvernhe, Marcabru and Bernart de Ventadorn', *Mélanges offerts à Charles Rostaing* (Liège, 1974).

Trojel, E. (ed.) *Andreas, Capellanus regius. De amore libri tres.* (Copenhagen, 1892).

Van der Werf, H. *The Chansons of the Troubadours and Trouvères. A study of the melodies and their relation to the poems* (Utrecht, 1972).

Westrup, J. A. 'Medieval song' in *The New Oxford History of Music*, vol. 2 (Oxford, 1954).

Wolff, P. *Histoire de Toulouse* (Toulouse, 1961).

Histoire du Languedoc (Toulouse, 1967).

Documents de l'histoire du Languedoc (Toulouse, 1969).

Zenker, R. (ed.) *Die Lieder Peires von Auvergne* (Erlangen, 1900).

Zorzi, D. 'L'amor de lonh di Jaufre Rudel', *Aevum*, XXIX (1955), pp. 124–44.

GENERAL INDEX

Abelard, 71
Agnes of Burgundy, 4, 71
Agobard, 34
Aimeric de Belenoi, 160
alba, troubadour dawn song, 5
Albigensian Crusade, 3, 241, 244
Alcher of Clairvaux, 36
Alfonso VII of Castile, 159
amar finamens, Raimbaut d'Aurenga's
term for Fin'Amors, 150
amars, Marcabru's term for venal
love, contrasted with Bon'Amors,
81, 83, 180
amor de lonh (distant love): Guilhem
IX on, 28; Jaufre Rudel on, 28,
49, 50–1, 56, 58, 61, 62, 63–5,
66, 69, 154; Peire d'Alvernhe
on, 164–5, 166
Amors, 18–19, 44; Bernart de
Ventadorn accepts the tyranny
of, 35, 36, 43, 112–22;
conflict between jois and 39;
as Fals'Amors in contrast to
Fin'Amors, see Fals'Amors;
juxtaposed with God by
Raimbaut d'Aurenga, 143–5;
no help in the quest for jois,
for Guilhem IX, 29–30, or for
Jaufre Rudel, 46–7; Peire
d'Alvernhe's poems on jois and,
161–72; relinquished by Jaufre
Rudel for Fin'Amors, see under Fin'
Amors; by the time of Raimon
de Miraval, has become a code
of courtly behaviour, 228, 231,
234; word used by Arnaut

Daniel as equivalent to Fin'Amors,
see under Fin'Amors
amour courtois, 122, 223
amour-passion, 150
Andreas Capellanus, 19, 122; and
courtly love, 174, 225; *De amore*
by, 233, 247–8
Aragon: Guilhem IX fights for
king of, 13; territories of, in
Languedoc, 243
Aristotle, 23, 244
Arnaud d'Aragon, 227
Arnaut Daniel, 195–6; accepts
rule of love, 198–205,
struggles against desire, 205–7,
experiences jois, suffering, and
hope, 207–13; Amors is
equivalent to Fin'Amors for, 200,
215–16, and is equated with
love of God, 216–17, 251–2;
courtly love not personal
enough for, 223, 234; full
development of troubadour art
in, 2, 244, and ultimate
expression of Fin'Amors, 235;
Jaufre Rudel as influence on,
206, 216; as metaphysical
poet, 183; paragon of love
poets for Dante, 25, 158, 196–8;
Peire d'Alvernhe as precursor of,
186, 190; Raimbaut d'Aurenga
as model for, 200, 206; rhyme
schemes used by, 154, 213–14;
trobar ric style of, 152, 217, 236
Arthurian romances, 5
Audiart, troubadour pseudonym, 220

283

39, 44, 71, 105–6; *Amors* and,
29–30, 39, 46–7; for Arnaut
Daniel, 202, 203; central for
Bernart de Ventadorn, 123–7,
173; controlled by *mesura* for
Peire d'Alvernhe, 161; of the
court, for Raimon de Miraval,
223, 228, 252, and of society, for
Guilhem de Montanhagol, 246;
displaced by *mesura* after the
Albigensian Crusade, 244; for
Marcabru, 83; quest for, by
Guilhem IX, 36–9, 44, by
Jaufre Rudel, 44, 45–9, 53–4,
and by Raimbaut d'Aurenga,
139–41, 144, 157, 202;
supplied by Fin'*Amors*, 59–60,
68, 173–4

Joufrois, North French romance, 18
Jovens (youthfulness, generosity of
spirit), 18, 19, 39, 71, 72,
105–6; Bernart de Ventadorn
as the spirit of, 136; Marcabru
on, 80, 82, Peire d'Alvernhe and,
186, 189; Raimbaut d'Aurenga
and, 157; for Raimon de
Miraval is the courtly code, 222,
228; word vanishes as innate
quality, 252

Kürenberc, 167

Lai dou lecheor, North French poem,
26
lassar (binding up of levels of
meaning in a poem), 26, 47,
152
lavador (cleansing place), theme of:
used by Marcabru, 100, 169,
and Peire d'Alvernhe, 187
Loba de Pennautier, famous *domna*,
227
love: courtly canon of, accepted
(from about 1170), 43–4, 111,
122; courtly terminology of,
39, 71; distant, see *amor de lonh*;
three planes of, in poems of
early troubadours, 26–7, 44–8,
see also *Amors, Fin'Amors*

Lyons, French poets of school of
(sixteenth century), 5

malvestatz, 20, 78, 79, 148, 156
Marcabru, 70–3, 107, 134;
Christian ethic in, 72, 74–5,
85, and Christian imagery, 85–6,
101; on 'coloured' words, 48;
his concept of Fin'*Amors*, 37, 56,
59, 99–101, 104–6, 112–13,
119–20, 121; Fin'*Amors*,
co-exists with love of God, 103,
183, 190, contrasted with
Amors (*Fals'Amors*), 19, 49, 73,
78–85, 234, defined, 84; on
fragmentary and integrated
thinking, 73–4, 83, 96–8, 100,
105, 180; influence of, shown
by Arnaut Daniel, 235, Gavaudan,
21, Peire d'Alvernhe, 165, 167,
169, 177, 178–9, 180, 186,
and Raimbaut d'Aurenga, 138;
Jaufre Rudel, and, 43, 51, 54,
57–8; on *mesura*, 87–8, 103; as
a metaphysical poet, 183; as a
moralist, 22–3, 24, 71, 72, 96,
104; and nature, 73, 74–5, 91,
103; his *pastorela*, 88–91, 99;
shows influence of Guilhem IX,
93–6; his 'starling' poems, 91–3
Marie de Champagne, 11
Marie de France, 35
Martial, 26, 151
Matfre Ermengaud, quotes Raimon
de Miraval, 220
mesura, 23; Bernart de Ventadorn
and, 127, 130; *jois* controlled
by (Peire d'Alvernhe), 160, 162,
166, 177; *jois* replaced by, 244;
key to life for Guilhem de
Montanhagol, 245; in Marcabru,
83, 84, 85, 86, 87–8, 91, 107;
Marcabru's ideal of Fin'*Amors*
inspired by, 247
mielhs (supreme happiness), 44, 56,
61, 62, 161, 186
Monk of Montaudon, 25, 195, 196,
219
Montpellier, court of, 2

INDEX OF VERSE-QUOTATIONS

(The figure following the first line of the poem is the number under which the poem is listed by A. Pillet and H. Carstens in their *Bibliographie der Troubadours*. The numbers in brackets give the line reference for the quotation)

ARNAUT DANIEL edn G. Toja
Amors e iois e liocs e tems
29.1 edn XIV (25–7) 202;
(1–8) 211; (17–24) 211–12;
(41–50) 212
Anc ieu non l'aic, mas ella m'a
29.2 edn VII (12–13) 204;
(23–33) 207
Ans qe·l cim reston de branchas
29.3 edn XVI (29–30) 206
Er vei vermeills, vertz, blaus, blancs, gruocs
29.4 edn XIII (8–9) 201
Autet e bas entre·ls prims fuoills
29.5 edn VIII (19–22) 204;
(46–54) 207
Chansson do·ill mot son plan e prim
29.6 edn II (10–18) 198
Doutz brais e critz
29.8 edn XII (28–32) 205;
(46) 206
En breu brisara·l temps braus
29.9 edn XI (9–16) 200;
(17–24) 201; (33–6) 208
En cest sonet coind' e leri
29.10 edn X (22–4) 206;
(1–7) 208; (19–21, 25–8, 29–35) 209; (36–40, 43–5) 210
Lancan son passat li giure
29.11 edn IV (33–40) 201;
(9–16) 202
Lanquan vei fueill'e flor e frug
29.12 edn V (8–14, 22–3, 29–35) 199; (36–42) 200
Lo ferm voler q'el cor m'intra
29.14 edn XVIII (1–39) 213–14;

(31–2) 216; (25–6) 217
Quan chai la fuelha
29.16 edn III (14–16) 198
Sols sui qui sai lo sobrafan qe·m sortz
29.18 edn XV (12–21, 29–31) 203;
(1–7, 31–5) 205

BERNART MARTI edn E. Hoepffner
D'entier vers far ieu non pes
63.6 edn V (31–6) 160
Lancan lo douz temps s'esclaire
(104.2) edn IX (17–21) 61

BERNART SICART DE MARVÉJOLS
Ab greu cossire
67.1 edn see p. 272 n. 1 (26–9) 241

BERNART DE VENTADORN edn C. Appel
Amics, Bernartz de Ventadorn
70.2 edn II (43–5) 126
Amors enquera·us preyara
70.3 edn III (56–66) 133
Amors, e que·us es vejaire?
70.4 edn IV (1–8) 115;
(41–8, 57–60) 116
Ara no vei luzir solelh
70.7 edn VII (1–16, 19–21) 121
A! tantas bonas chansos
70.8 edn VIII (36–9) 36;
(23–4) 127
Bel m'es can eu vei la brolha
70.9 edn IX (38–44) 132–3
Be·m cuidei de chantar sofrir
70.13 edn XIII (19–27) 127
Chantars no pot gaire valer

Index of verse-quotations